DAYS of DESTINY

COSMIC PROPHECIES FOR THE NEW CENTURY

THE EMERGENCE OF THE FIFTH WORLD

BY DR. ROBERT GHOST WOLF

SPECIAL CONTRIBUTIONS:

SIR LAURENCE GARDNER

CEASAR HUNBATZ MEN

MEMBERS OF THE HOPI SINOM

MANUSCRIPT EDITION

Days of Destiny
Cosmic Prophecies for the New Century
The Emergence of the Fifth World

by Dr. Robert Ghost Wolf
Published by Grail Publishing
Sante Fe, New Mexico

© 1996 - 2003 Robert Ghost Wolf
Wolf Lodge Cultural Foundation
http://www.wolflodge.org

Previous ISBN: 0-9660668-3-9

Voluntary Distribution by
Wolf Lodge Cultural Foundation
233 N Guadalupe St. #178
Santa Fe, New Mexico 87501

Cover Art
With Permission by my late friend
Susan Seddon Boulet

Cover and interior art/design by Quasi Construcs
Editing by Shoshanna Allison
Special *Literary* Contributions by The Indigenous Masters

This book is intended to provide information in regard to the subject matter covered. The purpose is to educate and entertain. The Author, Editor, and publisher shall have neither liability nor responsibility to any person or entity with respect to any loss or damage caused, directly or indirectly by information contained in this book.

Note for Librarians: a cataloguing record for this book that includes Dewey Classification and US Library of Congress numbers is available from the National Library of Canada. The complete cataloguing record can be obtained from the National Library's online database at: www.nlc-bnc.ca/amicus/index-e.html
ISBN 1-4120-0726-7

TRAFFORD

This book was published *on-demand* in cooperation with Trafford Publishing.
On-demand publishing is a unique process and service of making a book available for retail sale to the public taking advantage of on-demand manufacturing and Internet marketing. **On-demand publishing** includes promotions, retail sales, manufacturing, order fulfilment, accounting and collecting royalties on behalf of the author.

Suite 6E, 2333 Government St., Victoria, B.C. V8T 4P4, CANADA
Phone	250-383-6864	Toll-free	1-888-232-4444 (Canada & US)
Fax	250-383-6804	E-mail	sales@trafford.com
Web site	www.trafford.com	TRAFFORD PUBLISHING IS A DIVISION OF TRAFFORD HOLDINGS LTD.
Trafford Catalogue #03-0600		www.trafford.com/robots/03-0600.html

10   9   8   7   6   5   4   3   2   1

" In the final moment, if yours is the only voice to sing in the wilderness...sing then of your dream. For if only one voice still sings the sound of a dream it will continue... for your's is the voice of forever... and the angels that were there in the begining of the dream are there this very moment..."

Still Free

Otpemsiwak

Days of Destiny

Table of Contents

Days of Destiny, is a compilation of work done by Dr. Ghost Wolf during the years 1996 thru 1998. The prophecies in this work were 'seen' during that period. althoug many are today becoming regularly viewed events on the evening news.

Last Cry-Native American Prophecies and other Takes of the End Times.

Winds of Change, Visions from the last Ghost Dance,

Changing the Tides of Fear. A hand book for the Awakening, (Ascended Master Teachings)

Foreword by the Author

The work you are about to read was no lightweight endeavor and upon completing it I realized that of itself it is only an introduction to another reality. . When undertaking the compilation of this material, I realized it was a work to be ongoing for many years to come. Likewise, it is not going to be a lightweight endeavor for you while reading it, either.

A lot of the information I have presented here has in past times been reserved for initiates of the various Mystery Schools, serious Theosophists, and perhaps members of the Jesuit Priesthood. Much of the subject matter in this edition has not been available on the open market... The reasons are many, in the author's opinion. The fact that much of this information has not been available to the public was deliberate. However, times change and so do we.

Researching and compiling the information and editing the manuscript for form and content was no easy task either. The subject matter contained here in Destiny is compelling and pushes one to the borders of their reality. At every turn you will sense a strange familiarity, yet you won't find the words to express it fully to another. We are asked by the author to go into areas of our consciousness and heritage well beyond what is conventionally acceptable and considered appropriate for discussion at most family outings.

I will admit it is a lot easier now in this new century than it was a quarter of a century ago to speak your mind about spiritual views and to even find information on these subjects. In ways, through the chaos of the times, the opportunity for the creation of the new world is coming through the storm clouds of humanity's fears and superstitions. It is because of this changing of the paradigm you came upon this manuscript.

There are many issues and subjects presented in **Destiny** that explain 'how it is' and what will happen if situations remain the same. I honestly believe WE can change the ways in which we will be personally impacted and as well, change the ultimate outcome of any event. When and if we as individuals begin to realize that, "for real", in changing the way we deal with things on an everyday level for ourselves personally, the change takes effect unilaterally. This factor is the same philosophy and methodology being utilized by the Masters of Tyranny to establish a matrix of thought which controls the masses.

It has been said in the Judeo-Christian teachings that, *"In the beginning there was the word."* This statement, which is actually out of context and not the whole statement, falls short in my understanding and belief, of the truth, in *that "in the beginning there was the thought."* The thought created the concept and from that dream of a reality, our word decrees, in the human sense of it, and the condition of our realized reality is then experienced."

Understand, it is with no ill intent I address any particular faith in this work. I simply present the facts for you to make your own Divine decision. I would only ask of you to place your inquisitiveness on the message and not the messenger. Often what is written or represented in ancient artifacts, was created with the knowledge and intent of those who lived a very different reality. Their perceptions as well as their intentions may not correlate to modern beliefs.

This does not mean they are wrong, in fact from the studies of ancient artifacts we often find that we are the ones who have the wrong idea about things. Moreover it is important not to try to overlay our beliefs and perceptions over what they are saying, for we would only once again cover up the truth of things. And we are finding that so much of the ancient texts and interpretations were colored and edited by contemporary hands in order to fit them into a prescribed agenda of beliefs.

Through revealing numerous case scenarios, **_Days of Destiny_** tells us of the eventual unilateral outcomes that will have global impact. Many doorways shut to Western man for a very long time are opened wide in **_Days of Destiny_**. As my Hopi Elders and I have discussed, **'We are now in the end times and events cannot be turned around now; only the outcome can be altered based upon how humanity deals with each arising event as they occur.** " We can, in the reading of this manuscript, find ourselves in a perplexing situation where we feel the impact of the transition occurring within our core beliefs.

Please keep in mind that **_Days of Destiny_** is about potential occurrences. It is based upon facts beginning to be revealed to us in their entirety, unfiltered and uncut; these facts have been hidden from us for so very long. So many of you may wonder, where are the solutions? What do we do? What can we do? This is a monumental job, and must we face the opposing **world viewpoints alone. The answers to this and other issues can be found in my book _Through the Eye of the Shaman_.**

Through the Eye of the Shaman is essentially a master's teaching in technique and applied thought. It is mind-altering and shows us along the journey how to effect change, not just surface, and therefore temporary change, but true internal change. It is a compilation of **Ascended Master Teachings** with which I have been gifted, and I work with personally in my life. If you have read **_Through the Eye of the Shaman,_** this book will be easily grasped and understood. If you haven't, I suggest you do.

The answers to our dealing with a constantly and accelerated world of change around us are there. If you can't afford to take ten or twenty years to leave this society, your children and your obligations to the "condition"… and lend yourself to **Initiate Training** in a remote setting, then you need to read **_Through the Eye of the Shaman_**. It will change your life.

The outcome of your future condition in the **Dream called Life** is in your hands…It always has been. If we exercise compassion, forgiveness and allowing with discerning borders, I believe we will, as has been prophesied, enter into a Golden Age…We are already morphing '**within**' in a living experiential transition into a new humanity. As you come to know yourself, come to terms with yourself, you will come to know God, the true Creator of us all.. For we are but extensions of the same God realizing itself…God after all is beyond form and definition from our limited perception of the whole of reality and can only be realized from within when we allow our unlimited self to emerge and simply **BE.**

In the light
Dr. Robert Ghost Wolf

The Age of Aquarius

"When the moon is in the seventh house, and Jupiter aligns with Mars,
then peace will guide the planets, and love will steer the stars.
This is the dawning of the Age of Aquarius........."

The Zodiacal ages are determined by a cosmic phenomenon known as the precession of the equinox. Each year the Spring Equinox moves slightly against the backdrop of the heavens, moving approximately one degree every seventy-two years, or thirty degrees in approximately 2,160 years. It completes a full cycle in about 26,000 years.

Understand, this is a rough approximation. The real measurement of an Age is marked by the time it takes the Spring Equinox to move through the actual star groups of a particular constellation. The movement of the Zodiacal clock is backwards through each constellation; hence we have the Age of Pisces first, followed by the Age of Aquarius.

The last 2,160 years found us in the Piscean Age, as the fulcrum was in Pisces; previous to that, the ecliptic pointed toward Aries. It can get a little confusing to the layman, because there have been a few changes in the original calendar from which all prophesies and cosmic calculations originated. We will explain more in a further chapter in this work. (The Manipulation of Time)

We entered officially into the Age of Aquarius, in January of 1997

Looking back upon humanity's experiences during the Age of Pisces, we reflect that Pisces (as a personality) is usually the martyr of the Zodiac, and when in a negative energy influence, Pisces is the immortal victim, the one who sacrifices ego and dreams for earthly obligations. On the up-side, Pisces surrenders the Earthly pleasures for higher aspirations, such as art and Spirit. The greater good and striving for divine values is always very important to Pisces.

It is calculated that approximately 2,000 years ago occurred the birth of **Yeshua Ben Yosaf** (Joseph). He was also known as **Yeshua Criost** (Jesus Christ) destined to become a great Master who, like **Krishna, Buddha, Ramayanna, Quetzal Coatl Amaru, Deganaweda** and other masters before him, radically changed the views of humanity towards realizing its spiritual truths. His history and ministry here in the Americas has yet to be fully realized by those of European influence. Though **Yeshua's** perceptions of sacrifice may not have been followed in the ensuing centuries, they were certainly foremost in the minds of people.

As we are seeing the Age of Aquarius unfold, we are observing a unilateral search for the divine aspect within humanity becoming more personalized. Brotherly love, global communication, Quantum logic and the pursuit of divine reasoning are but aspects of our merging into the influence of Aquarius. The emergence of the computer and its becoming an intricate part of our lives also falls under Aquarius

The Internet, along with its networking capabilities, is perhaps the most Aquarian invention to date, affording us the ability to instantly connect all over the world. To our ancestors, this would have seemed as possessing God-like communication skills. Now the Age of Aquarius comes into its own and we are making yet another quantum leap as we enter the digital age, where we will learn through experience to move at an even faster pace. This is being introduced to help us speed the very vibration of thought and being.

We presently are witness to a universal raising of the awareness of the God within, the God I AM, and this is most definitely an Aquarian attribute. Violent revolution and dramatic upheavals and radical change within all structures of our humanity also seem to be attributes of the Aquarian Age.

We could say of the Age of Aquarius that it is indeed the "Plutonian era", but not in the sense the classic Greek Philosopher had in mind when he wrote about Utopian existence. We are in a time when everywhere we turn we are witnessing as well as experiencing mass destruction. We are experiencing almost global upheaval on most every level and Humanity is in the midst of Chaos. Enlightenment is arriving side by side with regressive and sometimes violent reality. Therefore, the image of divine beings arriving from the golden mists of the clouds is not exactly what is unfolding. We have rather the image of a cloud of a subtle holocaust, which changes everything in its path….......Aquarius it would appear entered as the Warrior Wizard.

Prophecies about the Age of Aquarius seem to have to do with Earth Changes, the consequences of catastrophic weather, cataclysmic occurrences causing dramatic and decisive change. Apocalyptic occurrences, it would seem, are very Aquarian, as is our romance with them. One would hope the millennial fantasies we are seeing played out and the consequences of humanity's dreams of destruction would die out quickly, like the raging of emotions in our adolescence.

Technology has become a combination of both the monster and the deity woven into one. We are struggling daily to keep up with the speed of delivery of our computerized information sources in what is developing into an almost instantaneous occurrence. There are no more secrets, and everyone, including the once infallible government, has left fingerprints at the scene of the crime.

We are dealing with what appears to be a time of science fiction reality as we witness the effects of the genetic modification of our food, as well as our bodies .In our endless search for immortality, we are witnessing on television the open cloning of man and beast... exorcised from our divine right. Diseases are rampant and out of control and we are even attempting to control the global weather. All this, while we are dealing with what is being presented to us an inevitable environmental poisoning of our entire planet.. a tangible end to life as we know it physically. No wonder our stress levels are so high.

One other feature of Aquarius that deserves our attention: That is the relative lack of emotion and compassion of this sign. Watery Pisces, alas, was awash with emotional storms, but too cool Aquarius is noted for its attributes of cool logic, and enjoys being aloof to the point of rudeness, while preoccupied with self-adulation for its reason and rationality…—and the self-worshiping of its intellectual and technical prowess.

Aquarius is a thinking sign, not a feeling sign. That translates into the fact that Aquarius is a male-oriented energy not a female energy. Therefore, mankind in this Age of Aquarius, has within its consciousness the tendency for slipping into apathetic reality potentials. If we neglect our better half, our feeling half, the emotional part of us, we could wind up like those who come from the stars we call "the Grays", and evolve into a race that eventually dies off from our own lack of exercised emotional capabilities.

Could this be the reason we are seeing so many passionate, yet ultimately emotionless temporal relationships that are capriciously formed in the cyber-reality of the internet, as well as the overnight rise and fall of information gurus? Could this be a sign of the times? The Age of Aquarius definitely has its problems before it. We, as humanity, must endeavor at all costs to exercise our humanity and follow a path of Compassion, Love, Forgiveness and Reconciliation. This, for the sake of the unification of our divine aspects, and the awakening to the oneness of it all, must be, if we hope to achieve any degree of divine realization. It is called 'walking in balance'.

If we do not choose the higher path, the Prophesied Golden Age of Aquarius could become the darkest hour we have ever endured as a living, thinking species. We are advancing in our mental abilities. Yes, that is certain; but without the balance of Heart-felt spiritual awareness and the development of a foundation of strong feminine attributes, we will only evolve into unbalanced Gods of the lessor kind.

The following is an article from CNN news -
Taken from their web site in January of 1997

Astrologers: Age of Aquarius dawns Thursday January 23, 1997 [star] — Web posted at: 2:22 p.m. EST (1922 GMT)

(**CNN News Report**) —

An exceedingly rare planetary alignment will take place Thursday, astrologers say. For the first time since the Renaissance, the heavens will briefly line up in a perfect six-pointed star—a galactic Star of David. While astronomers say the alignment is nothing out of the ordinary, astrologers hail the event as a symbolic representation of the long-heralded dawning of the Age of Aquarius. And across the world, events have been planned to usher in the new era.

The new era or Age of Aquarius, is said to be triggered by the alignment of a series of planets, which will center on the first degrees of Aquarius and be joined by the sun with the moon opposite them all. The last time the alignment took place was in 1475. Thursday's alignment was happening between 12 p.m. and 4 p.m. EST. **CNN NEWS**

Again, of this time of the Age of Aquarius, we are told in:

Isaias 11:6 " The wolf also shall dwell with the lamb, and the leopard shall lie down with the kid; and the calf and the lion and the sheep shall abide together, and a little child shall lead them; The calf and the Bear shall feed together upon the land, and their young ones shall rest together; yea even the lion shall eat straw like the Ox....."

I could not help but wonder while reading this if it might be a prophecy referring to the genetically engineered foods being fed not only to people, but to our animals these days. And then I also realized, we are for the first time in the history of our planet, witness to the virtual captivity of almost all the world's wild life; 'they' are even trying to control the oceans.

PEGASUS

I bring attention at this time to Pegasus because Pegasus is playing a key role in the unfoldment of the prophecies of the Aquarian Age. Pegasus can be found within the zodiacal sign of Aquarius. 'This is the Age of Aquarius' holding with its coming the promise of a Golden Age and a time of Great Peace upon the Earth and also of great wonders that arise out of mankind's awakening consciousness.

THE STARGATE FILES

"...We are told there will appear a mysterious light, which will be like a mist. This mist will engulf the entire Earth much like a giant cloud. We will be lifted from the wheel of time, and in the new energy we will be unable to determine its passing... and from the center of the mysterious light the great Star would begin to emerge. The light from this star would begin to swell and eventually become brighter than our own Sun. It would appear to take form as an eight-pointed star as it comes closer and closer to the Earth. It would become so large it would block out most of the heavens from our view... There shall come a day like no other, for all the creatures of the Earth in that moment of forever shall be as one, and man and beast shall communicate as it was long ago, for fear shall be a no-thing where we are going..."

From... **Last Cry** *- Native American Prophecies, Tales of the End Times*

The Vision
of the Star Knowledge

Let us compare the history and perceptions of the indigenous masters, to those of Western Mythology, the Bible which is a Roman invention, and as well the Eastern understandings of Hu-man existence. We will look at some inevitable events with which we will be dealing, while we enter yet another phase of awakening along our journey back home to the Source of our beginning. Now before you start your journey, remember that he who isbeing referred to as Jesus, was himself an indigenous master...

Being one who was born of mixed blood, I contain within my being the genetic all the encoded memories of all the cultures and races from which I began. This is the fate of all 'Metis People'. I am a man who remembers my connection to Source. Coming from two worlds blended together within one being, my life has been a living commitment to bridging the gap between worlds and cultures.

Words of truth often are not heard or understood in their own times, nor is the Prophet and Seer often recognized in their own land. My gifts, which I receive and share with you, are from Great Spirit, the Source, I call WAKAN TANKA. Over time these words will remain . . .For they were given to me for the enhancement of Hu-man consciousness and in the service of the Light; they come from the living word of Source.

(GAJA) LAKSHMEE

What is presented here is a humble attempt to clarify the meanings of prophesied events. Some of these things I was told by my Elders and teachers, and some, which I share with you, are my own visions. It is hard to tell where the separations exist after one has become one with the wholeness of it all. . Life is after all a tapestry of sequential events and experiences, creating an energy field we can choose to access or deny.

My venture into Prophecy began, when, being invited into ceremonial circles of Indigenous Elders, I would often be asked to interpret the prophecies and messages handed down through the generations telling of events. I have been interested in the ancient Spiritual Practices of the Indigenous people of the Americas since my youth. And after 30 plus years of being in those circles a certain trust level as well as an evaluation of one's abilities is established. So I guess to some I passed the test.

Much has already begun, and the wheels of destiny are turning of their own accord and can no longer be slowed by the actions of mortal man. Much of what we have come to know and discern as real will change forever over the next decade of our Hu-man experience. Much of what we see today in physical reality as well as Spiritual reality will never be again.

It is a time to begin to view our existence upon this Earth plane "***Through the Eye of the Shaman***". For in the higher reality there are no differences between Peoples. It is all so much game-playing by children to conceive that there are. The understandings of origins and purposes here upon the Earth plane are all parts of an holistic epic. It is a journey of the human species.

The differences we perceive between us began when we separated, one group at a time, for various reasons, from the original teachings and started to make our own customized adaptations and editions of the original story. God, the Creator, was remolded and shaped to fit our designer religions... supporting the differences rather than the commonalties, which defend one perception against another. Whomsoever has the biggest army wins the argument.

Our memories are once again merging in commonality despite the illusionary differences we have created. Deep within our beingness we all feel the ***Winds of Change*** blowing across our personal field of dreams.

Nothing here is intended to create fear. Rather, it would open the doors to a new broader understanding and hope to those who dare to awaken and take the responsibility for being. It is presented to nurture those who would choose to walk the pathway of peace and exercise compassion, as we as Humanity pass through the gateway of tomorrow, into an unlimited and uncertain universe.

In many ways we are ***beyond*** the Quickening now. We are experiencing the shifting of the Heavens and the shaking of paradigms as well as dimensions. We are emerging from the comatose state of illusion, and the former synthesized reality, like a dream, is beginning to fade. We are witnessing the birthing of something unexplainable, something mysterious, as we experience the dawning of a new consciousness…… ***All things hidden shall be revealed, and the truth will set you free***.

May you have compassion for all living things, and may you see the Creator in all whose eyes gaze into your own. May you know the God within you, and may you remember this when you gaze into eyes that do not.

May you recognize the living energy of the God force within all things even if you cannot explain them, for truly this world is a grand mystery that has never been able to be put into form. That idea has proven itself impossible, though we have tried for tens of thousands of years… for Spirit is formless.

What we have found is that without love and compassion we wither and die; this is the nature of the War of Valued Life. Without love and compassion we simply will fade away with the old dream…For all we ever were was a dream conceived in love in the first place. LOVE is the very glue that holds together the fabric of the dream………and that is an ***absolute***.

The Journey

There are many prophecies held by the Indigenous Peoples of this planet. I have written about those with which I Am familiar and which are pertinent to this particular time-line experience in the Hu-man drama. There are some, however, about which I have not written. I have alluded to others, but could not yet reveal the full impact of their meanings. This is because in the tradition in which the knowledge was shared, permission must be granted from the circle of elders in which the knowledge was shared, and not because I wanted to hold back anything. Anyone with experience in these circles knows this is how it is. And I might add, for a Metis those rules are even strictly applied.

I suppose that for me the Journey began in my childhood, and with the illuminated beings that used to play with me. I would often get lost in the woods and after several days of my parents being scared half out of their wits they, along with the local police, would search for me. The woods near the side of the freeway is usually where they would find me, content in my little shelter I had built. I was always so surprised when the adults came looking for me that so much time had elapsed.

I was so preoccupied with my friends from this other world that I would lose all touch with the 'other reality' in which my parents lived.   You could say, I suppose I was born with an affinity to speak with divas and fairies who to this day are very real to me. I am still bewildered when others cannot feel their Presence as clearly as I can, never mind that they cannot see them. I understand this now, although for the longest time I cold not. Over time, I found humans can only perceive the width of vibratory perception to which they allow themselves to be open.

One of the differences between us and those who remain in the elemental world is that those in the elemental planes have retained the ability to shift dimensional levels at will.   So, in a way, it appears that they wisp in and out of our reality — little lights in the corner of a room —something scarcely in our peripheral vision.

I have found elementals are fully conscious and have purpose and awareness in every movement and thought. We, on the other hand, seem to stumble through life like blind cripples leaking out energy with every mindless reaction and thought. They used to say to me that humans were like leaking lights. As a result of this leaking of light, we hardly have enough energy to maintain our balance of emotions, never mind perceive inter-dimensional levels.

We have fallen into such a slumber that we cannot even perceive our true selves and nature. Most of our existence is perpetuated either in living in some as yet unproven and unrealized future reality, or we are lost in reliving or at least dwelling in our past. We have created a world so over-inundated with pain and sorrow that most of us spend our entire lives trying to escape from ourselves, and exist in denial of the reality in which we do experience our lives.

I was never **unlucky** enough to be accepted by the herd.   I was a loner from the time I could walk, which I understand was about 8 months of age. I spoke my first words at 10 months, and by the time I was 14 months I was speaking sentences. I remember I could often see people with my parents and being told later they had no recollection of the people.

Also, I saw and communicated with beings I believe now were not in my parents' reality. I guess I was, as I can remember my father saying often to his friends, "a strange child." This continued long after I was in my pre-teens, so I cannot blame it on the lightning bolt that went through me and almost ruined the chimney in the house one summer afternoon while I was camped outside next to the chimney.

I remember I started having dreams of events which would occur weeks or months later. While in my little studio, I would draw pictures of people I would not meet until years later. Often times I would be talking to someone, a relative, my mother, or one of her friends and I would see them change form in front of my eyes and become other beings.

Then there was this strange accompaniment to this occurrence where everything would shift into slow motion, and sounds would disappear and then I could see them in what would either be past life experiences or future occurrences in their lives. This also could happen when I stared out the window or walked in the woods or as I would constantly get lost at the beach. (The greater portion of my life this time round, I have lived either on the beach or on the mountain, or a combination of both.)

Obviously school was torturous for me. I was diagnosed with everything from dyslexia, to A.D.D., of being too slow, being too advanced, with physiological disorders, (Day dreamer)…; and yet, when I would be dragged down to the counselors and the endless trail of psychiatrists to find out what was wrong with me, I would often end up telling them how to fix their problems. Now I know I was reading; I was psychically reading their consciousness.   And they would give me those ridiculous tests because they were stymied in that I always came out in the upper 2 percentile ratings on their IQ tests. Remember those? I was an enigma to my parents and the doctors, as well, I suppose.

One would think I would have outgrown talking to my childhood friends from the Spirit world, but as I grew older that reality became even more real to me than the reality into which I have always felt I was inserted. I could not relate to my own age group. I preferred to hang around the adults and they seemed not to mind having me around, for whatever reason. I remember spending my teenage years on the North Shore of Long Island. Friends of the family had a cabin near the beach, and one summer I was allowed to use it as a studio. No one lived there. It was just used as an occasional guesthouse…. a place where they would camp out when they were at the beach, and mostly, if not for me, it would have been abandoned.

The cabin was on the backside of an estate and up on a hill in a grove of trees. It was rustic and served as a small haven where I could escape from the world and just go off into another reality.   I would walk down to the beach where I would dig the white clay located in the hillside. Local artists knew about the spot and from time to time there would be impromptu gatherings down at the beach when a few of them would show up together.

That is where I met my friend Ernie. Ernie was older; he had a family, a big one from what I could see. But, then again, I was on the outside looking in. We met in the in-between place — the place just on the outside of the glass bubble. The beach of dreams was our world. I only saw his family from a distance, as through a filter.

 Ernie used to come down to the beach to let it all go. He would walk for hours up and down the beach, sometimes bringing a notebook and scribbling down notes. He said he liked to write stories. The beach was a place where ideas liked to hang out. Ernie had a boat; I used to see him out on it from time to time. He liked to fish and clam, too. He liked my paintings and sculptures. We used to talk about things and thoughts that most people don't discuss.

We found a place in the in-between world, and for whatever reason of circumstance understood it without words between us. It was more like a feeling we were after, a feeling where we could be free to dream. I guess that's why we called it the beach of dreams. Sometimes we would just acknowledge each other's presence out there on the beach of dreams, spending entire days without talking, but there were times we talked.

We would talk about things that reached into the depths of people's inner nature, the things that formed their beings. Or, he would tell me stories about Europe, things that happened to him during the war and, the war that no one knew about. When Ernie would go on a roll, he could go on for hours.

He would talk to me about my art, and I suppose I needed that. There weren't many men I talked with about my paintings, or many men I talked to period. I had grown up with art being such a solitary vocation. Even today I am used to spending many long hours in solitude. I don't talk for days at a time.

When I lived in the mountains near Taos, people would come and check on me from time to time just to see if I was OK. They wondered what the heck it is I do all alone all the time. "It's no good to be alone so much. It will make you strange in the head…". But I was always Ok, and I didn't mind the aloneness. The fact is that alone I was able to go somewhere beyond time and I wasn't always alone. I had this other world just on the other side of the glass bubble — this other reality I found out about, where I would actually leave time behind. I found out time only existed if you thought about it. I discovered that there was a place in-between time, or maybe it was beyond time, I'm not exactly sure.

Once you find your way there, many things can be achieved that normal people don't even think of, never mind experience. This really is a strange and mysterious world in which we live. Most people have no idea; they are so stuck in the matrix of the group dream, they believe the matrix itself is reality and the matrix is all that is there.

'On the beach or in the mountains the matrix is thinner' is how I explain it. The ocean and the trees can clean away the frequencies of the matrix. There we are not caught in the webs of everyone's chaotic thoughts. One can spend endless hours walking and collecting things that float up on a beach. Sometime you wonder how things get there. Collecting beach glass is an incredible hobby, and keeping the hands busy frees the mind. Along the way, that is a wisdom I picked up from the masters.

And speaking of masters, when I was older, (I was only about 16 during the beach house period of my life), I would find that Ernie was Ernest Hemmingway, but to me he'll always be Ernie. Yes, I have had my special experiences in this life. Little periods of forever memories. I guess I live in the classic movie section of consciousness.

I also found solace in the community theatre, although my parents never attended any of my performances. That did not bother me, for I knew somehow I was not really their child. I could not explain it then but I knew that I was from the stars and the Earth was my Mother and Father was someone I spoke to often; I did always look up, but I never saw his face.

My far-out ways seemed to upset my folks a lot; they wanted me to be like Ricky Nelson, and I was definitely not Ricky Nelson. . I related totally to James Dean, and even looked like him in my younger years. Like James Dean was depicted in the movies, in life I was his real counter-part stuck in the world of ego and illusion in a world of insensitive adults. I was the poor kid who liked motorcycles and sports cars, although most of the time I used a beat-up truck or old jeep. They were fun, easy to fix and you could throw things in them you found, or spill fish water, or load them up with beach lumber and rocks, and you just did not care.

When you are poor, you learn to be very creative and most of the time you live in houses that always need repairs. You learned how to do these things — that is unless you like water dripping on your head when it is raining. So old beat up trucks or jeeps come in handy for picking things up at the lumberyard. The back hills can be rough on sports cars, and bikes are for the open road. I was the kid that your Mama told you would be nothing but trouble, and if you were a girl, your dad would not let you go out with my kind.

I treasure solitude. I guess that comes from finding out early that this can be a cruel world, and if you are young and on your own, as I was, life can be hell. It is like you give out a signal or something they pick up on empathically, and they just gang up on you like ants at a picnic. People are unforgiving toward anyone who breaks out of the Matrix. Later in life I was going to find out how true this was, the emitting a signal part. You can be felt in the crowd.

People, I have found for the most part, live at least double existences. They are master role players and most have three faces if not more. There is the "them" they are programmed to be, and there is the "them," they would like to be, but do not have the courage to be. Then there is the "them" they never had the space to find out about being — the phantom part of their reality; the unexplored "them".   And that is the part of this reality I know very well…. What is just beyond the edge.   And last, but not least, there is the "them" that they think someone else wants them to be, whether it be their wife, their associates on the job, their boyfriend, their clan…they are caught up in putting on a face for approval.

Most people live on the inside of the glass bubble. For the most part, they are not even aware the bubble exists. Because they never live on or near the edge, they don't even know it is there. It's safer on the inside swimming in the Matrix. There is a safety one finds from running within the herd; it starts when you are young and are seeking recognition and approval.

In the noise and clatter of the herd you don't have to feel too much. You don't have to take chances, and you don't have to think. You just move down the conveyer belt, never knowing or caring who you really are until one day something happens and you get bumped off. For someone who is creative, life on the people farms can be a slow torturous existence in hell.

There is an invisible layer that keeps people caught inside that bubble. Out here in the frontier, well, there are scary things that live here — things that go bump in the night. One soon finds there are other rules one must learn to maintain if they want to stay free and keep flying. You learn to walk the middle road and not to get too close to the sensors of the Matrix. It is sort of like learning how to walk on a spider's web without waking up the Spider itself.

If you're lucky you learn about the forbidden zones. Those are the free areas where the other outcasts from this reality gather in the in-between place — where the Matrix does not exist. And upon your return from the forbidden zone, you are sure to get a lesson quickly about the fear those who are still in the Matrix will feel towards you, for your frequencies most assuredly will be intensified.

It is a natural thing, and if you have ever lived on a ranch or farm you know the feeling domestic animals have when they are around those animals from the wild. They fear them. It's a known fact Dogs never attack Wolves unless they are in a pack. And Wolves could care less about Dogs except to keep them at a safe distance from their young.

Most of us live in that other world, the world of virtual reality — the world of the Dog and that reality is always supposed to be the same. In the world of the Dog we establish routines that make us feel as though we know what is going on and we are in control. The players are like the fools that go to a casino thinking they can beat the system. The system doesn't allow for you to win, and in this game winning is breaking away and somehow becoming your own person. It is not designed for that. It is designed for group consciousness.

It's a crazy game, where the rules are never told to you; you learn from making mistakes, and finding out the borders that are permissible. It is a world where being an individual thinker can be hazardous to your health.   From the time I was young, I just did not fit into that mold and I still don't. I knew what I wanted to do and did not know why the world was so adamantly resistant to my accomplishing my dharma. But I was young and did not know what I was up against was the 'Matrix'.

What I remember of my parents……. Well, frankly, it is not a place I go too much….. Their's was an empty world, shallow and built upon being nowhere. They had no particular ambitions and no particular direction. I don't think they ever really had dreams, or at least the dreams they had were not important enough to make them want to risk everything to achieve their becoming reality.   In many ways my parents were completely alien to me; they could not see me and I could not fit the preconceived roll of what they wanted me to be.

They both wanted me to be different things, mainly because they lived in different worlds.   I don't ever recall my parents talking much together…and I never remember seeing emotional exchanges between them — ever. They were strangers, not only to themselves, but I was not in their reality.   And on my side of the glass bubble, I was always finding trouble. One thing for sure: They were right.   I was never the Ricky Nelson every one knew from television……. James Dean perhaps, but not Ricky.

By 15 years of age, I was **OUT** on my own. I found myself living with relatives or teachers who took me in, along with other misplaced kids. I was lucky enough to find others like me; it was that time…… Dylan songs, and Donovan and yes, a little later there was Cat Stevens, the pied piper of the highway. It was the end of turbulent 60's and there were a lot of people trying to break out of the Matrix and create little islands of free expression.

One thing was obvious: We kept outgrowing our borders faster than we could rearrange them to suit our new thoughts and desires. We were learning at an accelerated rate how to become some-thing else, and what that was, was not entirely clear.

Lots of times, the Music was our only touchstone. We always seemed to find someone's mom or uncle who had a room over the garage or behind the store. They were kind, benevolent souls who were surrogate moms and dads to us, and let the unwanted kids live there in exchange for work around the house or ranch…

It is amazing how many adults do not realize the extent of this situation. I remember just a few years ago when I lived on Orcas Island in Washington State. (Orcas is a small island with a population of 5,000 full-time residents.) There were some 36 teenage kids and younger who wandered around without homes and parents. They were just abandoned, ignored by their parents (who had dysfunc-tional relationships), so the kids were just extra baggage. I call them the X-generation. And in today's world this problem persists in larger and larger numbers; no neighborhood or social level is exempt.

Nowhere was there a voice to communicate with. In my final years of High School I remember winning several scholarships for my artwork, but my parents would always somehow mess things up and it would not mature. I do not really know how. I suppose it was my father.   He did not approve of my being an artist. I had to find a real career, "Do what men do," he used to say.

Then one day I heard the voices of freedom. **The Beatles** …It was "utopia". I found energy in the words that seemed to click in my head. They were friends…someone who understood the madness I was going through. Just the knowing that someone out there understands you, even if you just think they do, can help you keep it together when you lose the sense of wanting to continue.

Life in the Matrix can be pretty scary for teenagers and older folks alike. They are outsiders in our social order. They are the forgotten people in the social madness of the corporate world. It was a few months after I left home when God sent another angel into my life…… Bob Dylan. Another friend gave me a copy of Steinbeck's **_Travels with Charlie._**

I spent a long time trying to find out who I was, and with whom I belonged. I struggled to find out who my mother's family was cause dad's family, well, they just did not exist. I don't remember family gatherings…. I only knew that mom came from somewhere in upstate New York… Somewhere beyond a place called Utica, New York. I hit the Road at the ripe old age of 15. And what a long road trip it was going to be. I eventually found some of my mother's relatives. They weren't all that friendly except for an aunt. .

But my aunt told me some secrets that brought me to another cousin of hers and the story went on. From there through the broken links I gleaned the story of my family. I found that I had Native blood connected to the Iroquois. My blood Grandmother was a mixed-blood and part Gypsy, and her dad, I was told, was Sioux. Her mom was from the Oneida but I was strongly advised about speaking about it. In fact I was told to think of it as an accident…funny world wasn't it or is it ……isn't *it*?

The road less often traveled would lead me to Europe, Africa, even the Himalayas and India and of course South America. (I did not like India all that much…) Then one day while standing in front of a London record shop I heard a song playing from a *Crosby Stills and Nash* album, and that was it… I was on my way back to America, and the culture shock of my life.

Woodstock was over, that was certain. Freedom was on the run, and heroes were hard to find. So I was right back at home, the loner all over again. I had my paintings and my guitar, and I could always come up with a good tune or sell a painting. I was not appreciated back home like I was in Europe. Being an artist here is synonymous with starving for some reason, but I managed to stay alive by my skills.

Music was still magical for me and I stayed with that for many years. America was different from Europe; you could make it here by playing music in clubs, but breaking into the art market here was very rough and extremely exclusive. So music and I were a way of life. In the 80's I went to a blues grass festival, met a girl who was into country music and I have stayed with country ever since. Although the rock hasn't left me, it can be upsetting to the band when you break out with a Jimmy Page riff in the middle of a John Prine song. I would find, at least, with country music your public grows old with you, and they don't desert you. But the public scene changed a lot and playing out there just wasn't fun to me any longer.

I still have my Martin guitar, but no desire to play publicly, only for the spirit of it all and friends. I followed my native roots full-time after the California divorce. All the ripping of emotions and realities sent me to the mountains of New Mexico and Colorado to heal while staying with my Native friends and teachers. There is where my song writing skills became story-writing skills and evolved into the writing of the books which people now buy all over the world.

The road has never brought me back home again. I have remained within reasonable distance of the 'other reality' only because of a daughter I love very much, who was one of the miracles of my life. Through her birth is how I came to know about Sai Baba, only I did not have to go to India; he came to me in a garden at Stanford Hospital in California when she was born. But that again is another story, and for another time. Life came in the way again and her mother and I walked our separate ways, friends forever but no longer down the same path, as it did with many of us during that period.

During my time in the Taos Mountains I guess you could say that my Spirit opened up, or was opened, and I did not resist the opening. There was little behind me… nothing to which I wanted or needed to return. I was a long time up in those mountains of New Mexico near Blue Lake, alone in a log cabin, trying to figure out what happened to the world, and learning strange secrets, and sharing incredible knowledge with my Native friends — like how to pour water in sweat lodges, and how to find my way through the woods in the dark, time travel, karma cleansing, and dream walking. It was a time of learning how to journey in the spirit world, making it real and connecting to the magic that lies within us, if we dare to dig beneath the illusion and break the chains that hold us to the emptiness of the soulless world of the image.

I'd rather ride a horse in the mountains or get lost on a Harley, or spend time with the Hopi in Arizona. Spending my time finding old ruins and strange rock drawings. I had close personal ties with people in South Dakota and Minnesota up by White Earth, where I also spent a lot of time, but the winters there were too cold and the old fire that burned in people's hearts the 70's was not there much any more.

I took to the road once again seeing what else life had in store for me. Now that I was free of the "web", I wondered where do wild things go to continue their journey? I spent a lot of time during this period in reflection and perfecting ceremony, and in between there was a lot of writing and painting sculpting and construction jobs to pay the bills. I survived making contemporary Native American art pieces for galleries and even a few motion picture companies. I took whatever kind of work came my way easily so as not to get thrown off track, and though I was not certain where the road was taking me, I was aware I was on an incredible journey.

During this time I learned a lot about 'the way' it really is from my Lakota and Hopi friends and with their help and guidance I walked into another kind of dream. I was to meet and interact with incredible people. There was always a place to pull in the pickup or motor home. Native people for the most part never care where you come from, only who you are to them and they watch with a very keen eye how you live amongst them. After three winters you are either family or you are gone.

We are born to a physical family that is true, but I have come to believe that we often find ourselves searching for our spiritual family, our true family. I was eventually adopted by Hunka ceremony by a Lakota family, and to this day the Hopi at Hotevilla, remain family although to become fully Hopi one has to give up other ways, and I am Mother Nature's son.

Everyone and everything came from Creator, and life brings into manifest situations that direct your move from one place to another, or as a friend of mine once said "*from one past-life experience to the next*." If you did not experience this restlessness at one time or another in your life, then you were most likely in a coma or dead to your own spirit. Everyone has the right to begin again, and though people can be unforgiving, life is always open to us if we are willing to change and remain open. We learn from our mistakes. I never received a rulebook for this place and know of no one else who has.

People who do not receive their knocks in life worry me. They missed something along the way and never have the opportunity to become real individuals, with real stories, their own stories that is. They never come to experience real power, and for the most part have no idea what exists beyond the boundaries of what they are told exists. They are believers in someone else's story, and merely role players. When the Winds of Change hit (and they always do), they collapse quickly and morph into another character. These are the people who tell you everyone else's story, or lie about it and make it their own so they can seem important. You can get away with that for awhile but after time the rope runs out, and when we are faced with events causing us to call up knowledge or personal power and we find we don't have it, the fall can be pretty severe.

I learned the gifts creator had given to me were special it didn't make me more or less than anyone else, but they gave me a responsibility and were not to be taken for granted. Not everyone has 'the gift' and this is perhaps because the cost has been so high to receive and learn to use this gift effectively and selflessly. I have died several times along the way, and then I had a few more experiences through ceremony of what is called Shamanic death. In ceremony, if you are willingly give up your life force to Great Spirit, you can receive incredible gifts in return. It is a trust thing…sort of an exchange and a letting go where we learn the true meaning of surrender..

In order to progress along the path of the Spirit Warrior, it is essential we come to understand the relationship of what happens between our spirit and our character self, the role we must play out in life. We must come to know what the real relationship is about between spirit and flesh if we are to help others and fulfill our contract. This is so because many times along this path we will be tested, confronted by situations where the only way through to the other side is holding on to nothing, not even death, can be your link to here.

There truly is darkness in this world, born mostly of the fears of man, and as well some that were inherited from his brothers from beyond the stars. And be not so naive as to think there are not elements in the greater realities that do not honor the rules created by religion and man. Perhaps this is why some of the 300,000 children found missing in America each year are never seen again.

A lot happened to me since I was first hit by lightning when I was camped out by the side of my parents' house. Learning to lose at love and seeing the insanity of relationships breaking up was common with almost everyone around me as I struggled through the 70's and 80's; learning about personal relationships was painful. Life was a rough road to travel, and it did not get easier during the 90's. The world today is in many ways fractured, and often I think I simply experience what will be happening here on the Earth plane to everyone else next. I guess I was destined to be on the front lines.

There are ceremonies to help us get free of our past. Others realize it through the trauma of an accident, and an NDE experience. The deeper the trauma suffered in this life the more extensive the ceremony.

When it is decided a person needed this kind of ceremonial work, the person going through the initiation experiences actual conditions in consciousness we refer to as death, although not a physical death, and not always is this done under painful conditions. There are many ways to reach this point of awareness. Shamanic death experience is as real as dying. Sometimes it is more real, for we are aware of all levels of consciousness. Without the proper benefactors, I would not recommend this path for the amateur; you might not come back, most do not.

This is why we go to our Medicine People or to a Shaman. They are guides, not gods; we go to them because they have taken the hit and learned to move on and stay on the Spirit walk. And if they are real, truly real, they never command they merely advise. It is all about teaching you to walk your walk, which is as unique as each star in the Milky Way.

You cannot fake certain things. Going beyond death cannot be faked. These experiences do not just come from reading books. In my personal situation, these ceremonies took me from the place where I could not find a way out of the labyrinth of ritualistic repetitive suffering in which I was caught, to the place where I was literally able to release the pattern, or it was removed from my cellular memory by a higher hand.

It was through the quiet death of the old memory patterns, where my pain was too much to bear, that enabled me to find something else… another avenue, a separate reality. Life became my university, and the Earth was my campus. My teachers became the people I would meet along the way, and my textbooks were the texts of the ancients. . Today for the most part, I live in a world without borders, which I guess in some ways makes me an alien on my own planet.

Through extended periods of isolation and learning, and applying strict discipline, I received the gift of transforming my character forever as I became aware of a level of consciousness that most only read about. There was no prior experience of it, and no one to teach me about the nature of the chrysalis I would pass through and eventually emerge from as a changed being.

I became a fully conscious spirit without the break in memory of my origins with Source. I knew the body I was in was not my only reality, it was merely the vehicle through which I could experience my visit here in the third dimension. There was a permanent and powerful awareness and inner knowing that I came from a Source of inexhaustible power and intelligence, and that I myself was an extension of that Source.

My experiences and inner struggles were gifts of learning the process of a greater Matrix, the Matrix of Creation. I would come to understand the Universal laws dictating the conditions through which the life force itself is expressed. I would come to understand the unlimited ways in which this force is available to us, simply for the asking. I would be able to forgive my past experiences through understanding that without them I would not have been pushed beyond the walls of the Matrix. I realized my connectedness to all is literally and scientifically something the Maya call "In Lak'esh. I blessed my hardships, realizing without them I would still be a prisoner of my own limitations.

I would come to learn how to understand and later teach the process of letting go of those ties which keep us bound to our past and in a helpless reactionary state to the programming of our past. It was my first introduction to **the Kryah**, which I would write about later in my life in " ***Through the Eye of the Shaman".***

I never intended this work as a public work when it was conceived. It was intended as a workbook for the Ascended Master Teachings I was presenting in my workshops. It is sort of a handbook for the attainable miraculous; a pathway for those seriously wanting to realize more from this life then just eating, copulating and dying after a meaningless life offering no exit from the endless cycles of suffering and unrealized dreams.. We are all children of the same God playing upon an endless field of dreams. The work, since published, seems to have taken on a life of its own, much in the way the information came to me.

I was questioning reality, and the seeming futility of life, and relationships that always started out looking like forever only to end in frustration and heartbreak. I was distraught from years of endlessly trying to live up to ideals, which we seem always to be crucified for, and losing what we had created to the corruption that seems to dominate humanity.

Why was it that everyone who seemed to follow the spiritual path has to suffer and experience so much pain and loss? Why was it that the God of all things did not help us out more often? How come the miracles only seem to take hold when there is no tangible gain realized? Why can't we strive to be Godlike and have the creature comforts? Why was it that the bad guys always seemed to walk away with the rewards, the ladies, and the bigger faster cars? Can't angels work hard and have fun too? Even if they were fallen angels mending their ways.. is God not forgiving?

I was frustrated with my work with people and the way the workshops were going. Many people came. They all wanted to experience the enigma, the wonder boy of the Art Bell Show. It was like an endless sea of people appearing at my front door. And you should understand, at that time I lived on a remote island very hard to reach.

They would come; they would, it seemed, grasp the teachings and experience all sorts of wonderment and growth. They would continue to come and the drain on me was without end. I had no time for my own life, my own family was suffering, as I was always on call, always there for the public… They became, it seemed, more interested in the enigma than their own ability and what they had come to learn. .

They would go back to their life off the island and within a few days forget the Sacred they had experienced returning once again to the hum-drum of mediocrity, drowning in their petty conflicts and using the teachings to recreate themselves as manipulators of their friends and loved ones rather then expanding on their own worth into the greater reality.

It was fine when I was there, when I was performing; but, when I was not there it was business as usual for the wayward children of God. How does it go…What is not seen is soon forgotten, and if we can't see It , then IT can't see us…As though there was an entity watching and monitoring our every move.   Silly human thoughts... We are the God watching over us; we record every action in the akashic records of our DNA… We are never judged.

This occurrence that was more than occasional was not what I had intended. Was there something I was doing wrong? Was humanity really that shallow and self consumed? The whole purpose of what I was doing was to empower them to the wonders of themselves and their own relationship with the divine. It wasn't about me becoming a chief or guru… I was experiencing self-doubt, and realizing the truth of the human condition and what keeps us Earth bound, all in the same moment.

After a time I began to suffer from depressions of my own, and saw the whole situation as a trap....One which imprisoned me and kept me from the experiences I had once had on my own that lead me to touching and knowing this reality of enchantment and magic. One day I elected to quit and go for a long walk, a very long walk.... one that would take me almost three years to complete. I spent a lot of time out in the woods and mountains, riding my horse, and hiking sometimes for days, not wanting any kind of public interaction whatsoever.

Well, that was not what Spirit had intended. The visions did not stop, and the awakening within my own being continued to unfold. I was filled with questions of my own, and suffering from an extreme lack of self-interaction and personal experience. I had many long arguments with my teachers from the higher planes. When the call came, and it did often, I would lay out my questions and demanded answers…NOW!

The answers came and flowed through me emerging as a series of dialogs with God. Almost like conversations with God, the advanced class. As far as people? Well, I would come into contact with a most remarkable circle of people, and a new journey was unfolding before my very eyes… a grand test in manifesting inner desires.

Today, I no longer do what I would call public sharing of ceremony, or the divine teachings except through my books and occasional radio and television appearances. The river of madness connected to that has been slowed. I work extensively on my Archeological projects, still perhaps on the walk that took on a life of its own.

Through the Eye of the Shaman is an amazing living teaching when experienced, and there is a sequel being written. Mankind must fend for itself for the time being and there are many teachers with whom I share intimate relationships who have come to similar conclusions. We were for a period of time given an amazing amount of information freely and without limit. Now the time has come for us, all of us to come up to the mark and own and practice what we learned and shared,

Humanity has the answers, but they will have to seek those answers out for themselves. For the moment at least the 'Show' is over, and the time for personal responsibility and commitment to our own individual walk is at hand. My work now takes me to extraordinary realizations as well as places.

Through the in-depth study of the Spiritual Myths of mankind and discovering for myself the truths lying behind those myths, I have stumbled across another form of miracle. And this tale I begin to open for all to see here in ***Days of Destiny.***

I believe with all my heart that in the realization of humanity's past, we will come to understand all that we were, and all that we represent. In this process we may come to understand what we are not, and in this way we will truly come to own ourselves, and become our true selves. Simply put, in order for us to find out what and who we are, we must first come to understand and know what, and who we are not…Then all that we are will be revealed.

We have been lied to for too long about our heritage, and the real circumstances leading us to where we are today. We are amazing creatures and closer to God than we ever could think. If only we grasp the power to remove the veils and break the chains which have imprisoned us for centuries, we realize there is nothing to attain; we have already attained it. We are divine children of a loving and allowing Mother / Father/ God and are limited only by the thoughts we think.

So during this time of transition in my life, I would often ask Grandfather (my physical elder teacher at the time), "Why am I experiencing these things?"

"Spirit is seeking you out big time," Grandfather would often tell me. "Trying hard to get you out of here, to a place where you could hear, and learn to see things as they really are. These things happened so you could make choices and perhaps learn to use your true powers. What happened to you does not happen to everyone. You should be very grateful and go and leave an offering, thanking Spirit that you have been chosen for this task."

What I learned was: What is real and what is contrived….What of reality is created by mankind, and what is not. So many of us do not see this level of reality clearly. We take so many things for granted and walk through the dream in a sleeping state not feeling the tangible threads spirit is extending to us, which sustain us. We allow the illusion to take the place of what is real and we become easy targets for those who would play with interpretations of our true spiritual consequence.

For me, all this was the ultimate Sundance, and I chose once again the Spirit path. I wonder sometimes if I ever actually had any other choices. At the time and due to circumstance, it was the only way I could see to go. Along the journey I found nothing else in this world is real except our relationships with others, all things and ourselves; that our thoughts were what we carried, and what we dealt with, and our thoughts were the memories of our experiences.

Everything in the human drama is being played out for our experience. It only happens for you in the way that it does. For the next person it will be different, for theirs is a different lesson. I know this now. In the core of my being, I know that we are all just hanging out in Grandfather's dream. All that matters is the quality of our experience of the dream; each dream is individual and unique, specifically designed for us. It is a dream game of realized virtual reality and we are the architects spinning the dream we dream, and attract the trials in accordance with those dreams on a daily, and sometimes moment-to-moment basis.

The Arcade

Most people's lives are lived playing out a game, never knowing of feeling who they actually are in essence. Most of what people hold on to, and think is so important, they lose along the way anyway, in this game of virtual reality. The nature of the game can flux and alter in a moment. What you are willing to carelessly tear out someone's heart over, in one moment, becomes lost and meaningless in the next. It can be the sound of a child crying, an accident killing someone close to you or a friend dying in the battlefield in your arms while you sit there holding their guts in place waiting for help you know is never coming. Life can be a hurricane, or it can be a quiet mountain meadow. It can be the lightning storm, or it can be the perfumed breeze that moves through the flowers of spring.

We spend far too much time not thinking, but reacting to every thing around us, and not caring about the consequences of our actions and thoughts. Words can scar, and even kill. They can wound a heart for what can seem like forever. And your heart can only be mended so many times. Then the process begins whereby we automatically rebuild a new personal Matrix. We too often play with each other's feelings, never truly realizing how gentle the human heart actually is. Sometimes I think the whole world is suffering from PTS.

For so many people, it has just been too much pain for too long and it's been too hard. Think wisely, my friend, before you steal or trample on someone's dreams; think very carefully. The consequences are severe. No one escapes the **Tunkashilas** (the Grandfathers). No one escapes dealing with the Spirit world. This dream is temporary but the Spirit world always IS. You are Spirit and thus you are part of that forever world, and we never outrun ourselves. We are the judges and jury; we elect to continue or to quit, and the price for suicide is not worth the exit.

And after the ride we realize that life is consciousness. It is our memories….. It is our feelings…… It is our experiences… It is our relationships. It is our children. It is those quiet moments we spent in someone's embrace. It is the feeling of a kiss, and the smell of her hair. It is about how we dealt with things along the journey.

We are responsible for the outcome, not the conditions of the game. The game is a dream, and we have the ability to change the dream if we choose to wake up and take responsibility. At the end of the dream….we all turn the robe into the dry cleaners for the next in line….and we take the journey. You can become the dream master if you choose…

Yes, I chose Spirit. I was released from the web of repetitive cycles. Which pathway do you choose? It is no different on either side of the fence. On one side you are numb and never taste the passion of life and therefore will not come to know the truth. On the other side, it is rougher. You get some bruises, but you learn the game and get out of the Matrix and you are free to become your dreams. On either side, you come to realize most people just pick the fence.

The road to here seems so multi-layered now; it is like following a labyrinth. So many pathways I thought were the highway to Shambala turned out to be only one path leading to another which led to another leading to several, which led to yet another. In our brief history as humanity, war and the ravagings of the centuries and cataclysmic events have broken so many links to our past.

I still struggle to calculate how to speak about some of the truths I have found. I find things about which we as humanity are in denial. We are a race lost in our own amnesia, yet the instinct for survival is strong, and we seem to know even against the odds that unless we find our roots we cannot go forward. We need to know what we are, and why we are before we take the next step…..The ultimate hallo-leap.

I have spent many years now with my Native American friends, teachers and families. It has been a long road from Wounded Knee to here. Many of the elders who stood by my side and guided me are no longer here. They have chosen to take the long journey, rather then be here in these times.

Others I know who were once treated like deities are forgotten and cast to the side. Some are paraded past by the media for people's amusement. They have lost the fire of the life force. Perhaps they stayed too long at the fair, victims of their own media hype. They could not have comprehended at the outset the coldness of this modern world.

It has become a heartless world this modern world of ours; a world where people have little compassion for themselves, let alone anyone or anything around them. We no longer realize the sacredness of the fish, vegetable, fowl, or beast.   And because of this, they cannot see the connectedness of all things. We see rather the separateness of all things. We live in a world where people are unconnected to Source… And as a result our dreams are dying.

I am the Walrus

I am Metis. That means I am mixed blood... one who walks between the paradigms of two or more different cultures. My father is **Ate Wakan**, Father Sky. And my mother is **Unchi Maka**, Mother Earth. When I needed someone to speak to or find reason to continue, it was he or she with whom I spoke. Perhaps it was a Woodstock Reality. It was that time; we were going back to the garden. It was painted vans and pickup trucks with campers on the back. I am no longer certain what it was any longer, but once there were many of us and each year there seemed less and less. Fear took them over or they stepped off the path one by one. Some became carpenters, wives, some became attorneys, some got jobs at Payless Drugs. I always seemed to be the one riding off into the sunset, looking for my next assignment.

On the road I found one has two choices: the towns or the mountains...I took the high road, and walked it with Spirit. Of my friends who took the low road, they did not seem to have much success. Most broke down, cut their hair and got stuck back in the Matrix and the journey ended for them. Others well may have gotten caught in the labyrinth of chemically induced highs and hallucinatory visions of a paradise only existing in their minds. They were lost in the canyons of the deep blue void......where they tried for the moon too soon and did not quite make the leap.

The rest of their lives became some sort of Pink Floyd nightmarish world. They hid inside and closed off their feelings, and let their dreams slip away. They closed up and withered and died, or became real-estate sales people for Century 21. It was better than selling drugs, and worked on the same premise...greed! Town was a much more cruel existence, and unforgiving. The Mountains were severe, but they were giving and non- judgmental. The lessons were harsh, and the Spiritual activity was high ....I was, for all intents and purposes, an abandoned orphan, a fallow child.

My Ancestors? I am not certain any longer who they really were. From what I have experienced and from what others have given me in bits and pieces of knowledge, or heritage, the history of this place is much more vast than has been previously thought. As I had no road map, I followed Great Spirit footprints. I have learned many things from Spirit. I know now that I am this land; I am the Rockies and the fire of the desert stone in Chaco Canyon. I am the laughing of the brook cascading down from a creek in the Kootnies, and I am the Eagle who flies trusting in the unfoldment of the next moment.

I am the lake that let Father Sky look upon his face in the morning, and Sister Moon as she prepares for the evening ceremony and dons her cloak of purple and blue. I am the mountain lake that offers refuge to the great Eagles who teach their young as they did hundreds of generations ago. I have awakened in the forest and had breakfast with them and shared Salmon upon my deck while I had coffee...I wonder how many of you who read these words know what that is like.....To sit within a few feet of one of these great beings; both you and the Eagle are at peace with each other's presence, as you look into each other's eyes, and **just know.** The energy that comes from their living spirit when they are willing to be that close to you, is like being close to a dragon .....This is the best way I can explain it. Can you remember that feeling? Did you think it was only a child's story.......

I have learned things about my two-legged ancestors from the pieces I have found which they left behind so that I would know. They had swords, and they wore leather. And some wore armor. They wore skins and danced with the Spirits. They wore feathers and sandals, as well as shoes and moccasins, and fine silk, yes, here in America, long ago. Some were very tall and I emphasize **very** tall.. Some lived in pueblos and others rode upon Elephants, we are told, in the messages they left behind… Yes, that happened here in America, and not some far-off land.

I see the world through the eyes of my ancestors; I can feel them feeling through me, realizing through me. The veils that separate the worlds are thinning. And in many ways I fit neither into their world, meaning the world of the past, neither am I part of this present world of material madness. To me this corporate society is alien to this Earth I love so deeply, as alien as the English language.

The native people today in many ways are as lost as anyone else, and some are as close as anyone else, now many calling themselves the First Nation's People. "We are not Native Americans… We are First Nation's People" they cry. Well there was, quite frankly, someone here before those who presently are referred to as the Native Americans. And there was even someone before that... so long ago they and the structures they built are becoming the Earth they were built from once again.

So when I hear the words in the news, **Native Americans**, and I look at the narrow perceptions about which everyone is busy beating themselves over their heads, I have to ask them what exactly is a Native American anyway? I know what Human being is.   I felt this with the Eagle and learned my lesson well. There are burial mounds here containing the bones of the Norsemen. Are they the Native Americans?

There are burial chambers I have seen holding the bones of Sirians and those from Betelguese (Grays) …I have held their bones in my hands. So I know it was not a dream, and now I ask you, "Are they the Native Americans we have imprinted in our minds?"

I have touched the carvings of ancient Egyptians in the New Mexico and Arizona deserts, in Colorado, and in Illinois. I stood in awe of carvings of Horus and RA that towered over me carved in the fire pink stone of desert caves… Those who carved these effigies, perhaps they were the Native Americans? I have seen with my own eyes bodies that were ten and twelve feet in height buried in crypts wearing armor, draped in silk and cotton cloth, and carrying huge broad swords…. Were these the Native Americans? Conventional history says they could not be, but there are things historians have neglected to include in the books we were taught from back in school. The family who raised me as a boy was here for at least three generations. Were they Native Americans?

therefore I would say this to you: It's all word games causing the problems with knowing who we are, and in our relationships as well. We need a new term, or we need to broaden the reality spectrum of the old perceptions and whom it encompasses. These are new times and they call for newly expanded realizations.   Our awareness of reality as a humanity has grown considerably in the past hundred years and at an accelerated rate.

This reality as it starts to take form and awakens within you will stir up a lot of emotion; there will be those who would like to silence my voice for bringing up this fact through the stones. All that does not change the fact that what I base the presentations on is "**bare bone**s" truth, and often not backed up by sanctioned historical accountings, mainly because it is not supposed to be here. And, as far as the spiritual writings? Well, they are not in accordance with nor approved by the Judaic-Christian corporations.

Therefore, before you indulge into your mental responses to this, know well from whence you come, my friend. If you get past your own judgments and look deeply into the picture, you may realize the greater truths; that is, if you have the courage. In order to speak the truth you have to see the whole truth, not part of the truth.

The greater truth is: there was someone here before them, and there was someone here before them. And they all came from the stars. Who built the pyramids here and who drew the ancient star maps? Who talked with the people from Egypt and knew the sciences of the cosmos? Who? Who talked with the Mayans and the Incas before them?

Who taught them the knowledge they possess which survives even until today, thousands of years after the supposed demise of their civilizations? You cannot live a conscious life and not ask yourself... WHO? To everyone, I say, "Truth is about to change in this regard. We are finding the bones of our ancestors, and their coins, and their artifacts and their buried pyramids beneath the forest and the field."

The proof exists. Tangible hard evidence of what I say. So let us turn this type of thinking around into the correct direction for once. I want you to have your own awakening here, not just my words. Therefore, I would ask you to consider...What if the story, the true story, was just lost in time, and forgotten or removed from our memory? What if somehow it was genetically removed from our memory? What if everything you were told was not the whole truth? What if you saw the physical proof, what would you base your foundations upon then?

Someone you Know? (unearthed in Mexico, 1926)

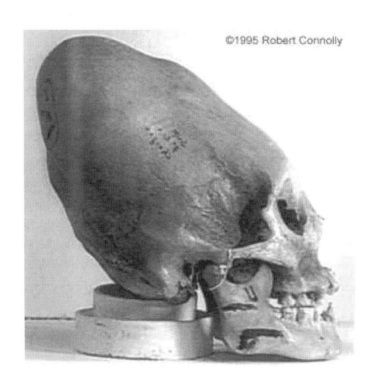

©1995 Robert Connolly

A Native American Awakening is at Hand

What you see here represents only a small token of the hard physical and written existing evidence, I present my case. What we have found indicates the Indigenous people of North America at the time of the arrival of Columbus and later when the English came upon the shores of the Delaware were themselves, for the most part, survivors of a series of apocalyptic events.

What if there were incredible civilizations here existing long before the coming of Columbus? And what if they were waiting for the return of those who said they would return. What if it were not mere myth?

There once existed here upon Terra a society that possessed a level of technology, and science that went along with a global system of trade and commerce that baffels our greatest contemporary minds. The why and how of its disappearance, along with the people who created it in their consciousness, can only bring wonderment. It is almost as if 'they' just vanished overnight, where in some instances, like Machu Picchu, they left their food in their bowls, the urgency for departure it would seem was so sudden. What could have occurred with such swiftness that whole races, and entire species vanished completely.

Here deep withn hte mountains of the Americas exist caverns with great rooms carved in living stone testifying to this lost Civilization, not a few minutes drive from Los Angeles, and as well not far from Washington, DC. These places tell a story of a people who knew much more than we know in many ways; there are rooms with giant tables where those who sat at those tables had to be at least twelve feet in height. They possessed a consciousness spanning the cosmos. Today we can't even come close. I speak fact not fiction. I come from the West where we still kick the dirt to test the soil. There are Pyramids in Tennessee larger than those of Giza... It brings up the question once again .....WHO?

Discovering the Matrix

Working closely with the Indigenous Elders of two continents, as I have and continue to do, can at times be very difficult for me. I find I have to deal with the paradox of my own personal exuberance to gift mankind with what has been revealed to me, and at the same time I must honor what my elders feel mankind is not yet ready to receive and understand.

Even as we become older and wiser and perform ceremony, we always have our mentors, or elders, whom we visit when the path gets cloudy. This has been an ongoing battle, where I have often wondered if one day I might be able to just break all boundaries and announce the bare truth of the entire picture disclosed to me through vision and ceremony. . Many of those elders are no longer with us, so the decision is no longer theirs to discern.

I have mentioned, like the larger number of the People in our contemporary world, I am Metis, born of mixed-blood, the result of intermarriages. This is not "new age"; rather it has been going on for many generations. For the last two hundred years people just did not talk of it… the subject was taboo.

In the Americas as well as the rest of the world we mixed bloods represent the major portion of the global population. Yet, we remain somehow the unseen and unheard voice of the consequence of an artificial picture of human reality, because the media does not portray the way life really is*… **The media portrays the way it is desired that we think life is**. We get a contrived picture of REALITY. Now the question arises — This presentation is therefore being designed by whom?

Oh, the subtle tricks of the mind…how stealth the real agenda of those desiring to keep the power. And yet we can sense its illusion… We all know it exists. We mostly just do not know what to do about **IT**…**IT** is the Matrix. We are caught in the web. The Matrix is what causes us to respond to pre-calculated responses, with pre-determined endings and results. The Matrix is how we are controlled. Those who design the Matrix know the outcome before it ever occurs.

The Matrix is a multi-leveled chess game, and **We the People** have become little more than pieces upon the holographic game board. It must be understood that thoughts are the building blocks of consciousness. Consciousness dictates the way and manner we perceive our reality. If one can control or manipulate the thought process, they can direct the nature in which life is perceived, even how we behave and think. And if it is being executed by technology (machines) and received by us as frequencies, well keep in mind these machines do not have to sleep and therefore the programming is relentless by its nature.

I have traveled much and experienced people with extremely diversified views of life, having many beliefs… and expressing through many cultures and hopefully I will continue to enjoy this blessing. Along the journey, I have come to see the beauty in everyone's truth, and realized the consequences of everyone's illusions.

All these differences were born of the disease of separatism. They are fired by fear, and those fears are what the political forces in power use to manipulate us. They know every button and every trigger we have. There is, however, a flaw in the program. It must constantly be reactivated, for every once in awhile we start to wake up naturally and that cannot be allowed. For if we did, then we would quickly realize the conditions of our life that control us are artificial. We would remember the Creator is within all things and all People. . Whether on this planet or another, through the dimensions, and levels of existence ascended or otherwise, all things living are born of the same mysterious Divine Source.

Yes, there is that part of me which remains wild and free. That part of me, because of my experiences and sharing of knowledge on almost every universal level, just wants to bust out of the corral and set *IT* all straight; after all, I am the Wolf. All my life I have been the warrior. When I walked away from the safe world of the matrix, I was cast out into the wilderness, abandoned and left to be devoured by the wild beasts and ravaged by the trials and tribulations of time. .

It was never calculated that I might survive long enough to figure out the codes to the Matrix itself. Yet, I was lifted and guided upon my journey **by the Great Mystery.** Let them throw their rocks at me; let them shoot at me in the dark and swing at my shadow. After all, everyone shoots at the Wolf don't they? Like Bob Dylan sang " **Everybody must get stoned...**" and things have not changed. Nor am I alone on this path any longer.

Then, there is that other part of me that has within its Divine essence the innocence of a wide-eyed child, the gift of the Magi...The child who hung upon each word coming from Grandfather's voice as he told me the stories of the **Canupa** (**cha-nu-pa**) the Sacred Pipe, and the way of life when we lived in dignity upon this earth. The Hopi Elders who would adopt me as family and shared with me in the sacred Kiva and told me mysteries of the other world shared the wisdom and compassion with me; and then there were the elders who brought me to the Temples of the Mayan.

In the Himalayas, I met the living masters, individuals who changed my level of perception forever...This boy who sat along side Anwar Sadat talking of the magnificence of Ancient Egypt as the sunset embraced the pyramids at Giza........The boy full of wonder who watched the sun play upon the steps of the Parthanon in Athens, and walked upon the same beach that Hercules washed upon after his ship wrecked in a storm. All these beings shared with me pieces of a mystical labyrinth of wisdom.

Grandmothers' Wisdom

When I speak of My Grandmother, I address also she who adopted me who was Nakota, who took me under her care and then by **Hunkpapa,** (Sioux 7 Sacred Rites _ making of relatives). I speak of my Grandmother who adopted me in Hotevilla; she was Hopi......I also speak of Ethyl...... She adopted me. Ethyl was black Cherokee. I speak of Kitty who was Nakota-Sioux.

I also speak of my Blood Grandmother who was Haudenosaunee and also a mixed blood, (from what we can tell she was Oneida and Hungarian Gypsy) whom I never knew; she who died when my mother was not yet one year old, yet through the spirit world I know she has touched me through others..

When I say my Grandmother, it also means every woman in my lineage, back through time, for it is through the woman the knowledge and the bloodline is passed. They saw the child and awakened it within me, letting me know I was not abandoned, and the great **Maka kan**, the spirit of the goddess that sustains all womanhood recognizes me and my struggle here in this dream.

I still remember the love in Grandmothers' eyes as she/they spoke to me of things that were ancient and yes, she/they spoke of the things women were not to speak of openly in accordance with traditional dogma that chained the women of her culture. It seems somehow women who manage hold on to their feminine aspect, (in spite of life's let downs) have always known the truth of these things for a silent eternity. They hold stories that have been kept within the Grandmothers' circles for generations — stories of how it was, not how it is. Certain things do not change about our humanity. They are just there sometimes and not there at other times.

Grandmother told me stories of what it was like before the coming of the disease of fear to this land, before the white man brought his demanding ways to all other Peoples of this Earth. She spoke of a time when knowledge shared amongst the Peoples of this land brought us in touch with the Stars, the Earth and each other and those from beyond our Sun…That child still remains, as does the living memory of their words.

Grandmother also warned me that the world we were going into in the latter days would be strange. The old ways were passing rapidly, and with them the ways of Sacredness by which the People lived. We would be entering a time of much confusion, and fear would be rampant. It would be as if I was mute, for I would speak and they would not hear, they would be so lost in their own fear.

She told me to always remember, "**This too would pass**". It was just a season, and we would be left always with ourselves, and our Hu-man feelings. One day I would find, when I reached the edge of the darkness, I was standing in the light…and Creator would be there beside me.

"Remember always grandson, our feelings are the gateway to our true self. Times change, and people change. The language changes…and life can become like a dream. Sometimes the vision is not always clear.

We can easily let fear come in and twist us around inside. Fear is the silent destroyer. Too many people walk on this Earth and think they know what the dream is all about…what Life is all about. They can never know, for life is a mystery. It is a story that is always ahead of us. Only Creator knows what might come in the future, for how we perceive the future depends on how we feel.

"So many wisdoms come from my memories. So many I can't even remember them all. Our People were not always as sad as they are today. No! Once they were a proud People. Once they were connected by an unbroken chain to their past. The memories were still intact. Now, that memory is scattered to the four directions. We see only parts of what we once saw. That is how I know this dream is fading. These are the end times…"

Yes, I still hear her voice as if she were right here with me, even now. I think of Grandmother often and our talks together remain with me as alive as they were in those moments. I think about her courage, always turning the day into a good day, despite the occurrences of the moment. I have always seen the heart of the People as she taught me.

Grandmother also helped me to understand that prophecy is a formless thing. That it is mutable and not written in stone. It is a glimpse of a potential future, not an absolute. I have always, to the best of my ability, tried to employ her wisdom in all my experiences and relationships: The principles of the '4-*D Reality*' being *D*iscernment, *D*iscretion *D*etachment, and *D*esire the basic ingredients for a well-lived and honorable life.

There are many things the prophecies tell us about and certain events appear to be inevitable. Once we had the science to know how the universe worked, and now that knowledge is lost to us. When we lose a part, then Spirit comes in and speaks to us. That is the gift of prophecy, a gift that compensates for our lack of knowledge. One thing I am certain of now in my maturity: Grandmother was correct in saying to me that the future will be very different indeed from how we experienced life as in the past.

In delivering the message of Great Spirit and the oneness that comes through me, I realize I am blessed by Creator in walking this path, this Spirit walk that I walk. I have come to see that more and more People today are ready for hearing the Real Truth — The Truth was once too hard for them to comprehend and accept because they were in my generation, caught in the webs of dogma and outmoded perceptions of separatism.

I have spoken about many things over the years to more people than I can remember, regarding Prophecy and the Wisdom of the Indigenous Masters. Much of what I once shocked audiences with now is being spoken about in their living rooms and written about openly and freely by many in periodicals and can be found in the book stores.......

The Thunder Prophecies

I have spoken often in my life about the Star Nations and our relationships with the star beings. In my Book **Last Cry,** this shocked some and inspired others. I have spoken about the plagues and told **the Prophecies of the Seven Thunders** in my book **Winds of Change.**

When presenting the prophecies I have recieved from the indigenous masters, I have spoken of geophysical Earth changes changes in cliamtes heat waves that would kill thousands, draughts and raims, and things like animal mutations and disease (the new plagues). I have spoken about changes in the international monetary forms of exchange, and within our sciences. And of these things that I spoke of, as we appraoach this third year of the new Century, many have occurred or are occurring.

The emphasis on my subjects dealing with change have always been with the more subtle forms of change, which in reality have the greatest effects upon us as a species. For what we think and how we think effects the outcome of everything — The Emotional storms, the dimensional shifts, the emergence of the new octaves of energy and thought effect life as we have known it.

We are now about to enter another level of experiences as we enter the Sixth and Seventh Thunders and witness the conditions that bring on the remaining prophecies before our eyes. . Much of what is occurring would have happened regardless of our awareness of it or our unawareness of its occurrence. However, the effect of what is occurring has everything to do with our conscious awareness, and the way in which we choose to deal or do not deal with the situations at hand. It is school after all..

Portions of **The Stargate Files**, presented here, are a partial compilation of visions of the elders of many nations and cultures. It is the dream of their children as well. The Mountain Brotherhood is comprised of individuals representing diverse backgrounds who are currently living on both continents of the Americas. The Brotherhood utilizes the combined knowledge and efforts of a complete circle. It is therefore multi-cultural and holistic in its mission.

The Mountain Brotherhood of which I speak is not an organization, corporation or political group or church. It is just that - a brotherhood, a sisterhood. If only there was a word like 'a Soul Hood', that was '*non-genderal*.' It is an ancient recognition of Souls who have been at this game a very long time, lifetime to lifetime. The Brotherhood is a living link to the truth of our reality going back thousands of years — back to the time of Hermes. We are runners in a race to save mankind, a race that is as ancient as the Pyramids themselves. The wariors are coming, and we are but the messcngers before tha Battle that will ensue as sure as you sit and read this page, this very moment. ANd like this moment the battle itself will pass into the dimension of memory.

This sacred mission and the message is exhortative, as certain events are about to occur that would be devastating to humanity as well as the planet. There is little time left to take proper action; however, what is seen can be avoided and at the very least rendered to occur with less intensity and contained to specific areas with lesser consequences.

If the spark of divinity can be re-ignited within the souls of mankind, we can and would achieve a unity through the principles of compassion, then the outcomes can be changed by humanity acting as a whole and exercising Divine effort.

We can, if we choose, bring about cohesiveness in consciousness as well as an understanding of the subtle energies of the universe and attain a positive outcome. Already, we are in the sixth thunder and the seventh is beginning to take form.

The seeds of destiny already have been sown; it is time to return to the fields and nurture our spiritual powers, awaken to our natural heritage, and claim our place in the cosmos. We are, after all, the Children of the Sun, born of a Divine ancestry beyond description, and the time is coming close when we will once again walk amongst the gods. And slowly the veils of ignorance are being removed from our eyes and our thoughts through an amazing life process called evolution. No one and no thing can stop the process, it would be like trying to reverse the flow of the river.

THE SIXTH THUNDER

As it is seen presently, mankind is coming into an experience where we will have to deal with the dilemma of making distinct choices on how life will be upon this plane. We are about to realize that, in fact, thought does manifest the nature of reality and that we are not the only form of intelligent life in the universe. We will either come to terms with our raging emotions and random thought projections, or face total annihilation of the species as well as the environment that sustains our life forms here on Planet Earth.

We can either succumb to the present matrix, which will evolve into implemented programs of complete enslavement of human consciousness and is a corrupted program at every level of expression, (It is caught in a cyclical pattern that seems to endlessly lead us back to self-destruction.)...... Or, humanity can choose to awaken and claim their heritage as living gods and take the responsibility necessary for being participants in a galactic universe.

To some, this is a strong statement… radical at least, perhaps offensive, and against everything people have learned to obey in the Matrix of their allowed perception of reality. Some might even see the truth of it, yet they remain imprisoned in their fear and confusion (born of living a partial life), where the only emotions they themselves have remaining are attached to denial, suffering, shame and pain. They are helpless to effect change of any kind; they are caught in their own patterns, like an insect in the spider's web.

Then again, there are some who would say this kind of thinking is lunacy, delusionary, and that Jesus will save them…they only have to give a little more to the church for extramunction and get on a payment program for special deals.. Yes, there are those who do not appreciate free thought and they come from all faiths, just as those who cherish Free thought exist in all faiths. When you are insecure, this is how you respond to something that you do not understand. When you build your house upon sand, well, there are going to be foundation problems. I would ask you, "Is it lunacy to choose a life based upon divine principals, following the understanding of the Universal Masters and following the pathway of divine love and compassion?"

Each one of us is responsible for our own journey. The choices we make, and the acts we commit. No one saves us; at best they can guide us to fulfill ourselves, and help us remember our life's mission and purpose. The Master Yeshua NEVER LEFT and is immortal to our reasoning, and the Christos is within all of us existing as a potentiality. The realization and attainment of that potentiality is a choice.

The existence of free will is rare in this universe, and was allowed to us as a species because of our Divine origins. For we are much more than we allow ourselves to think. Imagine everyone thinking and acting toward each other as a Christ… If thought truly creates the nature of reality, and it does, then it is a potential reality that we, as a species, can achieve that measure of Divine grace. Albert Einstein once said.. *"If the thought exists, then it is already a reality in consciousness…$E = mc^2$"*

If you think this is all such rhetorical Lunacy, I ask you, "Is it Lunacy to knowingly choose an existence of worshiping death and submitting to the necromancers whose only ability and talent lie in their capacity for living off the dreams and life force of others?" I ask you, "Is it Lunacy to live your entire existence enslaved to the Matrix that only perpetuates cycles of self-destruction and denial of the God force within us? Is it Lunacy to knowingly choose a pathway of existence riddled with fear, war, disease and the deliberate imposed suffering and even death of millions for the sake of the amusement of a selected elitist group of materialistic vampires?"

Is it Lunacy to think that what we are experiencing is the climax of what it seems has been an eternal struggle between the light and the dark... a war of angels perhaps?

.....Is it possible we are experiencing the culmination of a humanity struggling for centuries to complete its experience with the concepts of mortality and limited existence...?

That we have been living upon a merry-go-round where every orthodox religion seems to be little more than cults perpetuating dogmatic systems of mind control, designing our worship and our surrender to death?

When a self-appointed few exercise their power to control the masses and keep them in deliberate state of ignorance so the knowledge is known and coveted by only the select group....It is called a Tyranny.

When the system of social conditions no longer supports the wishes of the people and the laws of the Creator, it becomes decadence. When that society manipulates every living structure created by its consciousness from the treatment of the sick and less fortunate, to the deliberate desolation of personal liberty for all off its people, that society is condemned by its own hand.

When the structure therefore created engages in the deliberate destruction of universal truths, and the wholesale destruction of the Earth and its natural balance to such a degree that life as we know it can no longer be sustained...It is removed by that which gave it life.

There exists no structure, people, organization or military force that will escape the universal laws of divine providence. For there is a higher order, a supreme Source that will make its presence known, and that time is sooner in manifesting then we think, in fact it is already occurring.

There is no judgment; there is only choice and consequence for our actions or non- actions. You hold the keys to destiny in your hands. If you only knew the power you command, no one could ever enslave you again. In a moment you could change the outcome of eternity.........I am only the messenger.

May Great Spirit be with you.

The Seventh Thunder

" ..One day there will appear a great Star in the heavens brighter than even our Sun. This star will be so bright that there will be no nighttime when this star is seen ...and the skies will open and there will be heard a voice, and this voice will vibrate through the whole of the earth and every living thing upon it vibrate down to their bones. It will be the voice of Grandfather which has not heard since the creation...."

"Then we will hear other voices coming from the heavens, people will think that it is the Angels or Kachinas returning. This voice will sound like a great wailing to some and like a lullaby to others. At first it will be as many voices, then these voices will become *as one voice and the great oneness will touch all that is....these will be the sounds of the creation.... We will see appear in the sky the Great Bow the elders have prophesied.*

" It is said of this time that even the seeds that are still beneath the earth will struggle to rise to touch this great light that will appear...... The world as we knew it will be no more, but there will be a new world, where there are no lies and the suffering will be no more, for hatred and evil will have been wiped clean from this earth forever, the purification will be complete......There will be only the great peace. In this time we will learn to live once again with our brothers and sisters from the stars, for what once was will be again, when the once and future king returns..."

Shunkmanitu Tanka Wanagi
The Ghost Dance ...Yucatan 1999

CONSEQUENCES of the SolAR CyclES

Intense activity of our Sun is presently being demonstrated. The Sun is currently in the primary stages of a cycle, which comes about every 1150 to 1200 years. This cycle has been recorded throughout our history in many cultures. However, it is obvious there is very little surviving knowledge of these events easily comprehended by contemporary western science.

The Petraglyphs and ancient writings, which sometimes are encrypted in the very architecture of the buildings, have over the last 500 years been devastated by our own cyclic journey of war and self-destruction. This cycle left us only pieces and remnants of what was once a knowledge mankind shared for many thousands upon thousands of years. It is only to our contemporary civilization that the mysteries of the cosmos, and the technology of building pyramids has been lost. We are, as it were, gods lost in amnesia.

Here in America there is much evidence presently being recovered from these ancient civilizations telling us of a devastating series of events that, for the most part, totally annihilated the previous civilizations. These will be released in a future Stargate File on my website http://www.Robertghostwolf.com and a subsequent book. The 'They' I speak of are those who built the thousands of pyramids and structures remaining as ruins upon our shores. So complete was this destruction that some of those societies were totally removed from the matrix of consciousness, and their knowledge and genetic lineage along with them.

Much of the disasters we have witnesses in the news recently as horrific as they might seem will pale in comparison to what we will see and experience as a result of this present cycle of the Sun. Perhaps this could be the Great Star that so many Indigenous People prophesize is coming. Along with prophecies of three days of darkness, there is also that which speaks about fourteen days of light. They speak of a star so bright that the light of our little yellow Sun is neutralized by its brilliance.

We are presently in the cycle of the KaliYuga; the Goddess Kali is often times called the destroyer, and her husband, is Shiva. Shiva brings balance and wisdom and marks the end of the cycles of darkness. Witout the balance of Shiva the dance of Kali might destroy the universe. For who cna say where the wind begins and ends ? We only know of its presence in the moment that it is. Kali is also called the Mother Goddess of us all. She is the energy of transition and purification, a dualistic energy bringing the promise fulfilled of new life along with destruction or purging of evil. This is very like the Hopi prophecies telling about the coming of the Purifier and the purging of Evil from this reality. Whoever said the Purifier was male? Were the Hopi, when they appeared on the Art Bell Show, talking about the KaliYuga, and the cyclical seasons of the universe?

Before we move into the cycles of the Sun and the visions and prophecies of what will occur, it is important to understand the importance of the energy of Kali, for it is an intricate part in our remembering the original knowledge of why things are the way they are.

Entering the New Century _Thunder Prophecies

This new century will bring forth experiences that we as a humanity have never known before. Also it will bring on experiences we have known before as a humanity. We are at the final stages of this dream that is closing as a new dream is emerging and we as a humanity fulfill our divine destiny. We

are becoming and morphing from within. Every step we take, every thought we hold and embrace will come back to us ten fold, our trials as well as our gifts are right before us.

These times seem to many of us as a strange. We are awakening from a very deep slumber, where we seem somehow familiar with what is occurring. Many may find very often after an event occurs we have a feeling somehow we knew it would all along. We are sharing visions as well as thoughts. We are sharing emotions all in the grand sense of the God Force instructing us how to be individuals as well as part of the oneness.

Often those emotions surge and explode and we struggle as divine essences to break the chains that have enslaved us and held us in ignorance for a very long time. The friction means you are alive, the pain is in not understanding the circumstance and as well in not owning our part of the reason for all we see occurring.

Much of what you are about to read will have a kind duplicity in its effect on you emotionally. What is presented here is a discussion of sorts. A running dialog between minds — yours and the author's, and often the divine may intercede. You merely have to get out of your own way as the author did, and let the information flow through you, holding that which you feel and letting the rest go by, as it may not apply to you but might well be someone else's reality experience.

Nothing here is written in stone as they say, and your personal choices will determine your private experience as certain events occur in the unfoldment of the human experience as it is presently seen. Whatever is or may occur around you does not necessarily have a direct effect upon your personal being. How one chooses to deal with any situation in a given moment determines the impact that experience will or will not have upon that individual's life. Understand?

Presently the unfoldment of the human drama, at least here in the Americas, is seen as presented... If you don't like the potential outcome, then do something about it; you do have the power to change at least your own personal interaction with an event or experience. That is a God-given right and an immutable Divine Law. Miracles do occur if you create the space for them to occur. Let us proceed.

There will be many choices before us as a species, including the choice to persevere or keep on the path we are presently headed down — that of self-annihilation. We will come face-to-face with many challenges, and face some serious ramifications as we reap the harvest from our corrupted thinking and suffer the effects of duality.

We will also be entering a period of natural geophysical Earth Changes, and dimensional shifts. In the short view, it is going to be hard times; in the long view, humanity will achieve a state of plausible Divinity and grace at the other end of the tunnel. At the other end it will be a very different world and a galactic reality. We are reaching graduation time, and school is letting out.... now we must find real jobs.

There will be much upheaval in the family of mankind during the first three years of the 21st century. We will experience much social change and shifting paradigms, which seemed our very foundation. Many societies will crumble, as if built of sand. The amazing thing will be, as it is seen, the total lack of resistance to the apparent control by Big Brother policies and edicts that will be pressed forth by world governments, removing as it were almost all access to personal sovereignty.

Volcanoes and ' Thermo-terranic' activity

I know that you want dates... think of it this way: If you had dates you would manifest the when of things. If you rather observe the course of events, and the changing of conditions, you will develop greater powers of adaptability. This will empower your development of consciousness and as well, activate the DNA because of the energy you will be moving through you. You are like the earth, made from the same elements as she. She will mirror you and you will mirror her. What she is doing is, in the long run, for the advancement of the species.

The elements will respond to you and as you clear away confusion and indecision she will come to your aid in ways as yet indescribable. The opportunity for you to change in accordance to her frequencies all arise with greater and greater fluidity as you yourself harmonize with her already advanced vibratory fields.

The onslaught of the coming changes has been, in a sense, delayed and softened so that you might adjust and be better able to handle the shifting of frequencies and merge into the new consciousness that is and will result. Much like the mother ignoring the raging of their adolescent children as they go through their growing pains, you personally might ignore her interaction with us. She has never ignored her interactions with her children.

There will be severe tectonic and Thermoterra (new word) activity in the US. As it is seen there will be a series of major Earthquakes in the central US. They will begin in the Southern Mississippi Valley area, and continue for a five-year period with increased intensity culminating around the Yellowstone area.

The Eastern portions of Montana, especially the Helena area and south going towards the Eastern Borders and down towards Wyoming will be involved. There is a new mountain range being born here that will emerge towards the latter portion of the next century as the intensity of the Earth changes increases.

(Thermoterra, Rivers of flowing magma that move below the Earth's crust.) Thermoterranic: The movement of this magma will, as the Earth's crust begins to compress and fracture due to pressure from the plate movement and the building up of heat in the Earth's core, cause fractures to appear upon the Earth's surface. These fractures will cause at first strange behavior of the Earth itself.

We will see whirlpools of soil that will swallow houses and even large portions of land quite suddenly. This, as the infrastructure below begins to collapse and the energies released alter the physics of the geophysical compounds. Scientists will be baffled because they will not be able to explain such occurrences by former means and technology.

In many of the areas where this begins, it will only be a short time before the heat below the surface heats up the surface to the point that that which is combustible will burst into flames.

This will cause many areas throughout New Mexico to become volatile. You can expect existing water aquifers to disappear in many areas, as well many sources of potable water will become contaminated due to toxic gasses being released below the Earths surface through the labyrinth of existing tunnels that exist in that area. This was explained in Last Cry, for this will begin the 'fire storms' bringing sudden devastation where they ignite and are fueled by high winds which will be 'at times' better than 150 miles per hour.

The Fire Storms will destroy untold millions of acres throughout the Western states. Some will be the result of natural occurrences (including accidents due to human error). Others still will be the result of accidents and covert activities occurring in the secret underground complexes developed by the military along with alien (ET) forces.

The nature of these fires will be unnatural, and they will have extreme pulsating heat, at the core. They will seem to breathe and take on a life of their own, as helpless fire fighters and even the military stands by unable to do anything, due the intensity of the heat and the speed at which the fires travel.

In many places where these particular fires occurs the rock will fuse like glass and appear to have, in many places, a patina finish such as is seen on fine pottery. This will be beautiful to see after the surface cools down and the rains wash the ash and soot off the stones.

Whole mountainous areas will appear as colorful paintings in the desert landscape due to the mineral content and the different reactions to the flame and heat. It will be hard to remember during these terrible 'Fire Storms' that this is one of the ways that the Earth renews herself. The event is in a way a kind of forced reduction in human population allowing the forest to renew themselves over the next century.

However do keep in mind the Secret Complex reality. Some of this forced human population reduction to these forest regions will be intentional, and part of an agenda for the emerging of alien and human life upon the " New Earth'. Presently, the curious mind can discover for themselves documents detailing this strange Agenda wherein the forest and wilderness areas of the US are to be cleared of human inhabitants for a 75 mile buffer zone, this in accordance to plans to make all the forest and wilderness area part of predetermined globally protected regions.

We will see cycles of these earthquakes begin to build up in central Mexico. The Thermoterranic activity will cause the magma to move into areas it has not been previously. The Basalt and limestone near the seashores in Mexico will collapse with greater frequency.

Also the volcanoes will begin to become even more active than they are now. Those will start the movement of the Pacific Rim (West coast from Mexico to San Francisco, California to move in a Northward direction as the prophecies have foretold. See (Last Cry Native American Prophecies and Tales of the End Times).

Again in the South West we have problems arising in New Mexico and Arizona. This will encompass a very large area reaching as far south as 200 miles South of Mexico City. The sleeping giants are being disturbed (knowingly) that lie beneath the ground in the Havupi (Lava) tubes below the surface. The continued drilling for natural gas in the north, combined with the exploration for oil in Mexico will cause the giants to awaken.

This is an old prophecy, which has been ignored. There will be Thermoterranic activity continuing to intensify and we will see many strange things occur upon the landscape.

Fissures sometimes several miles long appearing overnight from which escape steam and toxic gasses creating a fog of death over the land.

By the middle of the first decade of the New Century we will witness many millions of square miles of the old forests turned to ashes from the enormous number of Fire Storms.

There will also be a strange kind of fire storm. fires that destroy thousands of acres beneath the surface of the land, where in places the surface temperature of the land itself will reach temperatures high enough to explode bushes and grasses into flame.

Once this activity has begun, the already existing Havupi tubes will become increasingly hotter. The heat will build up to such a point that thermo activity will be noticed strongly all along the Pacific Coast up into British Columbia. New hot springs will appear and there will be constant trembling of the Earth.

When Popo blows in Mexico, (there will be three or four eruptions before the big event) it will also trigger the mountain known as the Smoking Mirror. This will result in severe volcanic upheavals between the two and will, in a sense, rock the plate causing the escape valves that have protected this area from self-destruction, such as hot springs and other geothermic activities to respond to the movement of the magna below. The seventh time Popo Blows will begin the great devastation.

The faults offshore will open and the seas will be steaming pools of water; sea life will die quickly and the gases escaping from the underground passages will be extremely toxic. Raising the ocean temperatures as much as 15F degrees or even more.

Once the plates have been rocked sufficiently, there will be a response from the entire range all the way up to BC, Canada. In the Pacific Northwest, one of the Sisters will erupt. There will be three eruptions and then Grandfather...Rainier... will, as has been prophesied, erupt and it will be devastating. When this happens, the Sleeping giants will respond. We will see volcanic activity that has not been experienced for many Ages. There are details of the Rainier occurrences we can expect again in my book * Last Cry.

The Pacific area all the way along the Coasts of Asia, Japan and Indonesia will be devastated and will experience intense reformation of the land in that area. Many areas are already rising in the oceans there. And ancient cities are reappearing, bringing great questions as to the previously thought of historical accountings of the origins of mankind.

There will be a series of Earthquakes in Central Mexico,(8-10 on the rector scale) accompanied by firestorms and the spontaneous combustion storms in the desert areas. The ground will heat up and the volatile desert scrub will literally burst into flames. This will even be seen in the Southern Arizona regions East of Phoenix and all the way to Blythe, California.

This second series of Earthquakes will lead into the eruption of Grandmother below the surface of Mexico City. A dome will begin to rise and then what appears as a new volcano will appear to form. This will break open and the force of Grandmother's eruption will be felt around the World.

What was once Mexico City will literally be blown into the heavens and the Sun will not be seen for many days, due to all the debris that will be several miles high in the air. This will cause a huge cloud to wrap itself around the Earth's Girth, and the darkness will cause much panic with those into the Armageddon beliefs.

This eruption of Grandmother will bring a response again from Rainier, which will call to the cousins in New Mexico. There, many of the sleeping giants will begin to awaken and this will start to occur all the way up to Central Montana.

Yellowstone will become a flowing bed of Magma in many areas, and new rivers will emerge as well as new lakes. The granite of the Tetons will keep much of the seismographic activity limited to moderate effect. However, outside the mountains, in the flat land, there will be great swelling, and like the tail of the lizard, the ripple effect will cause some severe destruction.

Another result of the Volcanoes will be as it was seen in vision...cold weather in certain areas where it was once warm. Also, certain things will no longer grow where they once grew normally. New plants will begin to appear in many areas as we find ourselves moving into a new cycle of weather patterns that will be very unstable, at least in the transitionary stages which could last as long as 40 years.

We will need to focus on new methods of growing foodstuffs, and many things of this nature will bring people back to a more home-based system of self-sufficiency. However, it should be seriously considered that we will not be able to depend on the Natural weather to grow our crops and feed our livestock off those crops, as well.

As we near the mid-century we will see many new waterways appear, and new vegetation will appear as many areas begin to take on a completely different nature; temperate areas will become either hotter or colder depending upon the final flux of the magnetic poles. Think of the magnetic poles as being fluid and not solid. If one were to upset a large bowl of water there would be much rippiling before the water finally setteled.

The Emerging Anti Christ...

We will witness many social and economic revolutions. Social stress under the aging and decaying social structures will see the outbreak of violence worldwide. Civil strife with 'brother pitting against brother', in a new kind of civil action, a holy war... a War of the Human Spirit against a system that has no soul, no conscience, one that regards all people as a disposable commodity, to fulfill their corporate needs..

The rebellion eventually develops, as people can no longer find recourse to correct the condition imposed by the Corporate Governments and will tear this country apart. It will be a war zone and the ramifications will be such that we will see an eventual breaking up of the States into separate regions and governments.

The federal bureaucracy, already behaving like a dying whale that has beached itself, in attempts to hold on to control and keep its commitments to unholy alliances, will impose more and more regulations on everyday living. Eventually there will be a rebellion as the true face of our Governmental body is revealed. Expect the rebellions to begin around the year three of the new century and be the strongest in the Western States.

Which will begin to separate the amount of control the Federal government can exercise within a state's borders and be considered to be infringing upon the "Free Republic" status of that state.

There will be the appearance of a very bright celestial body in our heavens, near our sun, which will mark the switching of gears so to speak. (2003 - 2004) This will be the signal of the beginning of cataclysmic proportion geophysical changes headed our way. The influence of this celestial body will affect our planet very strongly, causing severe tidal waves, earthquakes and volcanic activity to result, from the pulling and stretching of the Earth's outer crust. Some will say of the celestial body " behold it is Nibaru, the Dwarf Star of old, returned..."

The present economic standards will change radically and we will see implemented a Matrix of the new order, whereby all finances within the matrix will be performed solely through electronic exchange... Mone, as we presently understand it will become non-existent as a means of exchange. Instead we will trans verse to an electronic means of exchange...(The Mark)

Within the first four to five years we will see the turning of events and social situation allowing for the emergence of that which has been prophesied as the Anti-Christ. The Anti-Christ is a dualistic manifestation in concept and in occurrence.

First, the environment must be manifested for the ultimate rise of this Emperor of divine rule over the Earth so that he can have a theatre in which to perform and a stage to play out his part in the drama.

When events mount and the drama of global financial collapse of the banking system is eminent, this stage is created.

Then we will see the actual actor emerge onto the scene. This drama, which is intertwined with the Armageddon illusion, will transpire during the first quarter of the new Century....

The rise and demise of his presence upon this plane shall last for two decades as it is presently seen, after the beginning of the geophysical Earth Changes. (Keep in mind this book will not be readily available during that period of time). This Anti-Christ is a real individual not a metaphor. The manifestation of this individual is the result of the consciousness existing that allows for the being to express. The condition always precedes the result.

He is already here upon this plane and is a dark-skinned individual, not necessarily black, but dark and swarthy in appearance, meticulously groomed and well-schooled. Remember, he has been schooled for presentation to the world since childhood, with the plan of getting him accepted and willingly placed into power.

By many, this one will be viewed as a spiritual savior for a time — A Grand Guru, if you will, and a successful and powerful businessman....For we are living in the material world, are we not? We are living in the corporate illusion of reality, are we not? If you have doubts about this I suggest a ride through the suburbs of the Bay Area in California... Silicon Valley to be exact.

It is Plasticville, U.S.A. Every town is the same layout. We shop in the same stores. Everyone wears the same outfits and goes to the same restaurants. There are rubber stamps of this scenario in every state now I believe.

We are lost in OZ, Toto... The land of the Golden Arches where on any Sunday morning one will find more cars in the Wal Mart Parking lot than at any church. There are no individuals, just the system that works for everyone and we have become beige in the process.

This Dark Prince of Islam is going to appear at first as everyone's savior, is he not? Remember this entity is already on the scene and is presently quite influential in the banking empire, which Islam has created and is centralized in Paris.

It is important to note that although this dark Prince will come out of the lands of Islam, he himself will not be of true beliefs of the faith of the Prophet Mohammed...he will be a true philistine...and his magic will be of the dark arts..

He heads a banking corporation, which has become quite a manipulative force in the Southern European (Mediterranean) arena, and has strong ties here in the South Western States. Keep in mind this a very old and karmic struggle going back many thousands of years and has its roots in the original empires thought of by most as merely mythical legends.

This physical presence of the manifested Anti-Christ is being felt even now by the Earth herself. She is reacting to this part of her dream of us, for he would desire to control even her desire, and there will be seven major seismographic calamities in the area once known as the Land of Islam.

His reign (yes, there is a female counter-part) will be precluded by the presence of a young leader who will acknowledge our tie-ins with Reptilian forces also known as the forces of Enlil/Jehovah. This has its beginnings in the Lands of Islam. It is all about an illusionary dance. The greatest ruse in the history of the world: the name of the play is "Armageddon".

The agenda is designed for the purposes of getting us to give up our dominion of this plane, and this Earth, by our own free will. Already preparations are under way for the return of the great ships of the Siriens and the Dwarf Star in the Land of Islam. This unholy alliance will manifest much tyranny upon this plane, and be the force behind the Anti-Christ's powerful reign that will not, at first, be opposed.

There will be an early attempt to stop this secret agenda in the Middle East. Expect a major war there within the first five years or so of the New Century.

This war will open an ulcerous sore in an already simmering pockt of discontent. There will be a rash of civil outbreaks, as the supporters of the dark one create pods, or cells of terrorist militia. These have the potentiality to expand into a war that spreads throughout all of Islam...and thus fulfilling the Armageddon scenario in its wake.

The Middle East is a powder keg of corruption and street gangs assuming their adopted roles in affinity to their spiritual myths and legends.

As I said it will be a failed attempt and back fire on its initiators, with terrible consequence to the US financially as well as politically.

During the reign of the Anti-Christ in America where he will fist appear as a Spiritual Leader, we will witness the struggle between the forces that hold to the original teachings as spoken of by the Hopi and Mayan cultures and in the Christian influence in Cayce's prophecies about the Law of One..

It will be as if the War of the Angels has touched the Earth itself. It is a very old war, and far from over; it has been going on since before the fall of Atlantis.

Many ships will fill the skies day and night, and will be visible to millions of people. The South West will experience many of these as much of that area ihas long been under control of the Earthly Alien Forces. Huge mother ships sometimes 2 miles long will be sited almost on a nightly basis.

These occurrences will also be fairly common in the North West in the regions of Washington and Oregon .

Within the first year of the new century there will be open fly-by displays. These ships will appear over populated areas in a show of strength, not much unlike the military parades of the Nazis, and the Red Guard in Moscow. It is the way tyrants do things.

It has been played out in every age of western civilization. And in the end of every trial run, the tyrant meets an unpleasant demise.... from Julius Caesar, to Octavian, to Justintine, Nero, to Caligula, to Napoleon, to Hitler, to ..... The list goes on.

And we will begin to see great auroras in the heavens indicating the battles in the heavens are close at hand, and the contest will have begun between forces of dark and light. The prize for the winner will be Terra and her peoples.

If the will of the People is not sufficient to oppose the will of the returning force who holds claim to Earth, then they will overtake us. They possess a superior technology and are instrumental in creating systems which presently control the state of reality they choose for us to perceive. Globally, weather will continue to become increasingly unstable and we will see massive crop failures, world wide, resulting. Then as it will become impossible to grow and harvest crops to feed the worlds' billions, the obvious will occur and we will witness the rise of little warlords as society regresses back into its more animal nature.

Travel will also become prohibitive due to the severity of the weather and governmental restrictions between states and a periodic intervals the international borders are closed off in the US.

Anyone who is not in submission to the reigning political powers will be viewed as a Terrorist, and the compounds presently being built across the country for this very event, will be filled quickly.

· Expect abnormal prices of the cost of goods in the marketplace will reach unacceptable proportions, such as lettuce for $5 a head, and so on. Water $2 a pint, coffee $10 per pound

Many will be unable to possess food or obtain supplies and fuels unless they are part of the system. All population will be monitored and read by computerized law enforcement programs. Much of the stress upon the legal system due to over population in urban areas will be handled by computerized systems. Even the prison system will show the effects of this, as prisoners will be kept in mechanized units with very little contact and interaction with other living beings.

As the exterior structures of society continue to break down the urban areas will become more and more dangerous, and as the systems of social order begin to break down and these beings once again roam loose, they will be a problem. They will not be as others and will be again mutated forms of their former selves. We will see the beginnings of whole generations being born and raised by the state in the new correctional programs presently being established as a wall of defense against the coming social rebellions that are foreseen by the NWO and our political leaders.

There will be flooding at the beginning of the century that has not been experienced since the time of the Great Floods. Whole areas will be washed away and lost beneath the sliding mountain ranges.

At the same time in the western states great draughts will be experienced for many years. Strangely this will give birth to a movement of a new form of Christianity being expressed by the people who will suffer hardship, and in that hardship have a need to pull together for survival. Survival of the economy, the livestock and to create a force worthy of controlling the tens of thousand of immigrants that will be flooding into the area from the South as well as foreign countries.

This form of Christianity will be influenced by the multi-cultural expressions of many faiths blending into one. And will be likened unto the original faith that spread from Judea throughout the Euro-Mediterranean regions at the on start of Yeshua's experience as the Nazarene.

This new faith will give rise to a strong resistance to the blind following of this new Messiah that rises from the East.

This Anti-Christ will appear in Southern Europe first, emerging from the Lands of Islam. Public notoriety will follow as he is brought out before the public eye in America. If America is stopped the dream of free will and enterprise will fall along with it, removing any resistance other than political debate

At first the political and spiritual forces behind placing this individual will be welcomed, and he is already establishing himself as a gifted being in solving problems between the European and Muslim cultures and economic situations.

He will present many cures for failing world economies; and, as the old standards of pride in nationalism fall away, the people will rally behind his programs and support him, for he will bring food and hope of survival back to those lost in otherwise inevitable demise in the rioting carcasses of our decaying world societies.

This entity will see a meteoric rise to power, his influence and the veil of fear and darkness follows in his wake. His rise to power and his tyranny will be seem unstoppable as it sweeps through the Mid-East and continues on into the western countries.

This will be made possible as the economy and social conditions deteriorate from the ravages of the severely erratic weather patterns and diseases caused through the monstrous experimentation with biological warfare elements.

Many will perceive that this individual possesses supernatural abilities. Remember he was trained since childhood for his performance, trained then as an adult in the European Market Place and then emerging as a spiritual being in America just prior to his entry into the stage of global politics.

The presentation and acceptance of this will be uncontested, as most are unschooled about the knowledge of the ancient schools. Everything about this individual will be based upon materialism and technology.

It will seem like an unstoppable wave of public opinion, as hysteria takes hold, almost like a traveling rock star. All the while his use of world-wide media to employ his desired belief patterns amongst the world populations will make him appear much more capable than he truly is.

Although, be assured that this individual possesses great abilities in the normal sense, and will have been schooled in the ancient wisdoms of the mind. However, it must be remembered also that this individual was specifically bred for his position...actually genetically engineered.

The realization of this fact will raise some interesting questions about what once was spoken about as the Secret Societies, as it becomes apparent, and yet at the same time we will be helpless in preventing the drama from playing itself out.

The ability of science to offer us new drugs enabling us to live-forever and hold on to youthful appearances. These chemical stimulants will only be available to those who can afford them. If your ability to keep purchasing the stimulants ceases (buy it on the debit card), so do the temporary effects of the drug-induced state of physical well-being.

We will experience many weather anomalies and see things occur in nature that are presently not yet describable in our language. Ice storms where actual sheets of ice will fall from the heavens and cover whole areas.

At first they will be small, say the size of a book. Then there will be larger ones. Winters in the North East US will be long and unbearable. There will be a pole shifting after the mid-century. Once this occurs most of the New England area will become encased in wintry weather. By the end of the next century the emerging of the new ice caps will begin to become obvious in that area.

The flooding of low-lying areas and the coastal regions due to the present ice caps and melting snow and the rains will change the shape of the land there, as it is presently known. This will happen quite rapidly over the first twenty-five years of the century.

The weather will begin to see-saw from drought conditions to extreme flooding. Winter and summer, no spring and no fall. Also the magnetic poles commonly used by pilots will change and shift directions without logical explanations

The activities of the sun during the first decade will also add to this transformation period, as we experience meteors falling like hale upon the earth. There will be much new substance for new life forms that come during the Solar storms which increase in both intensity and frequency, as we realize new weather phenomena resulting from the Solar activity.

The intensified activity of the Earth's tectonic plate movement and magma will cause deadly gases to rise to the surface. The effects will be devastating and some areas will become uninhabitable. The land will be too unstable and shifting and geothermal pockets will even make some areas volatile and explosive.

Oregon, Washington, New Mexico, Wyoming will be the areas where this will occur with continued frequency. This will allow for the 'under-waters'... space which is presently allowing seawater from the oceans... to flow into new openings.

This will also, it seems, cause rapid erosion of the basalt rock, which is the foundation of the surface land in many of those areas. We will therefore experience collapsing of land creating a new geophysical phenomenon. These conditions will be particularly bad in the South West region of the United States.

Europe will see devastating rains, and the effects of the storms in the northern regions and Mediterranean will be extremely devastating. High winds and ice storms will be major causes of the destructions that will devastate the crops, as well as their industry.

Africa will have been devastated by disease, and social revolutions due to the collapse of the ancient Spiritual infrastructures of the Indigenous peoples there,. Much of it will never recover, even after the time of awakening.

Chinese people will over a period of time become a major force in the western hemisphere.. Bringing much of their technology, ancient technology and culture to merge in the western lands. Millions will fell pollution and Cataclysmic devastation that will occur though middle and Southern Asia. This merging into this hemisphere will be subtle and a natural event. As it ill be discovered is a very ancient matter and has occurred before, tens of thousands of years ago..

NWO and their Digital Theatrics,
.... the selling off of the American Dream.

The ultimate method of gaining complete un-questioned authoritative control over a people is to create the conditions of an emergency — a war, an apocalyptic cataclysm, or a computer virus that threatens the world...

The New World Order is arising under the guise of restoring balance and prosperity to Earth and her People. We are being told that it is time to return to a period of normalcy and tradition. We must ask ourselves what is normalcy? Who determines what that actually is? Is it someone else's perceptions of normalcy or my own?

There will be many smoke screens, wars and volatile political situations deliberately designed and orchestrated to take our attention off what is actually occurring and the stress of complete unilateral financial collapse of the overgrown corporate structures which now control the entire world media, and Newspapers.

There will be untold Computer failures as there is an extreme attempt by those in power at the moment to re-take control over a situation wherein the entire world business is now being run by computerized communications. The system is failing at a very rapid pace. Much of this will be blamed upon Y-2-K at first, but in actuality it will be contrived.

Y-2-K is and was a contrived consequence to an impossible problem that stymied the progress of control of the world governments and the New World Social Order. The real matter at hand is the agenda for a global switching of all communications to digital sources.

Therefore be forewarned:

The New social order will be welcomed. I emphasize this for there will exist such misery and economic strife upon the Earth that when along comes someone to solve the problem, there will be no resistance.

Then the new Order of a one-world society goes into effect, for it is claimed to be the only solution. This concept seems like an unheard of dream to Americans who are still holding on to a fantasy that they live in the land of the free. That dream went out with FDR.

The power of the New World Order, which is the system of the Anti-Christ, has already been established. We are already under the effects of the consciousness and corrupted systems that will place the one in power.

The countries of this world are already giving up their own sovereignty and has joined the system created to destroy spiritual independence and eradicate forever the union between human being and their heavenly Father and Mother.

Many third world peoples are selling off their Spiritual items and turning from their beliefs...not to God and Christ, but to the violence of the streets. This trend will only continue to spread, and for the first ten years of the new Century life will be difficult for those who are aware of what is truly going on around them.

Those who created the NWO system are now literally entering into every computer system in the world under the cover of being Cyber Medics. As the existing sabotaged systems begin to fail (yes, they will be activated to fail) with more and more frequency the NWO system will spread throughout our global society like an uncontrollable fungus upon the face of the Earth. The masses will buy into the program, because they have been brainwashed into thinking they have no choice, and once they jump the fence they have been corralled, as they say in the West.

In essence, the new global political system which will take over financially at first, already exists and there is no way out of it now, unless we all become hackers overnight. The system will then move toward gaining unchallenged military control over certain social uprisings and calamities (Weather) giving them reason for employing Martial Law.

The NWO has already been accepted as inevitable by the bulk of populations in the Western societies, who already have surrendered their personal sovereignty. And the NWO System, through the propaganda techniques of the now infamous Y2K situation, was given carte blanche to do as they will.

There is now an open highway without restriction to implement their new programs into our cyber realities. The new Cyber aspect of their Matrix will only grow to unprecedented proportions as we are sold yet another package of goods which never comes to fruition.

Keep the population frozen in fear, and what better way than to create the aire of an attack from Phantom forces of Terrorists in our streets running wild, and acting without regard.

What percentage of what you see on the news is as it really is? Ask yourself this many times in the Days to Come.

The NWO will have the support of the masses, without question (at First), because of their apparent abilities in dealing with the diseases, (which they spread to the populous in the first place) and their ability for managing the weather anomalies (they are responsible for creating) through their new super technology.

This again, we will be told, is the only solution to correct what mankind has previously set out of balance in nature and her forces. Thus, the social order will arise creating the system through which the New World Social Order is already being established. It is this system that will allow the Anti-Christ System seemingly to take over the world politically and spiritually at an alarming speed.

For a period of time, there will exist a worldwide tyranny and those seeking personal liberties will suffer greatly. The blueprint for this plan is already in effect, and will be triggered into manifestation here in the US by the outbreak of many manipulated pandemics, as well as the contrived Y2K condition making it easy to shut down certain systems and initiate new ones that better suit the plan.

A "State of Emergency "of any kind, even "Acts of God" is all that is required to implement the program. We will see evidence of this in the very near and immediate future. Again, watch the signs, and compromise your liberty for no cause or being.

But how many I wonder will take notice of the complete changing over of the world wide media as they switch to digital systems, and how fewer still will wonder will stop to ask why...

Think about it. How perfect the plan has been executed, how we have been led right into the corral like cattle at the stockyard. Those who desire to control their brethren, those who are the new kings — the Bankers (the money changers) have created a plan whereby they gain access to almost every computerized system in the world.

The plan as well brings them into virtually every home in the world, with the exception of Third World countries. Just think of the script for TV shows and Grade B movies. Is it not always the intruder gaining entrance into the house by disguising himself as the repairman coming to fix the problem who gains entry into the inner sanctum.....and this time, through the beast: The Computer. You know, the beast with the ten heads. The disasters resulting from the strange and new weather anomalies just add spice to the plan. It is no less than Apocalyptic.

This New Social Order will appear at first in the urban areas of the US considered at first to be necessary to contain the disease and violence as humanity will, it seems, have lost all moral and social reasoning.

Much of the farmland will no longer be capable of producing food and combined with the natural disasters they will become virtual wastelands. People will desert them due to the total inability to survive. This will cause many areas to become havens for the hundreds of thousands of people fleeing the horror of urban conditions.

This will be particularly bad in the South West as tens of thousands of people flee from the horrid conditions that will prevail there.

These areas will become basically lawless as the main concentration of military forces will be required to maintain order and containment in the overgrown urban areas.

The US becomes the melting pot of Global Free Republic, but not until after several things occur. How these things are dealt with will determine the outcome. Good and bad become very abstract perceptions, depending from which position in the field of dreams you are observing the action.

Asia is corrupted in its political systems far beyond repair; then again, so is most of the world. Also, Asia is dealing with problems of severe overpopulation. There has long been a problem of struggle between the Orient and the Western Governments.

Enter the Dragon

There are various scenarios as to why this problem exists. Cultural, Spiritual, and basically on the Political front, this problem has everything to do to with " Gold." There is much ancient gold in China, Japan and throughout the orient, enough gold, it is said, to disrupt the present economic game and throw the present agenda for world control into serious disarray.

During the first half of the 20th Century much of this Gold was the power behind Hong Kong. This Gold originally was being filtered out through the Philippines (Marcos) and Taiwan. Aware that the treaty with Communist China would eventually run out, plans were made for Taiwan to become the U.S. stronghold. Hong Kong made its own plans looking far to the East to South America. What happened during this drama has been the subject of many books and some very popular motion pictures.

Over the second half of the 20th Century, many of the old Chinese families, seeing their future was not going to realize the liberation of China from the political restraints of the New World Order/Mau Dynasty operating as Communist China (and that Hong Kong would be sacrificed) elected to move their fortunes and places of residence elsewhere. Many of these families moved to Hawaii, Venezuela, and Belize, The Pacific Coast of the Us and Canada. There they could restructured their financial empires, carefully and calculatingly designing the program to establish an infrastructure in the Western society , and over the last half of the 20th Century, their wealth and influence has become well-established here in the Western Hemisphere. And most never knew that the Soft invasion had already taken place .

After WWII the U.S. entered into a short-lived period I call the American Heyday "Happy Days", where the good old U.S. of A. was the new super-power kid on the block. What the U.S. lacked in wisdom and ability it made up for with bravado and tuff-guy tactics i.e., the U.S. is well known in Third World countries for contrived assassinations and revolutionary activities. On the Surface, the U.S. took on single-handedly the salvation and liberation of the world's people, from what, exactly, still remains uncertain.

All of our foreign efforts, we were told back home, were for the American Dream, and they did a good job of keeping everyone in new cars and little houses and TVs and beer. America was fed its addictions and the pathway was laid out for the public to follow, turning them into a nation of consumers. Today the US holds all records for being the largest consumer country in the world.

Basically, The Yanks took over South America, which we always considered a satellite anyway, by deciding to use our Neighbor's resources to the South to collateralize our over-extended bank accounts, while playing our hand at taking over world banking.

We were as a society ruthless, cunning, corrupt and without long-established cultural and spiritual foundations, nothing was beyond our imagination. From drugs to coffee, to sugar to rubber, to pharmaceuticals, to oil… to precious metals, human labor through the economic enslavement of the People, we regarded the whole of South America as a US commodity. The Yanks went around with their heads up their *?*#!'s and as a people, we grew fat and lazy and were slowly sucked in to the already existing world banking systems. Today the foreign banks own us, ***livestock and barrel***.

Well, we learned the hard way that these boys in the World Banking Systems were smarter than the average bear, and about the time the 60's rolled around it was eminent that we would lose the whole game to our European rivals.

In that period we extended loans to the Third World countries, though BOA, CHEMICAL BANK, CHASE MANHATTAN, MANUFACTERS TRUST (all of which interestingly are now consolidating) and other good blue-blooded American organizations for the development and raising of the standard of living in these poor undeveloped and under-privileged countries.

Our technology came under the control of the former German Nazi scientists, and our factories became the domain of the Asians. The Arabs made a fortune off our consumption of oil and US development, and you can only spend so much money on camels and hotels. So, our swarthy friends from the Middle East invested back into America by loaning them money through the European banks that they bought up like kids playing monopoly.

Our friends in Asia waited until we got so full of ourselves in the 1980's it was costing Hewlett-Packard $80,000 a year for a janitor in Silicon Valley in California and the cost of labor got so prohibitive that US industry simply could no longer afford to hire US citizens. The computer, appliances and automobile manufacturers started to go overseas to create a cheaper means of production and keep their massive consumers well fed with new toys.

Meanwhile, they were gambling on the loans that they extended to Third World countries in South America to foot the bill while they developed a new industry here. It was a simple enough game of extending to them the funds to improve their ability to participate in the Game of Success, and become the labor and Natural resources reserve of America.

Further, we could insure our investments by locking every one of those countries into the economic enslavement policies that would insure them, in a manner of speaking. The US owned their natural Resources, and we would even be willing to forgive the loans.

We could reap huge profits from the loans and control the world markets. We would control the resources from South America, and use them to feed our factories cheap raw material. We could sell the whole world cheaper products built in our overseas factories in Asia and ship them in ships, planes and trains fueled with our own oil we controlled in the Middle East. What a fantastic dream and America would become the first nation to take over the world through the organized Retail System…imagine it… a world full of shopping malls.. Greed can be so blinding, can it not.

Well, there were many silent wars, and secret assassinations have occurred executing this madness; however, this is not the subject of this book so you will have to wait for another production. Besides, we all know that a lunatic in Dallas, acting solely on behalf of himself and his own personal agenda, shot Jack Kennedy, so we will just let that story be. This book is about prophecies and understanding truth, so why discuss why Anwar Sudat was suddenly relieved of his political duties as head of Egypt, again by a wild lunatic assassination attack where all the normal security people were conveniently missing from the scene.

We all know something about the Hunt Bros. in Texas and the wild stories as to their interest in working with the Kennedys to help secure the Independence of America from the World Banking Program, from Global Tyranny and creating our own self-supported currency. Just crazy rumors in a maddening crowd of drugged out people, I guess…… after all, it was the 60's and 70's when this stuff occurred…..It must have been the 'Jefferson Airplane' that flew off with the goods.

Well, while all this was going on and we were keeping our eyes on the European front and building bigger and better resorts and faster cars, and teaching our kids how to become millionaires by working less and taking more, we lost control of the South American front to those Asian families.

We also now had all our factories and technology in the Far East as well. These same families now will take control of the Panama Canal itself, *the gateway of the hemispheres*. Washington must be turning over in his grave, for we have forgotten all his warnings...... just as we have put aside the warnings of former President Eisenhower about allowing the military to get too powerful and autonomous. I won't even get into Jefferson and the rights of the common man to own land and keep our sovereignty and personal liberty.

Also, we lost control of Hawaii to this same financial empire and now the west coast from Vancouver, BC, to Mexico is also under the influences and ownership of these families, from the subtle Eastern Empire of the Sun.

After the collapse of Camelot and the Kennedy dream and the ruination of the Hunt bros. destroying any chance for American sovereignty from the European Banking Beast, we entered out first major changes, a complete shifting of consciousness you might say. We took on foreign investors and extended loans and inflated our economic systems so that today the inflated American economy is riding upon a hot air balloon which is losing altitude fast, Folks. It has been shot so full of holes and the fabric of what it was made has been steadily deteriorating as well. "Hello... Houston.... I believe we have a problem."

So, what do we do! The outcome is fairly evident is it not? Do we need to take a look at history once again...Well, perhaps in the next book, please.

We have choices here: We learn to understand what is happening to America right under our very eyes. We own up to the truth, and carry on with the new dream. We raise our consciousness and see that perhaps this lower labyrinth of games is really the result of a higher manipulation. America, the Dream is lost — Ozzie and Harriet are off the air. What we have now are memories of a dream that has been wasted away... All we have left is a *'Box of Rain'...*

HIP HOP "It's not just music"
The Special Effects Techniques
of a Holographic Movie

Yes "something is going on". Events are occurring and are about to occur which will change our present perceptions of reality forevermore. Some of these events are due to natural forces, others are due to the deliberate playing with these forces of nature and dimension by mankind. If a thought can be perceived it can be manifested. This is universal law; it is the law of the Kryah. All things existing in consciousness are potential realities. We are the architects of our perceived reality. We are the dreammakers constantly playing at creation.

We are experiencing the intensification of frequencies, the subtle and unseen forces dictating the order and levels of reality. There is a fractalization occurring of the natural order of energy and the holographic reality, which will result in the transmutation of our physical bodies in order that we can successfully merge with these higher frequencies.

"*The Quickening*", as I termed it back in 1992, is all about our merging with these new frequencies. We are experiencing everything being shaken up. We are adapting as fast as our little earth bodies can adapt to match the frequency band (known as the bio-sphere by scientists) as fast as it mutates. But, how it will manifest is still the question. Also, who is able to see these changes and frequency patterns and who cannot, can be a puzzlement.

The HIP-HOP Scenario.

These new frequencies are stimulating the DNA. This is being realized or received by our energy fields through energy waves or pulses, energy pulses — flashes of light if we could perceive them. This process is causing us to perceive things in a new way.

Our thought is influenced by our DNA and its ability to initiate and/or respond to frequency: the *thought, awareness, process* or (**TAP**). The aftereffects of TAP can be manipulated through/by the DNA for the better or the worse. It is a form of holographic communication causing specific results that I have termed HIP HOP.

Consciousness is stimulated by awareness, which causes an energy to result. This energy moves consciousness in a specific direction. Perception is the result of the expansion or restriction of the conscious mind — the ability of one to respond to and translate the *Holographic Impulse Projection* or HIP.

What we are seeing, or the manner in which we are seeing or feeling this new HIP, is the result of our response to the...overall holographic grid. We are reading the frequencies as patterns of light and as we respond to the new frequencies, our brains access new octaves of thought and we, like children in an amusement park, are playing and creating new visual patterns and new thought patterns. We are creating and responding to HOP or the *Holographic Overall Perception*. Remember this is all new and no one has a reference for these new frequencies. They are new data, virgin thoughts we are accessing.

As we develop our ability to HIP HOP we access the deeper level of understanding of the technique. It becomes second nature, we do not even think about the degree to which we perceive the matter. If we become truly adept at HIP HOP we can send frequencies and soon receive the desired results. This process can work in two ways:

> *Using the HIP HOP technique I project a thought matrix that radiates through my holographic field. Let's say I project the epitome of a perfect body. Well, if I think thin I become thin, if I think energy I become energy. If I learn to project not just as a visual, but include with it emotion, well, there is the trick to the trade.*

> *Remember the old saying. "I am having a bad hair day?" Well, when you do have a bad hair day, no matter what you do to yourself, or how you dress up the puppet you will not appear to yourself as you desire. Yet the moment you change your attitude or something happens which does: POOF! You're beautiful. People pick up feelings before they pick up thought. It's natural. If I learn therefore to project feelings and filter my own bad thoughts, you feel me before you see me. It's the old Hollywood thing. People see you as a result of your emotional broadcast; it overrides the optic nerve.*

• If I could somehow control the frequency in the air around you, say by the broadcasting of radio signals, I could influence the way you perceive things. "No", you say. Then why is it when you are in a bad mood everything takes on a negative outlook? Colors are not as bright, and we cannot hear the music the way it is played. We hear what people are saying differently than what they actually said. Is any of this familiar to you? Of course it is.

Now, imagine broadcasting this frequency with all the power of a satellite. People would see what you desired. Well, this is exactly how a shape-shifter works. They manipulate the frequency and you feel and you perceive them as they intended. Unfortunately this is not a Stephen King article it is actually occurring..

Beginning to understand yet? Good, then lets take it another notch upwards. What if I was not only projecting **HIP** frequencies that effected how you optically perceived me **HOP,** but I was able to **TAP** into you and read your emotional frequencies and project them back to you **HIP HOP.**

What if I was technically advanced and played with radionics such as HAARP and ELF transmitters I built in my garage as a hobby and played these things all over town? I could project frequencies that affected the neighborhood and whole groups of people couldn't I? Well, welcome to mind control and the image setting of our special effects department here at Imposed Realities, Inc. That is how it is done. We hope you enjoy our new **HIP HOP** subliminal mind games, and remember we have free upgrades every month.

OK, you think this is all **bunko**? Go invest in two 99¢ plants at the local Supermarket. Place one in a room and play only Rap music 24 hours a day. In the other room place another plant and play only Classical Music 24 hours a day. Given the temperatures are the same, and the sunlight is the same, take a good look at these plants 6 weeks later, and then you tell me the frequency does not effect consciousness.

Now, just because I know you have a defensive mind, I am going to ask you to experiment a little further with my **HIP HOP** theory, just to prove I am wrong about all this. Cause, if it can be proven I am wrong about all this, I would sleep better at night knowing I was just crazy. Practice with your emotions and project them around. See how people respond. Now you can't cheat, you have to be sincere, really make the effort…

And when you write me special notes about this I will take you to meet some of our friends, after I give you the course in shielding yourself against the broadcast emissions. But, you will have to sign a hold a harmless with Imposed Realities, Inc., because we cannot be responsible for the effects of what you will see when their makeup is removed.

The New Plagues

...and the emerging Biological Apocalypse

Feel tired and listless Lately? What about that cough that never goes away?   And what about that constant feeling of flu like aches and pains? Want to understand the bug that bit you? Read on...

Diseases will be rampant and it will be discovered, although at first it was thought that the viruses and pathogens were of multiple origins, in fact they come from a common source – that to which I referred as the "Green Mist" which would fall from the heavens and change all life upon the Earth in my book Winds of Change......

As it is seen, almost the entire human species is presently infected with these mechanical viruses that seem to have their own intelligence. They have the ability to mutate and change, sometimes even vacate prior to treatment by allopathic means, only to reappear in another part of the species manifesting as yet another aliment.

Medical practices will change radically as we are forced to deal with the nature of actual conditions, which are already rampant in mankind. There will be such an outbreak of disease within the next two years, that many areas of America as well as Europe will quarantine their urban areas. This will be accomplished through military policing.

Already the deadly elements are manifesting, going through a five to six year gestation period whereby they are slowly taking over the system of the body. We are already into the fourth and fifth year of the cycle.

Be it known that these are manufactured viruses, and not the curse of God. These are deliberate biological warfare tactics.   At first it was thought that there could be antidotes for the pathogens, yet that is now no longer an alternative with present allopathic remedies.

Behavior of the Pathogens: They enter the embodiment and we are aware of symptoms of a flu, a cold, aches and pains in the joints, lethargy, unclear thinking, which later manifests as irrational and psychotic thinking and behavior.

They commune in small colonies gradually wearing down the body's ability to utilize the immune system, are able to detect your weak points, places where the bodies energy fields are weak or out of balance.

The bug that bit you is, for the most part, undetectable, for they are lodged holographically in the protein itself; hence, they have been named "Stealth". The diseasement spreads and hospitals and Doctors are rendered totally unable to defend against the invaders. The message will be fear of the spread of the many deadly disorders causing terminal illness.

We will move into an understanding and level of dealing with the treatment of diseasement through the use of Quantum Technology. Many of the understandings of our medical and scientific community will realize the close relationship to the spiritual aspects of the causes for diseasement.

What first we will supplement with machines such as computers and radionics and broadcasting of frequencies, will actually be the tools by which we will learn to utilize the essence of our being, much as the Computer is teaching us to understand another level of consciousness through its utilization in analyzing data, and communicating through the Internet and will reach a place of a halo-leap when the whole system goes digital. .

The medical profession and scientific communities will begin to embrace techniques of healing which up until now have only been available through spiritual means such as Shamanism, Spiritual Healers, Ayurvedic Medicine, etc. The theorem that all of life is energy, energy expressing through light, will be embraced as it is realized that former methods of allopathic medicine are rendered useless in the face of the emerging new viruses that will plague mankind on every corner of the Earth.

One of the main concerns will be the outbreaks of plagues in such numbers that hospitals will become paralyzed and unable to render treatment to the countless multitudes of sick and dying who will come to their doors. There will, in many instances, simply not be enough chemical remedies to go around. We, as a species struggling for survival, will have to deal with the problem of the Stealth Viruses which will create their own immunity and transmute; the remedies and vaccines available will no longer work.

This will force us to take hold of alternative measures to deal with the situation. How does one deal with millions of afflicted people when there is only enough medicine for a few thousand at best? This will hit home when those in power fully realize the impact of the fact that they themselves have become infected.

Essentially, we are in what I have referred to as the **War of Valued Life.** Our very cells are at war with us. The very elements of life now hold the frequencies of cancer. Our consciousness presently is imploding. Consciousness holds the thought of perceived reality. If the consciousness continues to collapse at the present rate, within the next generation there will not be enough consciousness to sustain the hologram we know as perceived life.

As the consciousness degenerates and is unable to hold the frequency of perceived life, the life force itself dissipates and we as a human race enter a stage wherein our own bodies, in accordance with the laws of nature, release the death hormone. Nature has her own laws which we have too long ignored, thinking our technology could dominate even the very source of that which gives us our physical bodies through which our sprit expresses and explores the reality we have manifested.

Consciousness understanding is contagious. Thoughts connect to other thoughts and as the process goes at a certain point they reach critical mass and everyone is aware of the same thought, or understanding, much like the hundredth monkey theory with which most of us are now familiar. Imagine the effect of the greater portion of the human race going into the stage of degenerative consciousness and the death hormone is released. When this element reaches critical mass.... We could witness unbelievably devastating experiences.... Essentially, the race itself would enter into the death cycle. Only those outside of the matrix of consciousness that created the cycle would survive.

Be forewarned:

The technology and knowledge for the reparation and remedy for this condition manifested through our own misuse of knowledge already exists, yet contemporary corporate corrupted thinking and the invisible Matrix which dictates who shall be saved, and what social status, who shall be admitted to the hospital and what prescription shall be rendered, prevents this from manifesting

At first there will be an emerging of false hope from the pharmaceutical institutions. Massive media campaigns will claim to have the pharmaceutical remedies for rejuvenation and enhanced feeling of well being, and the reversal of the effects of the plagues; however, these can only be obtained by those who are in the system and have the means for payment. The social system, which is strongly connected to the drug companies and chemical companies, control our medical professions. Thus, they administer and control what remedies the insurance companies will pay for and allow to be administered.

The present medical structures of our Western society are based upon allopathic treatments and theories. They, for the most part, are based upon a method of treating the symptom of the disease, which never addresses the cause or the nature of origin for diseasement. In many ways it never did apply; it was an illusionary practice of masking the symptoms, creating huge industries that would be fed by an ever-growing population giving them an endless supply of patients. The goals were hardly ever to cure the illness but to keep the patients reliant upon continued health care, to insure the well-being of the industry.

We will be presented with many synthesized methods of dealing with diseasement, rejuvenation and sustained life force that will quickly turn into a nightmare reality as it is realized that:

The need for the synthesized chemical substances quickly becomes addictive and the intake is required on a regular basis to maintain a level proper for effectual balance. Also, the body itself will naturally develop immunity to the effects, requiring constantly improved more powerful versions to obtain the original effects.

Otherwise, the artificially induced condition of well-being will become rapidly regressive and even detrimental.. Adverse reactions and effects will also be detected as a result of the synthesized chemical enhancement of natural processes of nature.

Much like the plants one buys from the store at Easter, we will become chemically enhanced and genetically damaged from the extended use of these chemicals. The life force cannot sustain attack from outside pathogens that will continue to mutate and develop a consciousness of their own.

We will have to face the fact that "we are what we eat" and what we eat is taking us over both in consciousness as well as physically. The emerging viruses already have the ability to mutate and adapt quicker than the bio-organisms upon which they feed.

George Washington's Visions of America's Future

During the winter of 1777, shortly after the signing of the "Declaration of Independence" the American forces under the command of General George Washington, having suffered severe losses in the initial Battles against the British forces, took refuge wondering what the next possible action of the Colonialist might be. Washington and his troops were holding out in a obscure place called Valley Forge, through what proved to be one of the harshest winters in many years. Hungry and without sufficient supplies….. Hope was thin as to the outcome of events the following spring against the offensive action he expected to be launched by the British against him and his dwindling forces.

Not all Colonials were behind this war for independence you see; in fact, according to the records that exist, it was perhaps less then 10% of the population that supported it actively. Most, it seems, aided the British cause by giving them housing, and supplies feeling it was utterly hopeless and sheer madness to attempt to oppose what, at that time, was the most powerful country in the world. It was said that the Sun never set upon the British Empire.

There existed in the hearts and minds of the American people, a strong apathy. They were absorbed in self-interests, undecided about answers to the dilemma. It is well known that Washington was a man of strong spiritual beliefs, and he was renowned for his great courage and abilities at statesmanship. He had a good relationship with the Native Americans, without whose help and support Washington and his troops never would have survived. It is an acknowledged fact that it was the Native Americans who helped turn the tide for the Colonial forces in many a decisive battle against the British.

This is a story of something that occurred to Washington while at Valley Forge. Washington's accountings of these visions are recorded at the Library of Congress………

What follows ARE HIS ACTUAL WORDS transcribed from letters he wrote.

In his records, for he kept a journal, Washington said,

"*This afternoon, "as I was sitting at this table engaged in preparing a dispatch, something seemed to disturb me. Looking Up, I beheld standing opposite me a singularly beautiful female. So astonished was I, for I had given strict orders not to be disturbed, that it was some moments before I found language to inquire the cause of her presence.*

"*A second, a third and even a fourth time did I repeat my question, but received no answer from my mysterious visitor except a slight Raising of her eyes. By this time I felt strange sensations spreading through me. I would have risen but the riveted gaze of the* being before me rendered volition impossible. I assayed once more to address her, but my tongue had become useless, as though it had become paralyzed. "a new influence, mysterious, potent, irresistible, took possession of me."

"All I could do was to gaze steadily, vacantly at my unknown visitor, gradually the surrounding atmosphere seemed as if it had become filled with sensations, and luminous. Everything about me seemed to rarify, the mysterious visitor Herself becoming more airy and yet more distinct to my sight than before. I now began to feel as one dying, or rather to

"Experience the sensations, which I have sometimes imagined accompany dissolution. I did not think, I did not reason, I did not move; all were alike impossible. I was only conscious of gazing fixedly, vacantly at my companion. "Presently I heard a voice saying, 'son of the republic, look and learn,' while at the same time my visitor extended her arm Eastwardly.

"I now beheld a heavy white vapor at some distance rising fold upon fold. This gradually dissipated, and I looked upon a strange scene. Before me lay spread out in one vast plain all the countries of the world; Europe, Asia, Africa and America.

" I saw rolling and tossing between Europe and America the billows of the Atlantic, and between Asia and America lay the pacific. " 'son of the republic' said the same mysterious voice as before, 'look and learn', and at that moment I beheld a dark, shadowy being, like an angel, standing, or rather floating in mid-air, between Europe and America.

"Dipping water out of the ocean in the hollow of each hand, he sprinkled some upon America with his right hand, while with his left hand he cast some on Europe. Immediately a cloud raised from these countries, and joined in mid-ocean. For a while it remained stationary, and then moved slowly westward, until it enveloped America in its murky folds. Sharp flashes of lightning gleamed through it at intervals, and I heard the smothered groans and cries of the American people. "a second time the angel dipped water from the ocean, and sprinkled it out as before.

"The dark cloud was then drawn back to the ocean, in whose heaving billows it sank from view. A third time I heard the mysterious voice saying, 'son of the republic, look and learn,' I cast my eyes upon America and beheld villages and towns and cities springing up one after another until the whole land from the Atlantic to the Pacific was dotted with them.

"Again, I heard the mysterious voice say, 'son of the republic, the end of the century cometh, look and learn.' At this the dark shadowy angel turned his face Southward, and from Africa I saw an ill-omened spectra approach our Land.

"It flitted slowly over every town and city of the latter. The inhabitants presently set themselves in battle array against each other. As I continued looking I saw a bright angel, on whose brow rested a crown of light, on which was traced the word 'UNION,' Bearing the American flag which he placed between the divided nation, and said, 'remember ye are brethren.' Instantly, the inhabitants, casting from them their weapons became friends once more, and united around the national standard. "

"And again I heard the mysterious voice saying, 'son of the republic, look and learn.' At this the dark, shadowy angel placed a trumpet to his mouth, and blew three distinct blasts;

and taking water from the ocean, he sprinkled it upon Europe, Asia and Africa. Then my eyes beheld a fearful scene: from each of these countries arose thick, black clouds that were soon joined into one.

"Throughout this mass there gleamed a dark red light by which I saw hordes of armed men, who, moving with the cloud, marched by land and sailed by sea to America.

"Our country was enveloped in this volume of cloud, and I saw these vast armies devastate the whole country and burn the villages, towns and cities that I beheld springing up. As my ears listened to the thundering of the cannon, clashing of swords, and the shouts and cries of millions in mortal combat, I heard again the mysterious voice saying, 'son of the republic, look and learn.' When the voice had ceased, the dark shadowy angel placed his trumpet once more to his Mouth, and blew a long and fearful blast.

"Instantly a light as of a thousand suns shone down from above me, and pierced and broke into fragments the dark cloud which enveloped America. At the same moment the angel upon whose head still shone the word union, and who bore our national flag in one hand and a sword in the other, Descended from the heavens attended by legions of white spirits. These immediately joined the inhabitants of America, who I perceived were well nigh overcome, but who immediately taking courage again, closed up their broken ranks and renewed the battle.

"Again, amid the fearful noise of the conflict, i heard the mysterious voice saying, 'son of the republic, look and learn.' as the voice ceased, the shadowy angel for the last time dipped water from the ocean and Sprinkled it upon America. Instantly the dark cloud rolled back, together with the armies it had brought, leaving the Inhabitants of the land victorious!

"Then once more I beheld the villages, towns and cities springing up where I had seen them before, while the bright Angel, planting the azure standard he had brought in the midst of them, cried with o loud voice....

"...While the stars remain, and the heavens send down dew upon the earth, so long shall the union last." And taking from his brow the crown on which blazoned the word 'Union,' he placed it upon the standard while the people, kneeling down, said, 'amen.'

"The scene instantly began to fade and dissolve, and i at last saw nothing but the rising, curling vapor I at first beheld. This also disappearing, I found myself once more gazing upon the mysterious visitor, who, in the same voice I had heard before, said, 'son of the republic, what you have seen is thus interpreted: three great perils will come upon the re-

public.

"The most fearful is the third, but in this greatest conflict the whole world united shall not prevail against her. Let every child of the republic learn to live for his god, his land and the union. With these words the angel vanished, and I started from my seat and felt that I had seen a vision wherein it had been shown to me the birth, progress and destiny of the United States."

AMERICA *A-mira- ka el'* ... A Holistic Vision

(... the reflection of God)

It is the vision of the Masters that America be the forthcoming foundation of a universal republic; that this land, the Original Motherland of Humanity, become the birthplace of a true Solon's Republic. We will see the merging of the world's religions as well as the world's cultures. From this merging will come forth a new way of looking at our past and spiritual understandings.

Here will be the dissolving of nationalism that has separated the Earth's people for some 2,000 years. The presence of the Asian impact on our contemporary society is now obvious to most Americans, especially if you are located upon the West Coast. Also, it is quite apparent if you live near Vancouver and other areas of British Colombia.

The Asian cultures are much older than their newly arrived cousins here in North America. The blending of spiritual and social patterns is customary in most of China and Japan, as well as Korea. It is commonplace for those who work in factories or live in communities to gather for Tai Chi, Chi Gong or other methodologies for the harmony of body, mind and spirit. Many of these practices go back thousands of years in their societies.

It is accepted both in the corporate community and the social community as well, as being a necessary part of life. Also, there are long inbred threads in the people of spiritual fiber having lineage who practice understandings going back at least equal in time to the early Egyptian Dynasties and the time of the ancient Naga- Maya of the same period. What we are talking about is a post-Atlantis belief system.

They look upon the American culture from a very interesting perception. We are a fugitive consciousness. We do not work together; we resist communities and survive in an economic system that teaches us the world is dog against dog, the name of the game is **survival of the fittest**. For the most part there is little Spiritual understanding or philosophy applied to the corporate systems here, the emphasis being placed upon greed and the most for your buck.

The present western society is structured upon a base entirely materialistic and without substance, lacking severely in true spiritual substance. Most of our elderly are cast off and forgotten to fend for themselves. Our young are ignored and there is no apparent place or hope for them to achieve what has been pushed down their throats as the basics of the American Dream: 'To own their own home, to live under the guise of living free.'

Protected not by their culture, but by some documents called the Constitution and the Bill of Rights (which these days are apparently ignored and overruled as Government infringes its will upon all levels of personal liberty), Americans for the most part have simply allowed themselves to become slaves to their own economic system.   This travesty now threatens to destroy even America as a conceptualized reality.

Even within our corporate structures we are being presented an illusion; nothing is as it appears. The bottom line is that there is no security unless one plays into the patterns of the previous corruption. It is a cycle of self-destruction.   This system has, of course, spread across the face of the Earth.

Those who participate in this synthesized societal order are in many cultures now, and the disease is Malignant. However, in the ancient culture such as China and Japan underneath there is an infrastructure that sustains a way of life yet to be developed by the adolescent American Culture. Families here, for the most part, do not support other family members, and most see each other only in the hypnotic ceremony of holidays void totally of spirituality, and at funerals where they tear each other apart over the spoils.

We are lost in momentary reward and the characteristics of selfishness amongst the employed adults in the prime of life — 25 to 35 — who are caught in the spell of decadence, finding their pleasures where and when they can. The result of this madness is to be seen all around them. If only they could stop long enough to see the world around them, they would see not only the youth, but as well the millions of senior citizens living in motor homes or are being placed in hospices. Here they feed an even more corrupt program satiating the medical society simply because they are doomed to an existence that, at best, is below the poverty level.

Emphasis here is being placed upon the momentary gratification of materialistic pleasure and elusive sexuality, more than often non-existent in execution of the fact.. Very little emphasis is placed upon Spirituality and the streets are rampant with crime and homeless people. In China, for instance, are you aware there are no homeless people to speak of; isn't that an interesting condition?

This shows us once again the unity in the ingrained patterns of the culture of these people acting as a united force rather then separate entities. They are hive consciousness, highly developed over centuries of practical application.

The People of the Dragon shall seek out new lands, and there is little standing in their way here, for the Fugitives run like scattered sheep; they are victims of the very system they have created. Without the foundations of the family center here, her people are helpless against the oncoming changes in these **Days of Destiny**.

The family structure of the Orient is far superior to that which presently exists in America. They support each other, and they act as one. The whole family invests in a business; they invest in each other's success. The whole family helps the newlyweds build a home. The success of this policy as an applied science in America has reaped them quite a harvest. They jointly own many business chains; they have major holdings in US real estate, enjoying huge holdings in the American bond market and the stock exchange. America became a nation of consumers, and we are lost in our addictions.

Yes, the American way of life has become that which supports and develops a Fugitive Consciousness. We are islands alone, able to depend on only ourselves. It is a bitter lesson of the Fugitive Breed when they find that there is no place to turn.The dream has always ben about the Union, the Unity of the People. For the People can only be rendered by the People...

All around you the vast ranches of the Western Saga no longer able to support themselves being sliced up and sold to the highest bidder for 30¢ on the dollar. And what of the Great Family Owned Farms and Ranches which once covered this land. Today in actuality, the bankers, who are by the way mostly foreign entities, own them. Scarcely can be found land which the people themselves actually own. Our farmers are little more than indentured servants to the global corporate systems.

We must begin to integrate and accept what is inevitable: the emergence of races which eventually will develop into a universal society with at least an harmonious, if multi-formed, spiritual understanding. This present American society shall understand the full effects of the coming emergence first. It shall be felt from internal upheavals of our physical beings as the species itself transmutes, self-adjusting to merge with the new frequencies. It will experience much social conflict and total transition and restructuring of our way of life financially, spiritually, socially, scientifically and geo-physically.

America = A Miracle

A message of Hope from the Ascended Masters

America will be given the opportunity to evolve beyond the density of third dimensional conception. The test will be severest where the hope is the greatest for achieving the Emergence. Here is the opportunity to join together and overcome the limitations of the past existence that has so long crippled our world and kept it from waking up and achieving its true conscious capabilities.

If there is a willing acceptance of all races, all nations and all creeds; if we can recognize our connections to Mother Earth and all that is, then we shall see the dark energies be turned around. We will stand witness to a new energy realized through our actions. Once activated this new energy will initiate the most incredible growth of human consciousness ever experienced, and we will surely know a **Golden Age**.

If America refuses to accept the natural flow of the emergence and chooses to remain stuck in the old paradigms, then equal to the energy of resistance shall be the energy of opposing events causing her to become a conquered land. Then surely will she see the invasion on both her shores from those whose destiny also depends upon the outcome of these events. We are involved in global change; the whole of humanity is getting ready to alter completely.

Many things will be at her aid including the discoveries of her ancient heritage. Stories will unfold of the lineage of Sun Kings and the many races who once lived upon her blessed shores when she was still an Island Kingdom hold true, for once upon her shores did stroll the Pharaohs of Egypt and Lords of Sumeria. Here the Mayan Princes taught in the Mystery Schools, the Schools of Isis, and great armies and cities existed now even lost to the confusion of legends. But remember all legends are based upon truths.....

Those who are called to this place, America, are returning to their source, for from this land did the people come forth after the destruction. And, from this land did the Earth's people repopulate after those destructions of Atlantis. Like migratory birds they are returning to the place of their birth as spirits that dwell upon this Earth. Deep within her recesses shall the evidence be found and revealed to us of a greater truth than once was thought to be of humanity. Our divine origins will be traced to the last destruction, and the events following that experience during what is known as the War of the Heavens.

The Earth is alive and all upon her is moving. It is a phenomenon, but this is not the first time this has occurred. It has happened many times before, only perhaps not on such a grand level since prior to the time of Atlantis. It is the cycle of the Serpent energy. This cycle is known as the time of the Dragon. America's children, as well as the children of everywhere upon this Earth, are facing new frontiers, as the whole of the world merges with its new reality.

Kuthumi

The Arrival

" .....We will receive many warnings allowing us to change our ways....... from below the Earth as well as from above. Then one morning in a moment, we will awaken to the Red Dawn.

The sky will be the color of blood,. Many things will then begin to happen that right now we are not sure of their exact nature. For much of reality will not be as it is now. There will be many strange beasts upon the Earth in those days, some from the past and some we have never seen.

The nature of mankind will appear strange in these times when we walk between the worlds, and we will house many spirits, even within our bodies. After a time, we will walk with our brothers from the stars, and rebuild the Earth. But not until the Purifier has left his mark upon the universe...."

...Last Cry - Native American Prophecies, Dr. Robert Ghost Wolf

It is hard, if not impossible, for one who has not been raised with the influence or experience of interaction with the First Peoples of this land, to understand their use and comprehension of the English language. Harder still for those of us caught within the web of **social consciousness** to understand those who are still in the natural state of Hu-man consciousness.

It is often difficult to understand those who live close to the Earth and understand her mysteries and still feel and understand the mind of the Mother of us all. Being caught within the web, one is too busy rationalizing and justifying the illusions of our synthetic reality.

It is impossible for these individuals to feel the truth of this Earth as being their Mother. They look upon this statement, at best, as being merely a metaphor for they are caught in the atrophy of their own stagnant Spiritual awareness.

In Genesis 1:4 ... " Let there be lights in the heavens and let them be signs."

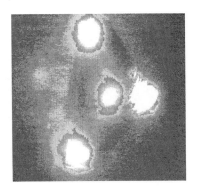

The ancients knew of future potentials and the turning of the seasons of the celestial clock because they understood the keys to understanding the way things worked was in the stars. The wise men who came to witness the coming of the Little King knew where to be because they knew of the event prior to its occurrence, due to their understanding of the Star Knowledge.

The prophets and sages throughout time memorial from all cultures have had an inner understanding, if not a formal education, in the mechanics of the celestial geometry of the universe. Many keys to this knowledge are encoded with the Judeo-Christian Bible. We will investigate several of them as we progress upon our journey into the realms of higher understanding.

The Bible, Pegasus, and other a-musing stories:

In New Testament from the surviving texts of the teachings of Yeshua we are told of the second coming of the **Universal Christ**.

Revelation 19:11" And I saw heaven opened, and behold a white horse; and he that sat upon him was called Faithful and True, and in righteousness he doth judge and make war."

Is it merely a coincidence that in the Scriptures it refers to **Revelations** and the Native People speak of the Purification and the Purifier?.... Coincidence that the Bible talks of the **Prince of Peace**, and the Native People Speak of their **Peacemaker** when referring to the Pale Prophet? ... That he will return upon a white horse, and the Native Peoples reference is that the Peacemaker will appear as a plumed serpent in the heavens? We are also told of the return of **Kate-Zahl** in the Mayan teachings (also known as the Prophet or Quetzalcoatl.)

Revelations 1:07....." Behold he cometh from the clouds; and every eye shall see him, and they also which pierced him, and all kindred's of the Earth shall wail because of him. Even so, Amen... 8 "I AM the Alpha and Omega, the beginning and the end- ing, saith the Lord, which is, and which was, and which is to come....."

As many of you are now aware, we here upon the Earth are in fact receiving some kind of mechani- cal signal sequence emanating from something out in the depths of space, and that signal is coming from within the constellation of Pegasus. If you are not aware of this, I suggest you research this very interesting web site.   http://www.lunaranomolies.com   There are many other interesting bits of information, as well.

It's a great site!

Revelations 6: 03 " Come see......and I saw, and behold a white horse; and he that sat upon him had a bow, and a crown was given unto him; and he went forth conquer- ing, and to conquer.."

We are told again in the Christian Bible about the Second Coming as it refers to the **White Horse** in the Heavens, which can be none other than Pegasus, the winged horse of Greek Mythology. Pegasus, we find upon deeper investigation, is not limited to the heavens but in the ancient teachings Pegasus is also referred to as "Hippocampus". In the human body this is the place of memory where the Gods speak to us and we connect to our source. This place is none other than the Pineal Gland in the human brain.

Now, take into consideration our bodies are comprised of about 98% water, which means we are basically sea creatures carrying our own private ocean around with us. OK, Interesting don't you think? We also find upon further investigation that the word "Hippocampus" actually translates to Sea

Horse. The father of Pegasus was Poseidon the Greek God of the Sea. Also, he was one of the Atlantean Kings. If we are a little left-brained, we would suggest looking up Hippocampus in Stedan's Medical Dictionary and we will find that " ....the hippocampus of the human brain is a white eminence..."

This information, therefore, makes Pegasus the White Sea Horse of the body; it is the White Horse of the Bible, upon which the Second Coming shall commence, and it is the White Sea Horse that is the memory of origins within you and I.

NOTE: We must understand that a vast amount of symbolism and parables have been used in all teachings to explain information and deliver messages. Often they were tailored to fit the level of comprehension, and/or fit into the cultural understanding of the times.

This insured that the information would be understood at least enough to be brought forward through the telling and retelling of the stories, legends, lore, petraglyphs, and hieroglyphs, until such time that Humanity would arrive at a point where the consciousness would be able to comprehend the information and it would become applicable.

Recently, Archeologist, Scholar, Historian , Author Zechariah Sitchin revolutionized our understandings of ancient Sumerian "Myths". Sitchin realized that eleven of the 'Gods' described in the Sumerian records were actually bodies in our solar system (the planets plus the Sun and Moon).

Sitchin further realized that the Sumerians had a knowledge of the outer planets that by all rights they shouldn't have had, according to the conventional historians. He proved this to the world by submitting to NASA detailed descriptions of the outer planets as found in the Sumerian records BEFORE the NASA space probes had yet reached these planets. Images sent back by the probes confirmed that in fact, the ancient Sumerians indeed knew what these planets looked like and the calculations of their size and orbital paths were correct.

What makes the scenario with the constellation Pegasus, and the signal coming from this part of the universe at this time even more interesting, is Pegasus' connection to the Goddess energy. This is more than a coincidence if we take into consideration the present awakening of the feminine energy and consciousness in today's world, especially here in the Western Hemisphere.

We are told by conventional historians that Native Americans did not have the convenience of the Horse until the arrival of the Europeans. (There exists hard evidence to show this is not correct.) We are brought to the Prophecy of the White Buffalo Calf Woman...**Pti san wi**. (Her name in proper Lakota) These Rites are brought to the Lakota and Chief Hollow Horn, 19 generations ago as of this writing, by this sacred woman, who appears to them as **the White Buffalo Calf Woman,** and also as **the White Buffalo. IS** there a connection here between **the Goddess and Pegasus**, between **Pti San Wi** and **the White Buffalo**, or am I reaching for the stars?

REVELATIONS 12:1- "..And there appeared a great wonder in heaven, a woman clothed in white with the Sun, and the moon under her feet, and upon her head a crown of twelve stars...."

In the story of **the White Buffalo Calf Woman**, which is about the history of the Lakota/Nakota/ Dakota People, one might say it is their Biblical accounting, we are told again about a radiant feminine being from the heavens...

The Vatican and Wormwood

And a Letter from a priest

by Rev. Dr Joseph Puleo

In December of 1996, some of you might remember an unusual letter that was received by Art Bell. It was a purported letter from a Vatican Priest, which created quite a stir. In the letter the priest indicated that while working in the Vatican in a high security position with their data files, he stumbled quite innocently upon files which clearly indicated a direct connection to the Hubble space telescope. Not only it seems were they directly linked but the telescope it turns out was directly pointed towards the comet Hale-Bopp.

The data discloses, as the letter goes on, that the Vatican was very aware of the companion which was of major concern to them. The letter further tells us that they were very concerned with the whole idea of Wormwood, which ties us into Zacahriaz's information from the Dead Sea Scrolls and the Sumarian information about the planet Nibiru also known as Marduke, and sometimes recognized in ancient script as the Wormwood Planet.

I have made some startling discoveries while investigating this Wormwood issue and the letter from the priest. Several times I tried to send faxes and letters to Mr. Bell about my discoveries concerning the priest letter and having to do with my work decoding the bible. There was no response from Mr. Bell and I was about to give it up as a lost cause when I met Robert Ghost Wolf. A friend had put us together after seeing Ghost Wolf speak at a seminar in Spokane, Washington.

When I told him about my research and trying to contact Mr. Bell on whose show he is a frequent guest, I was further shocked. Apparently the priest had E-mailed the very same letter to Mr. Ghost Wolf some two or three days before Mr. Bell spoke about it on the air. Ghost Wolf showed me his copy of the E-mail and it was indeed the identical letter dated prior to Art Bell releasing the information on the air.

I disclosed my findings again to Ghost Wolf and asked if he could get the information about the decoding of the information spoken about on Mr. Bell's show. He said he would try. The information, in my opinion, was of the utmost importance for the world, as it tied in to what was going on presently and related to ancient Bible Prophecy. If our forefathers, who were men of God, wrote their information encoded for the benefit of future generations who would need the information in a time of need, all indications were that this was that time.

Ghost Wolf, it seems, was also unable to get Art to speak on the matter and so to this day the information has only been known to a small circle of people. When Ghost Wolf came to me and asked me to write this article for the Wolf Report I felt that perhaps at last I can get the information out. I feel that if we know the truth of matters it will help us through these troubled times.

Even if we must face certain calamities and Earth Changes, perhaps some of us, if we have the information, can be effectual in helping our fellow human beings to get through these times. I firmly believe that "the truth shall set you free." Knowledge is the only defense we have against the dark, and the only pathway where we can hope to alleviate the suffering that seems to be spreading throughout the planet and our people.

We wish to present the information for your consideration.

May it bring understanding and courage to all of God's children that it reaches.

In the light of the Christ,

The Reverend , Dr. Joseph Puleo

THE FOLLOWING LETTER WAS READ ON COAST TO COAST RADIO ON THE ART BELL SHOW AND WAS SUBSEQUENTLY CC: ALSO SENT TO DR GHOST WOLF

Dear Mr. Bell,

I have listened to your program off and on for around two years now, whenever I get down-time". I have some disturbing information and I fell that your program would be the perfect vehicle with which to distribute what I have. I have been under the employ of the Vatican for over five years. I have done what could best be described as counter-intelligence work, for the church. I am a man of God and please believe me when I tell you that the information I have is genuine, and very serious. Without going into too much detail about my former employers, I will briefly tell you that I have had a Top-Level security clearance in the Vatican for quite some time.

Most of the work I have done regrettably falls into the realm of "black-ops", and I will not go into detail about that now. Around six months ago, I was working at a data terminal in a highly restricted area following a case that I had just completed, when I stumbled onto something that nearly made my heart stop. Please pay attention here, this is where it gets strange. I uncovered a heavily encrypted sub-system that was surprisingly well hidden.

I found that it was only accessible through the terminal I was at, and one other terminal.(I must point out that the area I was in was not an area that I routinely used.) After two minute of trying to get into the system, the whole lab shut itself down and I was booted off the terminal.

Not wanting to raise any eyebrows, I decided to leave and come back later that night. The strange thing was, when I came back, there were ARMED guards standing sentry outside of the lab. I must say

that it is not unusual to see guards roaming the Vatican, but it is very unusual for them to stand sentry at a lab, much less while armed. Over the next month, I managed to slip in unnoticed only once. And after I had found what I came for, I understood the security. It took me a good deal of time to break into the system, and when I did, I wished I hadn't.

When I entered the system, I came across a file titled "WORMWOOD?".(Yes, with a question mark.) Thinking it to be a text file, I brought up the file with the intent of copying so I could read it later. What happened next was truly remarkable. The file sort of "deteriorated" into a series of command lines that lasted approximately two minutes. Once it was done running, there it was. I had found a direct link-up to the Hubbell space telescope. Not only that, but it was pointed directly at the comet Hale-Bop.

The program was running some kind of analysis. Taking directional notes, projecting path of travel, etc. After realizing what I had discovered, I started searching and came across an e-mail data trail that led directly to the office of the Pope himself. What was discussed, I cannot know.

Over the next two weeks, I began to uncover evidence that the Vatican is very aware of the existence of the companion, and is VERY worried about it. I began to copy files and pictures that were present at the terminal, when I found a report from the United Nations to the Vatican, as well as a report from NASA regarding their concerns. It is very obvious to me that a great many people and entities know of the companion and are doing their best to keep quiet. VERY quiet.

As the next part of my story illustrates. I had found another file that I wanted to look at, but it was independently encrypted. At the time that I discovered it, I had already been online at the terminal for some time, so I decided to copy the file encrypted, and decode it at my leisure.

As I was leaving the lab, I was approached by two of the Pope's top aides and was asked to meet them later in the evening. I didn't feel comfortable about the situation, so I agreed and told them that I needed to shower, and would join them later. I haven't been back to the Vatican since.

I found out about a week later through some old friends and contacts that a contract had been placed on my life. Two days later my mother and father were killed in a car crash in France. Three days after that, my brother and sister were killed when their single engine plane went down on the East coast of the U.S. I've been on the run for a very long time now, and am still trying to decode the file that I have in my possession. Approximately ten copies have been distributed to friends in the field in the event that I should disappear.

I do not fear for my life, as I am very adept at not being found, however I believe that the world needs to know of the information that I have. I would be willing to share all that I have with you Mr. Bell. But you need to understand that your life could be in danger if you were to go public with what I give you.

I apologize for being so vague, but I feel it necessary at this point in time. If you would like the information, say so over the air when you get this letter. If I am not listening, someone will get the information to me, as there is no safe way for you to contact me at this point in time.

I await your response.

PRIEST–

What was the priest really trying to tell us? Did he encode a hidden message in his letter........... "**If they have the eyes to see***..." view the following with an open mind and decide for yourself .*

Secrets from the Bible codes

King James and Mr. Webster: A rather strange alliance

The information before you comes from an understanding of the encoding of the Bible that is accessible to anyone. The King James Bible is very important, and attempts to alter it for its content have been somewhat successful especially over the last forty years. No longer available is the Apocrypha which is the key to understanding certain links between Old Testament and the New Testament, also telling us certain predictions about events that will be occurring in the future which is now the present.

King James was a Mason and knew certain secret understandings of the Bible that were only privy to the Masonic order at the time of his incarnation here. He rewrote the Bible The King James Version making certain that the encoding was correctly placed and positioned and not easily detectable. So that again future generations would be able to have access to the information when the time was right and it was needed.

The numbers and encoding of tone, words and frequencies are to be discussed in a book that, with the grace of God will soon be published. Referring to it here... the encoding and knowing where it is.....is not quite enough to unravel the mystery. Along our journey through evolution and different world powers and government we find that words change and sometimes the meanings are lost to antiquity; other times they are altered in today's perception and sometimes they have been eliminated entirely.

So to the well-intended seeker, the answer can remain unattainable for a lifetime. This is where Mr. Webster comes in. How many times have you picked up the dictionary and looked up a word in your life. Well, we usually find the correct spelling and then take up with the first meaning of the word. But how many times have you actually picked up the dictionary and read it. Not many, correct? Read it so you understood it... Its structure and how it works? Are you getting my drift here.

In my first book, *'Bible Codes and the coming Biological Apocalypse'* that I shared co-authorship with Dr. Len Horowitz and a subsequent book that will soon be released, I go into detail as to the incredible information one can find by utilizing the dictionary properly. Worlds of knowledge will be opened up to you if you learn to use the dictionary properly. Again, what this has to do with this article is that Webster was also a Mason. One with proper guidance will quickly learn to understand how to cross correlate between the Bible and Webster's Dictionary where the dictionary becomes a living guide to decoding the King James Bible. They work hand in hand.

When reading the letter from the priest, certain things become both very disturbing and apparent about what is going on in the world. Why there is so much sickness, and epidemic respiratory diseases. Why there is so much circumstance that is leading all of us headlong like a cattle stampede into the **Armageddon Syndrome**. Presently it appears that we are being lead like sheep to the slaughter, but it does not have to be that way if we take advantage of a little knowledge, a little effort and make the choice to alter the outcome.

Remember when Ghost Wolf spoke on Art Bell's show about the Seven Thunders, and the green mists and the three little devils that would fall from the sky in connection with Hale - Bopp. And they would cause the waters to be polluted, and the fish would die. Then after this we would see the same in humans. Then there would be many abnormalities appear in the animals that lived by the waters, first by the rivers and then in the great oceans. Then we would see this happen amongst humans.

Then the crop failures, and the strange burning of young crops before their season even started, and the hundreds of thousands of acres of US farm land that now lie dormant, and wasted with crop failures...The strange viruses and funguses afflicting millions of Americans with respiratory illness, and flesh eating anomalies. The mutant animals are being born first by the waters and then upon the land, and now those same anomalies being found now in humans.

Well, what Ghost Wolf spoke about in the **Seven Thunders** is also spoken about in the Bible, and referred to in "the priests letter" to Art Bell if one can pick up on the encrypted codes he placed there...

Now put the puzzle together for yourself. Figure out the code...remember Webster's Dictionary, and King James Bible...watch the numbers, and look up all the meanings, and their roots... and remember, I did not say it wouldn't take you time...

In the name of the Christ, Dr. Joseph Puleo

So let's make this a little easier. We will locate the phrases in the King James Bible and cross correlate them with Webster's Dictionary...Let's see how it all unfolds

King James Bible:

Revelations 8: 9 And a third part of the creatures which were in the sea, and had life, died; And the third part of the ships were destroyed.

What is happening to our planet and its oceans this very moment?

Revelation 8:10 And the third angel sounded, and there fell from heaven a great star from heaven, burning as it were a lamp, and it fell upon a third part of the rivers and upon the fountains of waters;

What fell from Hale-Bopp? Is this the green mist that Ghost Wolf Spoke of that would kill the life forms on the planet?

Revelations 8:11 And the name of the star is called Wormwood: and the third part of the waters became Wormwood; and many men died of the waters, because they were

made bitter

What has happened to our waters? The viruses clearly are being carried by water. And, 90% of our water in America presently tainted and non-potable.

REVELATIONS 9:10   ...and they had tails like unto scorpions, and there were stings in their tails; and their power was to hurt men five months.

Are these Apache helicopters in the Gulf War?

REVELATIONS 9: 11   ... And they had a king over them, which is the angel of the bottomless pit, whose name in the Hebrew tongue is Abaddon, but in the Greek tongue hath his name Apollyn

That turned the place into a place of death with no escape?

REVELATIONS 9:12   One woe past, and behold there came two woes more

Does this refer to the three little devils of the Seven Thunders?

REVELATIONS 9 :14   ...Saying to the sixth angel which had the trumpet, Loose the four angels which are bound in the great river Euphrates.

Something from Iraq?

REVELATIONS 9:15   ... and the four angels were loosed, which were prepared for an hour, and a day, and a month, and a year, for to slay the third part of man

What is the date, where are the stars on this encrypted date?

REVELATIONS 9 :16   ... And the number of the army of the Horsemen were two hundred thousand; and I heard the number of them

Two Hundred Thousand?

Now we proceed and connect it all for the date..

Four angels: ... Is the fourth month ... April...

...The third Angel: is the third day...

... the horsemen were two hundred thousand: The year is 2000. So we are looking at either the millennium or somewhere near the turning of the millennium

Websters Dictionary: By following the root and the original language and meaning in that language we find the following facts through cross reference.

A pol lyon   Bible in Revelation, *the angel of the abyss;*
Abaddon Rev 9:11

Etymology Gr. **apollyon**, destroying, ruining <**appolyein**, to destroy<**apo**-, from+**lyein**, to loose

A bad don   Bible

1 the place of the dead; nether world: Job 26:6
2   in **Revelation**, the angel of the abyss;
Apolloyn , Rev 9:11 etymology
Heb. Destruction, abyss

Looking up Wormwood throughout the Bible we also find;

Jeremiah 9:15   ...therefore thus saith the LORD of hosts, the God of Israel; Behold, I will feed them, even, this people, with wormwood, water of gall to drink

Jeremiah 9:16   ...I will scatter them also among the heathen, whom neither they nor their fathers have known....(are not the people of the west are considered the Heathens 'Infidel's' in Iraq?)

Lamentations 3:15 He hath filled me with bitterness, he hath made me drunken with wormwood.

Amos 5:7   ...Ye who turn judgment to wormwood, and leave off righteousness in the earth

Amos 5:8   ....Seek him that maketh the seven stars and Orion, and turneth the shadow of death into the morning, and maketh the day dark with night: that calleth for the waters of the sea, and poureth them out upon the face of the earth

Deuteronomy 29:18   ....lest there should be among you a root that beareth gall and wormwood;

Deutronomy 29:22 ...and a stranger that shall come from a far land, *shall say, when they see* the plagues *of that land...*

Deutronomy 29:23 ...*the whole land thereof is* brimstone, and salt, and burning, *that it is* not sown, nor beareth any grasses...

Deutronomy 29:24 ....Even all nations *shall say,* wherefore hath the LORD done thus unto this land? What meaneth the heat, of this great anger....

Hebrew and Chaldee Dictionary

894 Babel (baw-bel) *from* 1101; confusion....

1101 Balal (baw lal) a prime root; to over flow, (spee with oil) *by impl.* To mix;also. (denom. from 1098) (to fodder:-anoint, confound, X fade, mingle,mix give provender, temper

3939 la anah (lah-an-aw) *from an unused root supposed to mean curse;* wormwood,(regarded as poisonous, and therefore accursed.) hemlock, wormwood

Webster's again

I-raq a republic in SW Asia. N of Saudi Arabia and W of Iran, centering in the Tigris-Euphrates basin of Mesopotamia.....

Summation of Dr Puleo's findings

Few people remember that one day on world television after the occurrence of Desert Storm, Sadam Hussain, while standing in front of the world's news cameras, said with a smile on his face as he turned the switch which allowed the oil to flow again, "The world will never be the same."

There is fungus which grows in the oil (wormwood).   It is then transported to America, and upon processing and use in our automobiles is releasing into the air the new viruses now plaguing us as a humanity and are killing millions of people.   It is in the fumes of the gasoline as we self-fuel our cars; it is in the exhaust of jet airliners that fly in our skies and fill airports in major metropolitan areas.

We were given a little gift from Iraq, a subtle revenge for the tens of thousands we had murdered in Operation Desert Storm.

People are degenerating by the day. People are becoming more and more lawless and violent and desperate to survive. Relationships are deteriorating and children are committing suicide by the thousands in our country. These are facts, not just someone ranting with delusionary visions of an accursed world.

Our waters are so polluted, and in many areas around already the only source of potable water is reconstituted Ocean water. With the coming of the first decade of the new century, these areas may well become wastelands of death, unable to sustain life. (Written in 1998 ***Winds of Change***)

The fungus is already in our waters and in our food supply. It causes crops to burn up and wither before they grow to maturity. It is in the rain that falls from the clouds. Horrible? Yes it is. What is worse, if we do not pay attention to the problem we are a conquered country, and the death that could result would fulfill yet another prophecy - one that I do not want to think about.

I pray we wake up in time, that we turn to our spirituality and begin to pray to whatever God we call sacred, because it is going to take a miracle to turn things around now. We have ignored the warnings for much too long.

My Indian friend had a dream and in the dream all the animals had vanished from this earth; only man was left...the only solitary life form. The only one left to watch
the end time, as all of humanity passed from this plane and then the Earth was reborn.....without us.

Expect a Miracle.... Soon!

There is after all the other side to the prophecies if our intent and actions are

impeccable and pure...

Dr. Joseph Puleo

Social Disarray and
... and the Methodical Enslavement of the Masses

For the most part, urban cites and communities will become little more than death camps for the afflicted as well as those individuals who are considered dissidents and dangerous to the official policies of the state in the maintaining of order. As the situation escalates, there will be little hope for those caught in the inner cities.

Already plans are in effect and have been for some time to deal with this situation as it develops. Our penitentiary systems are being geared to be turned into large labor camps that will compete with the labor force on the outside. This will, of course, create a problem because, essentially, the labor force, (those individuals who are caught in the gears of the system), will be slave labor...economic competition will be impossible.

We will see the formation of a special Federal environmental program and as well a security program that raises itself once again above the law. This organization will be formed to deal with problems resulting from the abnormal weather conditions. This organization will have carte blanche power to take over cities, when dealing with technology to cope with the environmental problems.

There will be no way to intervene with this organization and in many areas they will render dictates of martial law. This organization will create a new interpretation of National Emergencies, allowing the President to act with dictatorial powers.

The Soft Invasion
or Third World and Assimilation of the US society..

For a period of time it will be such that Third World people and countries will suffer greatly at the hands of technologically advanced nations that have the upper hand in controlling the governments of those countries. Their already shaky economies will feel the effects of the echoing of economic collapse from the Western powers that are the present conquerors and Lords of the Land. These will be replaced at first by an international NSO group, which eventually will allow *for the emergence of the Intergalactic representatives who truly run the game of illusion.*

This will occur before the quarter-point of the next century. The old power lords, orchestrating the recent emergence of the corporate reality, have set up a Matrix by which they are in total control manipulating the actions of governments and those placed into key positions, to comply with the program. This is the subtle, often unseen but all encompassing Matrix for world enslavement, and eventual termination of the masses by the few elite class members who believe they would have the blessings and protection of the Galactic Order....

As it is now, the world is manipulated by illusion on almost every conceivable level. Those in power are very few in number. This small group of self-appointed elite control all the media and thus they control the banks, as they once controlled the Churches... Thus they could control the population. Now they would seek to control the heavens themselves, and yes, even our Sacred Mother through HAARP, ELF and other frequency- oriented technologies.

Those presently in control of world governments have little or no fabric of spirituality, save materialism and the desire to live forever in their lust. They have their agendas and take their orders from those from above. Nothing has changed in 10,000 years, only in external appearances. What occurs today was seen 10,000 years ago, for there are those who understood the nature of time and used that knowledge for their own means. We are simply playing out the scenario of every possible potential. We have reached the end of the purpose of limited experience, and there are those who would hold on to this dream even at the cost of destroying themselves.

Also, it will be admitted, many of the pathogens and emerging viruses will have somehow infected nature itself and that they thrive and are spread through the waters and the vegetation as well as animal life.

Oceans will become great pools of death and there will be devastating realizations that in fact our seas are devoid of life forms as we have known them.

There will appear many mutated life forms; creatures will appear, although microscopic at first, having the ability to change and develop rapidly into more advanced versions of themselves. What we call monsters will be seen with increasing frequency. There will remain pockets of the oceans of our worlds that host life as it was known in the previous centuries. These will become sacred places to the people of Earth in those times...

There is much presented in my book **Last Cry** about social changes. It all still holds true, and is not off the mark. So if your questions are concerning this subject, I suggest you go look there. We are in for tumultuous times, and the whole of society the world over is being affected. As you view things and events in the near future keep in mind that **All might not be as it appears**.

Vision from the past _the Days of Destiny

We will, despite what we want, experience a collapse of the global economic systems of the American Money Machine. The game player since this the **Last Dance of the Tyrants**, where we will experience the fanaticism of religion going mad, and America will receive a hit in the beginning of this new century the ripples of which will have profound long rang effects.

The corruption of the corporate systems and the enslavement of an entire world's population to feed its need for endless growth and increased profit is going to explode.

'The Beast' will try to consolidate in a last ditch effort to gain control over the entire world media. The large corporations will in a last attempt to hold on to their empires of lies and thievery of the world's resources, including the people, will form "Super Corporations" So much for the anti-trust.. the way of American business.

The fall will be swift and without mercy as America the beautiful falls into America the Shameful. And the corporate gods are carried of to the dungeons of time, allowing for the even further unveiling of those who would enslave the whole of the world for the sake of the 'Greenback' and a system that is already dying on the vine.

However this, despite its 'For the People' reality tone, is not a communistic or socialistic prophecy. For it is the genius of the Free Enterprise System, unrestricted by tyrants regardless of whether they call themselves emperors, or bankers, or CEO's that allows for it to rebirth itself through creative powers of the human mind. When The Supreme Court took the words " Under God" out of the Pledge of Allegiance, and declared it unconstitutional, it also took the Spirit out of the American Matrix. We have become a Godless Nation, merely a political system

Below is a heiroglyph from the Temple of Abydos, Egypt, about 800 BCE

Necessity being the mother of invention, many of the 'boy geniuses of the twentieth century' will come to the calling and create a new and different corporate system. We will see an actual attempt to create ' Positive' Corporate ethics, as many of the leaders, or heads of these world corporations are as well affected by the ever-rising pressure of an awakening world.

I would expect the first of these to come in the field of medicine due to some very real issues that the whole of the world is now facing.

The Thick Plottens as the cover ups are exposed through the science of genetics, as mankind begins to understand the nature of the Stealth Viruses... and the emergence of the 'Great Dying" These new plagues will be brought on through irradic weather and the breakdown of the immune systems in all species plant as well as animal due to the effects of no consequence explorations in wholesale genetic engineering.

What is Presently Foreseen:

Centers will emerge throughout the world where new and alternative methods of healing will be employed. Traditional medicine will make an all-out effort to bridge the 'GAP' between natural and Holistic and Allopathic procedures of medicine.

These will be the beginnings of what the masters have referred to as the Temples of Rejuvenation. Here thousands will come to receive the healing and relief from what was formerly considered terminal and untreatable.

Viruses are crystalline in form. Crystals, especially manufactured crystals, are not affected by the use of vaccines and serums. They are affected through vibration and frequency. I will explain this in this manner. The vaccine upon entering the body totally disrupts the chemical balances.

The virus senses the invasion this time by the supposed good guys and has the ability to enter a state of a suspended animation. In that state, much like the caterpillar, it senses the conditions around it and has the unique ability to transmute while safely tucked away in its chrysalis. It then changes form waiting until conditions are right to reactivate within the chemical environment of the body.

IT - the "Bug" - is not gone, it has simply entered a state of dormancy and while in that state it is constantly sensing the environmental conditions of the world around it. So in a way, the consciousness is still alive. The Virus, while in this state, is interacting with our biophysical and energy fields, causing the body to alter and create for itself an environment to accommodate its required ideal conditions. When the chemical or frequency conditions become compatible with its frequency range it is resurrected into a new and improved version of its former self.

Therefore, as long as you are walking around, so to speak, with the frequency of the virus in your embodiment, you have the potential of that disease proliferating in the body. The symptoms can be arrested, or slowed down, but the potentiality for it to move to another location, or manifest in a trans-muted form always exists. This is why when a cancer patient goes in for an operation and even though the cancerous tissue is removed, the cancer can suddenly reappear in another art of the body at a later date, or the condition suddenly and unexplainably reproduces itself and the patient has a relapse.

If you can, imagine viruses not only having the ability to do this within the realms of biophysical conditions, but also having the ability to attach themselves to your consciousness, having the ability to actually become a part of it. Imagine, as well, that they can enter and exist in both animal and plant life. If you can imagine this, you will be at the beginning understandings of the nature of the new plagues currently emerging. Welcome to the holographic world of quantum physics.... Because this is what these viruses do. They make the body's natural defenses think that they are part of the natural matrix, and in doing so they remain undetected, hence the name...***Stealth.***

The Awakening of Self..... a global process of becoming

Did you ever stop to ask where does your consciousness exist? Where does it express? Where is its domain? How is it that knowing can be passed through the mother to her child?   Remember the story of the Magdalene and the link from mother to mother to mother, all being a part of the one?

Yes, it is in the soul, but is that where it exists?… Do we pass our souls on to our child?   NO, but we do pass on the blood. The consciousness resides in the blood. Through the process of the next decade the masters implore you to work on the disciplines to purify your bodies, so that you can become conduits for the new energies. The emphasis of this cannot be overstated.   For the serious initiate, it must become a way of life.

Keep the vehicle clean. Eat only natural foods and supplements whenever possible. Cleansing of the blood as well as oxidation of the blood is extremely important. This enemy lives in our blood, and it has been unleashed through the chemtrails and fungus now running rampant through our ecosystem and has infected the food chain down even to the precious plankton that lives in our oceans.

 The plankton are dying, as are other life forms in the oceans.   As the plankton die off so does our supply of oxygen. For the plankton, the bazillions of tiny life forms filling the oceans; when they are healthy, they are the beginning of the chain for this element in this incredible Alchemical Garden.

 This enemy of which I speak exists within the electron, of the protein cells of our bodies, within the very protein of the molecular structure. This is where it cloaks its presence within our temple. It enters the bodies through a variety of avenues…through the air, in our water systems, through our food chain; the beast is formless... has no form of its own. It borrows form, in a manner of speaking. I should think that the best way of describing this is through illustration…

Footprints of the Beast

There has been, over the last century, much experimentation in the field of biological and chemical warfare, as well as a lot of experimentation with nuclear energy. All of this has taken its toll upon the ecosystem and even our atmosphere. We are the earth and we are made from the same elements; what happens to our mother happens to us. Remember the lesson of the Magdalene.

One of the most diabolical ways the beast has worked its way into our beingness was through the petroleum. It was placed in the petroleum that was shipped to the western countries from the Middle East. Originally it came from Iraq and was created in the very biological labs established by the US. There we created holographic viruses that responded to frequencies. Understand, we are masters in synthesizing nature. Our entire pharmaceutical industry is built upon synthesizing the chemical components of nature.

These were further researched so that they could have their own intelligence. In other words, we designed viruses that could specifically seek out a particular genetic pattern, a specific age group, and gender and genetic composition or race. The Hunta Virus, the Navajo Flu was specifically engineered to seek out Native Americans of a specific blood type between the ages of 25 and 35. Well, this virus had its own intelligence. Publicity in the newspapers blamed it on field mice and squirrels. Problem solved: kill a few million rodents and the situation will go away before the cause is found out. Well, this was not the case with Hunta Virus. The cause was found out. I know it sounds too Kurt Vonnegut, and I wish it were just a dark fantasy.

Yesterday's news! Today we have the West Nile Virus, and Ebola appearing randomly where accidents and deliberate intent were at play. And what about Anthrax?and the dreaded Pox ?

It appears the virus, or the spore of the virus, found a place to reside and exist prior to its finding a living host. It was found in the grain shipments of wheat that came from Canada and was shipped to the Native Americans living on public assistance on the reservation in New Mexico and Arizona. It went to a few other places as well, but most of the outbreaks were in this area. The grain was grain from fields being experimented on by highly classified Corporate Chemical conglomerates, which shall, for the moment, remain nameless; there is plenty of information out about that part of the story now.

The experiment had to do with working with the cross-breeding of human genetics with that of plants. Well, in the results of that experiment the farmers were left with huge fields of now contaminated wheat and grain. Following the prudent policy of waste not, want not, solutions as to what to do with the grain went into high gear. There were some problems with the grain. One of the big problems was that you could not make bread. From the first group of grains it was decided to market the grains as cattle and livestock feed. Also, it is common for some poverty stricken indigenous people to use these grains for their own food supply — fry bread and tortillas do not need to rise.......

This later created other serious problems throughout the American West as the livestock feeding upon the contaminated grain in other areas caused the breakout of Brucillosus Virus which was then blamed upon the innocent Buffalo of Yellowstone Park.

The point we are going to here, with all apologies to the environmentalists, is the nature of this new strain of mechanical virus. All of us here at Wolf Lodge, myself included, have been avid supporters of the Buffalo in the Buffalo Wars…trying desperately to stop the senseless killing of thousands of Buffalo who were never the carriers of the disease in the first place.

This type of mechanical virus has its own intelligence. It will seek out your resonant frequencies and find those that resonate to diseasement.... What we can call the carrier frequencies. You may not actually be showing the symptoms of the disease but you can carry within your holographic field, in your actual physical system, the frequencies that can manifest the disease.

This may be hereditary or induced by some life condition; the frequency can lie dormant within you for years until the right set of circumstances appear and then **Wham**… As if out of the blue, the disease manifests into physical reality almost overnight and it advances with extreme speed with devastating effects.

Only the implementation of very advanced technology of another order will be able to help us deal with the numbers that will become afflicted in these times………Much of this technology already exits but the knowledge of its availability, it will soon be found out, has been kept from the general public.

STAY TUNED TO OUR WEBSITES: http://www.wnho.net The World Natural Health Organization, http://www.wolfreport.com and http://www.robertghostwolf.com, for further information.

PLAYING WITH TIME

" WHY THINGS MAY SEEM A LITTLE SURREAL…
…AT TIMES… AND AT OTHER TIMES…"

Many of the preceding prophecies will happen and there will be more occurrences. At this time it must be understood the timelines are fractilized due to continued experimentation on the time/ space continuum. Levels of realities are being manipulated to perpetuate those false timelines wherein alternative realities have manifested.

How can this be, one wonders? What if, in the next moment you were to be consciously aware of every element within your perceived reality from the Star above you to the insect crawling upon the ground you stand upon, to the sounds of life that are registering in your ear, to the smells, to the thoughts you were having, to the feeling you are sensing; all that and more comprises the canvas of reality.

Everything you perceive in that instant is a part of your consciousness. If you somehow had the ability to transfer your essence to another level of consciousness, or another time line, all that you are would become part of that level of consciousness or time line as well.

It is a transference of reality. If you further had the ability to move at will in and out of that level of reality, you could then alter things to a great degree. Remember that part of achieving time-travel is to move through a vortex point of NOW. Once achieved, mobility is attained and there is no difference in moving backwards or forward through time. Time itself, remember, is fixed - it is stillness. You are the mobile essence that moves through time, even in the present condition of limited existence.

Therefore one could exist in a place wherein time did not exist and take advantage of entering time and merging with the frequencies of that expression.

In other words, it would be totally feasible to be capable of going back to a targeted time-encapsulated event and return with something from that sequence of time experience, whether animate or inanimate. Each event of this nature alters the time/ space sequence. If enough of these events occur, or if the event is powerful enough of its own accord, you would alter future events. Also, you would be imprinting your frequency in that particular time/space experience, thus altering the moment and future events as well.

You corrupt the matrix and cause a mutation in the process, thus creating mutated results and weakening the matrix that holds everything together.

Do this with repeated frequency and you will knowingly or unknowingly shred the fabric of that time reality. There is a geometry that enables each and every thought to exist. Each and every element is affected, simply because everything is connected.

So if you kept traveling to let us say June 15th 1943 and interacted with that target agenda, then everything — every soul, every tree, every bird in your awareness would be affected. If you did this repeatedly you would rip that time sequence out of natural order. Therefore, that time experience and everything connected to it would repeat over and over. All the elements, animate and inanimate would be caught in a time loop, having no beginning or ending, just playing over and over again, caught in time, so to speak.

In our particular situation, meaning dealing with the whole of our perceived reality, an alternative reality has been created through such experiments as the Philadelphia Experiment, Montauk, The Phoenix Experiment and other time-related research. Time is no longer *time* as we knew it. Time again is a bubble, *a tensile bubble*. It expresses within a particular frequency band, neither stretching beyond that frequency band nor to another frequency expression unless manipulated by external forces.

When this occurs, you destroy the fabric of the specific time expression itself and it becomes corrupted. It is like…when you cannot read a disk you copied information onto from your computer hard drive. Well, the disk has an element that is programmable through frequency imprint.

If the bio-physical composite of the disk is manipulated or if you run a magnet around it a few times, you destroy the configuration of the disk and you can no longer read it. The disk has lost the geometry of the original frequency register…then the disk needs to be reformatted in order to be usable.

You could say that this is one of the conditions affecting our reality at this moment. We have corrupted the nature of time and destroyed the geometry that once made it functional in the matrix of our perceived reality. The information can no longer be accessed; we are losing the memory and ability to connect the dots.

If this occurs, then you are in an emergency situation; something must be done before time devours itself and becomes a no thing. If it becomes a no thing, then that which expressed within its reality also becomes a no thing.

It is the LAW that in the Nature of things all which expresses within a given plane of reality are connected to everything else in that plane. Therefore, if one thing is affected it effects the whole, even if the consequence of the event cannot be immediately seen.

This LAW of Reality has been spoken about throughout the ages, utilizing various terms to relate to the oneness of everything. The term I choose to use to describe this Web of Life, the unseen, yet eminent force interconnecting the sacred grid that sustains thought form and which determines the expressive nature of reality, as the *Matrix.*

That the *Matrix* exists, can be proven in that everyone reacts to the reality of a flashing Red Light which means stop on the highway. Yellow means caution and so forth. Everyone agrees that the sky is blue, and clouds are white.

The conditions of acceptable thought of the present human consciousness is creating a *Matrix* that dictates a commonly accepted common reality. If that reality were to be perpetrated by a force contrary to the geometry grid, or the *Matrix* of the reality expressed….. If, for instance, those who come from other dimensions and who had the ability to express in this plane suddenly started to make appearances within this plane of expression ...the *Matrix* would be altered, for there would be a shock to the perception of reality. The ripple in the perceived reality could, if conditions were severe enough, cause an alteration in the *Matrix*, which could remain altered forever.

This is the case with time travel and the manipulation of the time space *Matrix* by which we have perceived life. Our present existing condition is due to experiments with which we are familiar such as The Philadelphia Experiment, and the Montauk experiments.

Similarly, experiments that cause the manipulation of time to merge with this or another time-line experience, such as going back through time, affects the nature of the time Matrix forever. Where this has occurred on numerous occasions in the last fifty years, the time lines are now shredded, and as a result many fragments of the time line remain in a state of flux. They are no longer a part of that from which they come — they are more or less suspended in-between the fabric of time.

That means exactly what you are thinking. That which is connected to this time line experience is, for now, caught in that moment of time; everything that is connected to it is also caught, at least in part, to that time-line experience, for as long as it remains a fragment of time, it will remain a separate reality.

We have altered time more than can be discussed in this writing. We will pay the price of that calamity and all it has affected. For what was most overlooked in the games of those who would play at being God is that there is more to this Great Mystery than their egos could have imagined.

Like children at play without knowing the full consequences of their actions, it could not be foreseen. What is now occurring in this present experience of time could not have been foretold. The knowledge of the cycles of the universe has long been lost to the people of this earth. They are now returning.

The consequence of what was done through the manipulation of time will soon be realized. The sadness in this is that once the window has been broken by the baseball, it no longer functions as it formerly did, nor can it be glued together. It must be replaced by a new one. They forgot why...... My Native American Brothers and I call it a Great Mystery.

I was talking with some fairly prominent people once who were involved in experiments having to do with time travel and the altering of reality. We were speaking about how what everyone was involved in had changed reality forever. I listened, and to a degree I agree with them; however, I brought to them another aspect to consider....

What makes you so sure that while you and those involved in these experiments were playing in your reality that someone else was not playing with reality from another aspect totally.

If you claim that you have changed reality, is it not also possible that the Avatar on the mountain in deep meditation, or the Andromedan visiting Earth, or the Mayan priest in the Andes, or Sri Sai Baba might have been playing with reality on a level of understanding that you either could not, or have not even taken into consideration yet?

Time is a funny thing, dear reader. It has within it "its" reality, yet in the consequence of the whole, it is separate, and unique unto itself. If reality and the matrix of time have been altered, perhaps it will only affect those caught within that reality.

Or another way of putting it would be: If I were caught in a particular web of consciousness, then the realities of that web, or holographic perception and expression of time, would have profound effects upon me.

However, if I were not caught in that particular web of consciousness, then the outcome would not be the same for me as it would be for those caught up in that frequency, for I would have my own separate reality, and I would be the creator of my own reality. It might get lonely, but at least I would not go down with the **ship of fools.**

I   And I can hear you asking, "Have I been involved in these experiments?".... I'll never tell.

The Hyper - Dimensional Stargate

The future is upon us. The days to come, they are now the days that are. We are at the threshold of a dream. We are no longer what we once were, but we are not yet what we are to become. This is a time for New beginnings, as well as endings to that which cannot fit the new expanded reality of our eminent future experience, for the future is being born of the now.

Time itself is devolving, going through an involution of sorts, as it slowly **destructures** from our consciousness. Our perceptions of reality and our place in the cosmos is fluxing with such velocity that even the simplest of us is aware of the quickening other futurists and I have spoken about for so many years.

This is the essence of **the Quickening**; it is the gathering wherein we will move into new frontiers of experience as we flow along in the river of life. It is a river that is never-ending and seeks itself without judging itself. Reality has now moved into the mode of free flow. We must develop our ability to adapt quickly to changing circumstance and changing perceptions, for we are entering the depths of transition as we become the new race.

CHANGE is our natural circumstance. When one attempts to reason out why we as a Hu-manity live in fear of change is a Hu-man anomaly. To many, the fact that we live in simultaneous realities has already been realized and owned; it is inevitable that soon this realty will be realized by the multitudes. Over the next eight years Hu-manity shall pass through the threshold of the dream they are dreaming individually and as a collective.

There is no judgment coming in the Judeo-Christian sense at all. No celestial being is coming to punish us. We are not the bastard children of a heartless and compassionless God. God would not condemn his own creations to eternal hell. What ludicrous thinking.

It is saying that God would in fact condemn himself. Which means again in that moment God would cease to be. Fairy tales! We have been being spoon fed fairytales instead of truths. Our Divine Creation and heritage has become little more than distorted Myth filtered through the veils of many latter day Organized Religions. As Joseph Campbell once said of it. *"Religion is simply misunderstood Mythology..".*

History = His - Story ... Mythology = My- Story

Anything in this third dimensional plane that does not change will be out of step with life and all that is natural. This applies to Hu-manity as well. To resist change is to become rigid, and one can find out quickly what it means to be in conflict with the natural order.

The clashes emotionally can be devastating. Relationships break up, we become devoid of creative thought, the excitement for living withers away, and we find ourselves dwelling within an eternal cloud of darkness, seeing only the negativity in life. We lose all sense of the Divine that dwells within all things animate and inanimate in nature. We lose our ability to live in joy when we lose our ability to dream and see the wonder of it all.

This time is a time of change. It is a cleansing and a time when the essence of all that is upon this plane is rebirthing. It is the **War of Valued Life**, where all that is out of alignment with the process of that which is natural shall be removed. No thing living shall not be touched by the Light…...

".... The Spirit of God will be poured out on all flesh, and the,y the righteous, will not look on a man's skin, or his social status, but they will look and be shown the intent of a man's heart by the Fathers and through this method will they know how to gather the wheat from the tares...."

Last Days Admonition, The Book of Mormon

We as a Hu-manity are entering a **Hyper - Dimensional Stargate** where we are experiencing our perception of time devolving, and we are witnesses to the dimensions beginning to merge into the oneness. We are experiencing, at times, the future merging with the past, and we are finding ourselves learning out of necessity to hold onto, and **TO BE in the NOW**.

We are walking in two worlds and upon shifting ground. This, my Hopi elders taught me many years ago when we spoke about the Days to Come. We must understand that we are becoming Light once again, and we are remembering to be formless once again as well.

Thinking about these times, as we see the headlines or listen to the radio or watch the transpiring of events on the evening news……. I believe we can all agree in simplicity that they are strange times indeed.   We are taught to think of ourselves as the advanced civilization, masters of the Earth, the superior race. Well, I heard it has been said :

…*"Strange times are these in which we live when the old and the young are taught falsehoods in the schools of learning. And the one man that dares to tell the truth is called at once a lunatic and a fool..."*   PLATO

What we are experiencing is a transition, a complete transition — one that takes place in body, mind, as well as spirit. Such is the impact as we approach this particular millennium. For this is the time we have been told about for so many thousands of years by all the illuminated beings who have played their part in the grand performance of the Hu-man drama. We are, indeed, being prepared for our venturing forth into the unknown of a new reality, accessing a new consciousness beyond limitation.

This is the Great School. We are all masters in training being prepared for contact with the truth of our origins...For our ancestors are coming home. We are in the throws of a great awakening, traveling through the **Alchemical Garden** of **Hu-man** potentials. We are all traveling thousands of paths to come to the same destination. All of our stories are different and unique, yet there are similarities tying them all together into the Greatest Fairytale ever told.

" It is important to understand that these messages will be found upon every living thing... Even within our bodies... Even within a drop of our blood. All life forms will receive the messages from the twins....those that fly, the plants, even the rabbit. The appearance of the twins in our heavens begins a period of Seven years. This will be our final opportunity to change our ways. Everything we experience is all a matter of choice......

.......When we see the twins in the sky, we will know that we have about eighteen months before the appearance of the Purifier.... Not far behind the twins will come the Purifier. The Red Kachina.   When the Purifier is close in our heavens it will appear fixed in our skies, and the time of the purification the Hopi elders have spoken about will have begun...... The Earth, her creatures and all life as we know it will change forever"

Excerpted from

<u>Last Cry</u> - Native American Prophecies and Tales of the End Times

by Dr. Robert Ghost Wolf

CALENDAR MANIPULATIONS
Of Western Society and our Synthetic Perceptions of Time

Today we are struggling in our awakening to once again understand the exactness of the calculations of the Chaldeans and the ancient Mayan. They could calculate into the future and see certain events that would occur by the stars with an uncanny exactness, an accomplishment for what we were taught were such a backward people.

To this day, their precise methods remain unrivaled and a mystery to us. As well, it startles us at the preciseness of their calculations. We have had our method of telling time to the hour, as well as reckoning to the seasons so distorted for so long that today we are completely our of sync with the cosmos and cycles of the Earth Herself.   From the time of the Caesars we have seen the great understandings of mathematics and the sciences of Astrology and Astronomy dissipated into the dark ages of pretence.

Rome and the reign of the Caesar god Emperors had conquered the world known to them. The information they stole from the temples told them of even more great peoples and land they then sought to take under their control.

It seems the Romans vanquished the land and the people in their brief but dark dominion upon this Earth. Even though they were a corrupt and decadent society, they had successfully sacked and destroyed the known Mystery schools in Egypt and Greece. Only the Druid and their strongholds in Gaul and Britain were possible as a threat to their desire to not only rule the world but control the consciousness of the known humanity.

But they were thieves and not creators. The knowledge they employed was stolen and they did not possess the intellectual capacity to understand the workings of the mathematical calculations that had established many systems by which humanity functioned as a civilized societal machine.

The Romans had major problems even with their various methods of calculating time, and the calendars were in such array that the calendar as we are presently familiar was not created until the Rome of the Caesars was itself no more.

The calendars of Rome had to be literally reformed and created by the Conquerors of Rome itself. The civil year was found to correspond so little with the seasons that summer had merged into the autumn months, and the autumn months into full winter.

It was Sosigenes, a Chaldean astronomer, that would restore a sense of order into the utter confusion, by putting back the 25th of March ninety days, thus making it correspond with the vernal equinox; and it was Sosigenes, again, who fixed the lengths of the months as they now remain.

In this way Sosigens corrected the faults of the calendar as it was established under the Roman Emperor Constantine, bringing it closer into alignment with the original Chaldean Calculations. Although for whatever reasons, the original calendar was only known to certain orders of the priesthood and was never again used for the public.

Shortly after their arrival in America, the Spanish found the calendar of the Aztecs and of the Maya gave an equal number of days and weeks to each month. This was a very ancient calendar system. Like those of the Chaldeans and Egyptians of that time, any knowledge other than that which was sanctioned by the Holy Church in Rome, was considered sacreligious and punishable by death.

Further, the Papal orders from Rome ordered that anything which did not agree with their sanctioned doctrines and scientific outlooks be destroyed utterly and completely, providing, of course, that a sample was sent back to Rome. All such works were considered the work of the devil and untrue. It often is hard for me to believe what the Europeans called their Renaissance birthed this consciousness.

Over time, the mathematical accuracy used by the Aztec and Maya would continue to amaze the Jesuits and others who would come to this land of the Americas to plunder these ancient texts and artifacts that told of an ancient system of astronomical calculations.

To this day, we are hard-pressed to find error in their reckoning by subsequent verifications; and it has been over 500 years since the Europeans landed upon the shores of Mexico in 1519. They were, by the Julian calendar, nearly eleven days in advance of the exact time predicted by the Mayan.

Mayan Legend

Long, long ago, in the time of Quetzalcoatl, the head of the serpent fell asleep to the ancient moanings of time, while trying to express in manifested realities, only too soon to find its body held in bondage by the thoughts that created its form.

"Wake up, wake up," cried the Lord of Hosts, " For your truth is about to be revealed. Your eyes have seen the fire deep within your belly that consumes your desire to return to that you once were. Your heart has felt the yearning to fold into the reality you have created in search of the Great One Heart, the One Heart that gently guides you into the light of awareness of all that is."

Genesis 6.1- *"And it came to pass, when men began to multiply on the face of the earth, and daughters were born unto them,*

Genesis 6.2- *"That the sons of God saw the daughters of men and that they were fair; and they took them wives of all which they chose."*

The Mayan god Kulkulkan...at the controls of his Starship

Mayan Prayer to the Lost Children of the Sun
Concerning our merging into the 5TH World

Ee-chay-sa-gen-o-an
Omblay-swon-be-go-an

Hashi-men-blee-chon

English translation (This prayer message was, and still is sung today, as they repeat over and over sounding much like a distress beacon in their chanting):

Sons of all Suns,
Daughters of all daughters,
Creators of light and form.
You are the fabric which holds our galaxy together.
Come into yourselves before the time of Kaliquentali
(Time of Change and purification, the awakening).

You must recognize yourselves in order to hold the form you so dearly love.

The future of the creation in is your hands.

The decay in human consciousness is slowly tearing our world Apart, you are falling away from yourselves   .

You must find yourselves or all is lost.

Please come home...

You are only lost in your experience.....you are dreaming"

Consequences of the Arrival

Yes, what is going on in our heavens with Pegasus, by elements of circumstance and actual occurrence, might well be the fulfillment of the prophecy of Revelations. Also, we will attempt to show along our journey its connection as well to the Mayan People, the Haudenosaunee, Lakota, the Hopi, yes, even Tibetan. This is an occurrence of unilateral consequence.

We will attempt to show you this as we progress along this magical and inspiring journey, but fulfillment will not be without its consequences. It will be of a supernatural nature — it will be coming from beyond the present limited scope of reality. We will have to cross over with our consciousness into the realms of Super Consciousness and utilize our potential to tap into the unlimited potentiality of the Universal Christ Consciousness we all possess.

For by all indications, we are about to have an arrival the likes of which you and I could only imagine. We are about to experience a **Star Wars** reality situation, ladies and gentlemen. So best you prepare for **it has come... and like a thief in the night**.

Now the King James Bible tells us...

Revelations. 12:07- *" And there was a war in the Heavens. Michael and his Angels fought against the Dragon; and the Dragon fought and his angels*

Rev12.8. *"And prevailed not, neither was there place found any more in Heaven*

Rev:12.9. *"And the Dragon was cast out, that old serpent, called the Devil, and Satan, which deceiveth the whole world; he was cast out from the Earth, and his angels cast out with him..."*

This is not Lucifer they are talking about. We are talking about the Dracos...Those from Sirius B — the Reptilians, and they are talking about bloodlines, and ancient wars surrounding those bloodlines. We humans have a love/hate relationship with Dragons do we not?

Enter the Dragon

It is important to understand the true reality of the relationship between the Reptilian Consciousness and the one who will role play the Anti-Chris in our human drama. This is necessary to understand the prophecies of the indigenous elders concerning the Sixth and Seventh Thunders. The Alien relationship with our government is not a myth. Already world governments are straining to keep this biggest of secrets secret.

The Truth of what really **IS** leaks out of every conceivable nook and cranny almost daily. The ruse is about up, and as we are able to accept the greater truth so shall it be revealed. One day there will be many red faces in our worldly political circles as the truth makes itself known. Although I fear in the beginnings it will be used against the people, and as a wedge by the corrupted system creating the pathway for the Anti - Christ. Most are little more then puppets dancing poin a stage, automaticly playin g out ther roles.

We all a share in commonality a connection to the Great Reptilian Myth, and the truth to the Myth must be revealed if we are to hope to clear away perhaps one of our biggest misconceptions of our own truth as a humanity. If you think still that we do not have genetic connections to Extraterrestrial races, look at the evidence. If you think that Aliens are a mystical subject for Stephen Spielberg and the science-fiction artists who draw game cards, think again.

As a small token of evidence, I ask you to look at these pictures from the Maya in Yucatan and the Inca in Peru. Hybrids very larg 9 to 14 feet tall and very small some being less than 4 foot in height.. AAARe you asking yourself...Who? Where? How? ... did these various humanoid species below evolve and be born to flesh and blood.. there are things you have not been told. These only represent a small few from the eviden I alone have in my files..

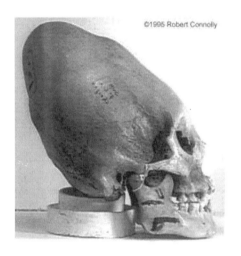

©1995 Robert Connolly

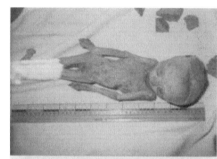

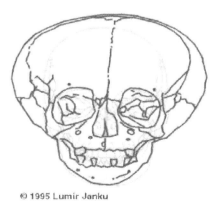

© 1995 Lumir Janku

© 1995 Robert Connolly

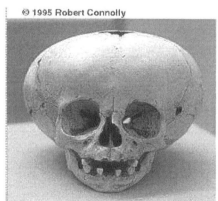

SPACE SHIPS OF THE GODS

A short explanation of Vrill Energy

Now the picture is not always clear. There have been manipulations and tampering with the time-space continuum and events along the way. How... You ask? Somewhere between the rumors and the reality of horrific proportions lies the truth. Time lines have and are being altered...here is presented at least a beginning point for you to research and discover for yourself why so many who have prophecized and foretold the potential of human events have suffered ridicule, been scandalized, or in some cases completely vanished from site.

Perhaps you may even figure out on your own why so many refuse to come out publicly ... Not all that is seen is of a pleasant nature... and the line between science fiction and reality grows thinner by the hour.

… The discovery and Science of Vrill energy is from all the research I have compiled attributed to a German scientist Victor Schauberger. Schauberger worked in close association with Wernher von Braun, the German physicist who oversaw most of the achievements of the U.S. space program until his death in 1977

As to the Vrill energy itself, it could be either hot or cold = electricity. I try not to think that it is something we don't have now. I just think it is a way of energy that we have not captured to our dominions use now.

Ball lightning is a globule of energy that is sometimes the size of a basketball and has very unique properties such that Vrill is rumored to have. This so-called plasma energy is probably closer to Vrill then any thing else.

I have heard of the cold current electricity which might even be closer to it, or a combination. A so-called ether electricity might have these properties but to really call into question "what it is" or "what does it do" you have to correlate the properties this thing we are calling Vrill energy has.

Properties of Vrill Energy:

It is cold to the touch- or makes components go cold instead of warm (super-conducting at room temperature with a inversion of temperature.)

It is able to propel itself away from a magnetic field thus being a type of antigravity force field Or shall we say creating anti-gravatational magnetic? Floating like the northern lights in the sky. Easier to achieve than finding out what gravity is or isn't.)

It can also be used like a fluid - plasma - in pipes. Moving mass has certain unique properties- Keely's taffy, Frogsteins, Saucers technology craft

This use of the Vrill Energy dates back to WWII and the German Circular Aircraft that was built in the physical or 3D during this time. There are 4 people who were involved in the designing of this type of craft. These were scientists whose names were Bellonzo, Shreiver, Habemohl and one other who I cannot at this time remember. I do recall the nature of his design which had to do with water, and the utilization of hydrogen.

It was discovered by the German scientists during the 1930's who were obsessed with ancient technologies the world over that this Vrill energy was also used in Atlantean and Indian aircraft which were used according to the ancient texts around 10KBCE

There is a book written about this which I highly recommend you read. It is called '**_SPACE SHIPS OF THE GODS_**' by a man named Henry Kroll. Henry Kroll is a gifted writer with a vast archive of real-world achievements.

It is suggested that you read about Henry Kfoll and research his credentials as well as his books. You see Evil does exist, it was created by Mankind ...
-

Space Ships of the Gods, is a collection of documented accounts of UFO, and extraterrestrial activity, formatted in one comprehensive volume. Kroll takes us into the secretive world of the World War II ERA, German Third Reich space vehicle, rocket, and ballistic missile programs. He also narrates the post war catch-up space programs of the United States and Russia.

What follows are somw Excerpts from Space Ships of the Gods by Henry Kroll

" Every 12,500 years our earth has an ice age. This is a well-documented scientific fact. There are evenly spaced, lay-ers of coal at Bluff Point in Kachemak Bay. A ten-foot-thick layer of glacier rocks and silt separate each layer. Some of the layers of coal are two to three feet thick. One warm age left a layer over four-feet, thick. 80 distinct layers of coal extending deep underground document a million years of ice ages. All the coal seams were peat bogs and forests at one time because leaves and the wood from the fossilized trees is plainly visible in the coal.

" We still don't know the reasons for these severe climatic changes. Scientists speculate that they have something to do with pole shifts brought about by the precession of the earth's poles or possibly the movement of the magnetic pole. Some of the numbers do correspond. A new ice age is due.

" Obviously the earth's biosphere is not a closed system. Objects that come from outside the solar system every 26 million years affect the history of life on earth. Rich Muller proposes that either a large planet or a companion star to our sun in a very long elliptical orbit enters our solar system every 26 million years disrupting the Ort cloud sending killer meteorites plummeting into the sun. Some of them impact the planets including our earth. Is this what killed Mars? This killer object is due.
-

" Not only is Life on this planet tenuous but subject to cataclysmic extinctions every few thou-sand years. It seems that life in other star systems is just as rare and must be nurtured. We must develop the capability to get off the planet and assist life in other biospheres. If cloning is necessary to create a being capable of making long space voyages to carry on our mission so be it. Even genetic alteration of the species to make it more adaptable to live in space may be necessary.
-

Unexplained Circumstances after World War II

"The Nazi party never surrendered after the war. The USSR and the US were afraid of a bloody Fourth Reich because Hitler promised the fight would go on from other places if Germany were overrun.

" If the last war with Germany was WW II, don't you think by this time the 'Third Reich' would have a contingency plan? What ever happened to the 'First Reich' and the 'Second Reich'?
-

"Admiral Durnet moved the last battalion of over a hundred U-boats to bases in Antarctica at New Swabia (Neuchwabenland) and South America. This was a complete series of U-boats not a random list. Nazi Germany staked Neuchwabenland in 1938 to 1939 prior to the war by dropping javelins decorated with the Nazi flag out of airplanes. The 20,000 square mile territory of Noise Swabbenland, New Swabia, or Neuchwabenland is reported to contain many underground caverns with hot-water springs, open lakes, and an undersea rivers allowing submarine access far inland. Many of the underground caverns were warm and only need the addition of lights to make them hospitable. Given the Aryan preoccupation with underground caverns it is quite logical that they would colonize such a place.

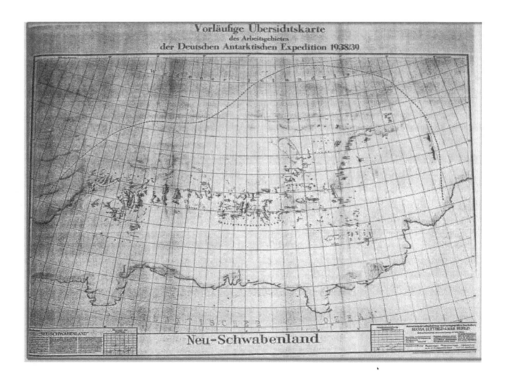

" I have a copy of a 1948 list of 261 German flying saucers. There are 84 Vrills of 11.5 meters in diameter and three Haunebu II's 25 meters in diameter and several Hanebu III's of 79 meters diameters. These have speeds of 2900 miles per hour and the capability of traveling to Mars. A Hanebu IV was on the drawing boards. Several Andromeda mother ships were constructed in the old Zeppelin *hangers at the same time as the Vrills. These could carrying six Vrills and two Hanebu models into space. The Andromedia mother ships are the long cigar-like shapes objects seen occasionally orbiting Earth and are pictured in a Russian photograph orbiting Mars. They were powered by six Vrill Levitation Power Units.*

-

" If the Nazis had 261 flying saucer craft in 1948 they could very well have built thousands of them since then. Even if all of their bases in Germany were bombed out of existence I am sure that some of them survived such as the Marcony plant located inside an extinct ten-thousand-foot, vol-cano some where in South America. Who knows what underground cities they have by now. They may have even joined forces with the ancient underground peoples still controlling the 'Vimana' and 'Asvin' technology.

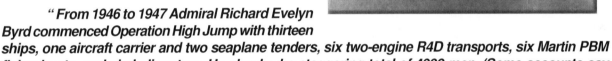

Some of the following information is from W.A. Harbinson's book: Genesis and other books on the subject.

-

" From 1946 to 1947 Admiral Richard Evelyn Byrd commenced Operation High Jump with thirteen ships, one aircraft carrier and two seaplane tenders, six two-engine R4D transports, six Martin PBM flying boats, and six helicopters. He also had a staggering total of 4000 men. (Some accounts say 5000 men). This seems to be a bit much for a "scientific and mapping expedition," don't you think?

-

" It was considered odd that when his force reached the Antarctic coast, they docked on January 27, 1947 near the German-claimed territory of Neuschwabenland, but then divided up into three separate task forces. Some newspapers reported the expedition was a huge success, revealing more about the Antarctic than had ever been known before. It wouldn't take much knowledge to make that statement because very little was known about Antarctica at the time. Other, mainly foreign reports state this had not been the case. Many of Byrd's men were lost during the first day, and four of his airplanes inexplicably disappeared. The expedition had enough supplies for six to eight months but returned to America February 1947.

-

" Admiral Byrd is quoted by a reporter as saying: "It is necessary for the USA to take defensive actions against enemy air fighters which come from the polar regions," and in the case of a new war the USA would be "attacked by fighters that can fly with incredible speed from one pole to the other without refueling." According to a Brisant reporter, after Byrd's return to the USA he was ordered to undergo a secret cross-examination. The USA withdrew from the Antarctic for almost a decade.

-

" During the war the Germans were sending ships and planes to the Antarctic with equipment for their massive underground bases. At the end of the war the flying saucer pilot team of scientists were taken from Germany to submarine U-530 and U-977. The Americans interrogated the crews of those submarines when they docked in Argentina. Upon hearing about the Antarctic base, the Americans organized a military task force disguised as an exploratory expedition. That expedition turned tail and ran when they encountered the German saucers. The United States pulled out of Antarctica temporarily, in order to build their own saucers based on the designs found in Germany after the war.

-

" Years after the war it was suggested in the socialist-leaning, Brisant the Democratic Republic

of Germany should claim back the rights to that part of the Antarctic which the Nazis stole from the Norwegians and arrogantly renamed Neuschwabenland.

German U-Boats in the Azores 1943 (image left)

WITHOUT A TRACE ..MISSING TIME, MISSING PEOPLE LOOSE ANYONE LATELY?

"Thousands of slave workers and their SS overlords disappeared in the chaos of the liberation and were never seen again." It is quite possible the Nazis continued to ship saucer parts, men, and documents to Antarctica throughout the war. Judging by the gigantic size of underground bases found in Germany after the war, with wind tunnels, assembly plants, launching pads, machine shops, supply dumps, accommodations, and adjacent slave quarters for thousands, it is quite possible they constructed similar bases in Greenland, Antarctica and South America.

" All this was kept secret even from the people living near by. "Most of the secret weapons projects were kept secret from everyone, even the historians as well as members of the military."

"That is exactly the kind of fanatical dedication it would take to travel to another planet and colonize it. As long as we have it so good down here on Earth why would we spend the time and money to develop the technology to move to another planet? This is why I believe the Nazi's actually did traveled to Mars and built a city. Perhaps they found a city already there that is millions of years old.

" Their technology was at least thirty years ahead of the United States when they were forced to establish bases off Earth. The ability to come up so quickly technologically suggests possible ET assistance. Some of their technology was retrieved from its Aryan place of origin in Pakistan.

"According to legend the white Aryan race came from the fabulous underground cities of Shamballa and Shangri-La. Germany sent several expeditions into Tibet prior to the war to gather up this technology. The Nazi Party's ability to exist and develop technology underground is legendary.

" Captain Heinz Schaffer in his book U-977 stated that in April 1945 an SS associate had offered him a demonstration of a "death ray" (laser weapon). Schaffer in his urgency to return to Kiel for his famous last voyage declined the offer. According to our mainstream scientists lasers weren't invented until the 1960's.

" -SS General Hans Kammler who pushed the development of the V-1 and V-2 rockets disappeared from Germany in April 1945, His whereabouts is a mystery to this day. The German flying saucer team members Schriver and Bellonzo are dead, and Habermohl was captured by the Russians. This may account for America's fear of Russian saucers after the war. Miethe who worked on Projekt saucer, went to work in Canada and America. The prototype of the AVRO flying saucer was handed over to the US. It was loudly condemned as a failure and now is located in the US Air force Museum at Fort Eustis, Virginia.

" The Kugelblitz (ball lightning Automatic fighter) was first flown in 1945 over the underground complex of Kahala in Thuringia. Allied bombers and fighters reported hundreds of sightings of flying fire balls hovering off their wing-tips. No matter what they did to avoid them they couldn't shake them. There were also reports of death rays.

" In July 1952 a fleet of flying saucers flew over the White House. They were seen by thousands of people and document on radar. Jets were scrambled three times but the saucers easily outran them each time.

The Germans were already developing Antarctica heavily in the latter part of WW II

. " On August 27th, 30th, and September 9, 1958 the US dropped several nuclear bombs on Antarctica. How many bombs were actually dropped during those infamous three days is anybody's guess. Could this be the reason there is a hole in the ozone layer over Antarctica today?

" It seems the Cold War between the United States and the Union of Soviet Socialist Republic was a front designed to squeeze money out of taxpayers. They needed money, lots of it, to construct tens of thousands of nuclear bombs and advanced tactical weapons, enough in fact to kill all the people on Earth ten times over. All this time the real, perceived threat by our government was the Nazi Party's saucers.

" Shortly after the war the Nazi Party sent a Haneubu III to Mars. This was a daring pioneering venture. After they had established radio communication with Mars they sent two Andromedia ships each carrying six Vrills and two Haneubu II's. Since 1948, engineers and scientists from all over the World have steadily been disappearing from major development corporations.

" Many of them went willingly from a society, which discourages scientific discovery to one, which encourages it for mankind's survival, and many of them went to Mars. Infrared satellite photographs of Mars show underground tunnels and a city the size of Los Angeles."

SPACE SHIPS OF THE GODS ... by Henry Kroll
.... end transmission

This documented information found in Henry Kroll's book has been referenced by many individuals in the global scientific community, and has been the topic of conspiracy writers for well over a generation. Much of it has been recognized as being authentic, however due to the environment surrounding such information as considerable portion of the information which came out after Henry Kroll wrote his book has been laced with disinformation and creative conjecture.

We may never know the full accounting of the truth, but the cold blade of treachery feels real and the story resonates with the souls of those who have found out enough on their own ...and met the cold hand of the Silent Powers that control the information flow to the mainstream media, and the global public. The ancients had technology far in advance of today's meager attempts at super-technology.

This information has been kept secret for generations and the most extreme measures have been taken against anyone who would dare to bring it out to public access. So I leave you with a question, "If all this was just so much bunko...then Why?"

The truth lies somewhwere between fiction and surreal accounts of these events. Read research, and you make up your own minds.. Life is often stranger then what others call fiction. The photos below depict actual German operational craft... below.

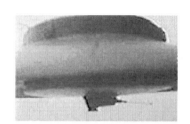

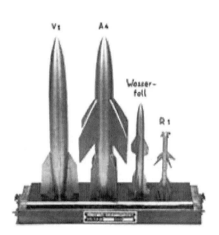

Could this artist rendition above have been a posible actual scenario... Why Not?

The Nature of Reality ...   Understanding Alchemy 101

In becoming the ***initiate***, we learn to become the empty vehicle, the hollow bone through which the God-Force expresses. Therefore, we become servants unto the Supreme Cause, which is the Christos. There we realize our true cosmic purpose and destiny… to consume the unknown. We are excited when we learn and employ new knowledge and technology… Humans prosper in the growing cycle, they degenerate and fall into decadence, in the accomplishment or down cycle…It is a pattern that repeats itself in every accounting of the history of any civilization. Think about it! Reason it out!

We are ***voyagers upon the light***, learning the laws of creation. This we do so that we can serve the purpose of the God-Force that is within us. For the God-Force has no other purpose but to perpetuate and to fulfill Itself. From this basic principle, all we call life is created as pure thought potentiality.

The God-Force can be no secular thing, for to elect to be one or the other is a form of judgment. The moment that the God-Force judged, It would no longer be. Therefore, it would be ludicrous to think that the God-Force would express only through a specific gender or a specific elemental species, for the God-Force is all these things and more. Likewise, the Creator can neither be good nor bad.

For in the moment that God would be either good or bad, judgment is born. In being the supreme elemental force of All That ***IS***, in that moment of judgment, All That ***IS*** would cease to be. Life as we know it would end.

You could say that the God-Force is Lawless, for there are no fixed rules the God-Force follows, only Divine Principles. Rules create form and structure. The God -Force is formless. Hence the essence of our Being is also without form and cannot be contained in the rigidity of dogmatic thoughts. For in the moment our thought realizes itself, thought changes. Like Father like Child.

God is the infinite unknown we call the void. Space itself, as we conceive it, is the river upon which the thought of God Supreme travels through the millenniums of universal existence. And like a river it has its sounds and nature to be understood. It is ever changing, and thus remains the constant from which All That Is springs forth into being.

The God-Force cannot be measured in terms of ***Light*** and ***Dark*** for in truth there is no darkness, there is only God. And what are we? We are the expression of God manifest upon this physical plane. We came from God, because we came from the thought of God. We were born of the Light and remain the Light into our foreverness. We as particums of light travel through Divine thought and manifest upon the various planes of reality as thought evolving.

We are eternal lights expanding into every part of the Universe. When we pass this plane, we again return to the thought, the Supreme Source. Thus the cycle continues in its forever process of God realizing Itself through creation. It is endless, for God is unlimited.

The process called creation is the Divine gift of The Source, initiated unto the children of God, Children of the Sun, we that are the Christos. For Creation is but a thought of Itself in a constant exploration of Its own potential, always seeking Itself, moving like a serpentine energy through the cosmos.

Evolution and growth is presently realized through one's ability to create reality. Hence the time/ space continuum is perpetuated so that we can identify with that essence that we are. Experience is our touching stone, our remembrance of ourselves.

The thoughts of our creation reach out into the cosmos, through the planes of realized experience. The Divine thought seeks us with full passion, just as in the end of each cycle of our own creation, we return to the Source Itself. It is called valued life, all things seen and unseen. All things potentially, unrealized and realized are born of God. All is Divine, for all is from God's purpose, and born of Love in a state of perfection unto the thought of God

The God Force is eternal and touches us through the breath. The Breath of God manifests always into perpetual life. It can and will transform, but it can never end. Thus, God as we perceive It, is **Egoless**. For we can know not the true nature of **EGO** until we are no longer **Altered EGO**. We have become the reflection of the Light, believing that of itself, **IT** is the Light. Thus we walk in darkness, for the true Light is within, not without. We have created a reverse polarity in our manufactured state of consciousness.

God is the purifier. To perceive that **the Source Of All That Is** would judge, is not based upon the Laws of the Supreme Being. It is based upon the laws of man, man in his state of limitation, living in an adopted state of reality, what could also be termed an **Altered State of ISness**. What we have perceived through limitation as **Ego**, is in fact, the **Altered Ego**.

God of Itself is **pure unaltered Ego, I AM THAT I AM**. Man in his floundering has perceived himself to be, "**because**." But, there is no **because**. There is only ISNESS. This then is the perpetual state of God, ISNESS. BECAUSE, is the reaction too, and not the CAUSE of.

The manifestation of the miraculous is seemingly unknown to most of us simply because we deem it so. We deem it to be beyond our reach. It is out there instead of in here. Because we are living in denial of the Supreme Being as being a part of us, it is illusion.

For God is all that IS. "**Because**" is born of judgment. In the state of judgment as most of us are, we have separated ourselves from the Supreme Being. Thus, we are in denial and being so, we negate our own creations. We are lost in this state of illusion from which we perpetuate our existence, through pain and limitation. The cause is that our Dream Creation process remains unrealized.

We have, as Hu-manity, allowed ourselves to fall into patterns of behavior whereby we are creating the nature of our reality from an incomplete perception of the Universe, thus manifesting reality, in conflict with its true nature and ourselves.

Through this process we have become the **reaction to**, rather than the **supreme cause of.** In our altered state of reality, we perceive the Source of Life as being external, rather than internal. Thus we are trying to create from a portion rather than from the whole.

We are the participants in all that is, Co-Creators in the game of life. In most cases, what we have come to call miracles are simply the experience or witnessing of something we do not yet understand. This is because in most cases we do not yet possess the knowledge of what is making things occur.

We no longer understand the **Kryah**. The reasons why we do not have this knowledge are simple. There no longer exist the great schools of life. We are not taught the Divine principles of life in our present educational institutions.

Look anywhere in the educational structures of western society, it becomes evident very quickly that we are not being taught the fundamentals of the Life Force, and how Universal Law applies to our everyday life. Thus, we have become graceless and stiff in our expression of self. We need psychiatrists to tell us who we are because we have lost touch with ourselves and our connections to Source have been broken.

We are being bred to become little more than feed for the corporate machine that in the end devours us and cannot allow us to have our own individual expression. "Everyone is expendable and no one has a real friend."

In our neoteric society, we are becoming almost completely reliant upon the use of technology to solve our problems. We continually seek the answer to a situation by going outside of ourselves. For the most part, the majority of the people working with modern technology do not have the slightest grasp of how or why anything works in the first place. They are operating in a space of robotic consciousness.

Our neoteric society is built upon the premise of logic, rationality and the explanation of things through intellectual **Mind**. Everything is linear; our thought process goes from point A to point B without question, like a horse with blinders. The Universe is spherical, as is time, as is the true nature of our Spirit. Our Spirit-Self is not linear.

Linear thinking is two dimensional, as is intellectual **Mind**. There is something beyond **Mind** called Consciousness and beyond Consciousness is **Awareness**. The explanation of this phenomenon is easy.

For example, let us suppose that you are involved in some sort of trauma, say an automobile accident. You suddenly awaken in a hospital room. You know that you are in a hospital, but you do not know why or how you got there. Further, you are unaware of what is going on or why these strange Beings with masks are hovering over you. At this point you have come back into third dimensional consciousness.

You are not yet in possession of your **Awareness**. Awareness occurs when you remember what event or events brought you to the hospital room. Consciousness becomes utilized. This activation of Consciousness, where it transmutes into Awareness, gives us the ability to achieve action. You could say that **LIFE is a Verb** and not a noun, for this indeed is a great truth.

What is occurring around us, in the experience we call **LIFE,** is the result of Awareness activating Consciousness. The entire nature of our perceived reality is the result of this process. These ancient laws we are talking about are infinite, and therefore imperishable. The elements that are constricted to this temporal plane have little affect upon them. So, the Universal Law that was in effect fifty thousand years ago is just as applicable today, as it was then. What Merlin accessed and drew upon can be utilized today. The understanding of this Mystery is achieved by opening our *Mind* to the realities of Metaphysical Truth.

We then enter the world of *Quantum Reality* through right use of *Will*. We quite literally become contemporary Alchemists. The problem for the most part is that even though these very basic principles of *Kryah* exist, we are not aware of them and we take little responsibility for our actions and words.

We have little understanding if any of the Universal Laws of cause and effect. We feel we are hapless victims of chance circumstance. We are caught up in the results. We are unaware that reality is being manifested unconsciously and constantly by our thoughts. Creation is a natural law that is occurring with or without our conscious participation. It is akin to breathing; we never stop to wonder why or how it occurs, do we? Therefore, one could say most have fallen asleep at the wheel.

There is a limitless Source of Divine Power that is available to all of us. It is waiting there at our total disposal this very moment. We just have to learn how to tap into it. That is the purpose of this revealing of the *Kryah*, to show you how that can be achieved.......not in some distant future, not a nebulous tomorrow, but right now.

These simple understandings can completely alter your life...if you are ready to accept the responsibility of reclaiming and owning your own Divine Power. Excerpted from *Through the Eye of the Shaman*

THE SECRETS OF KRYAH
The Acceptance of Metaphysical Truth

The first step is to understand that *Kryah* is a process. Universal Laws dictate conditions for experiencing, as well as perceiving the Nature of our Reality. The participator transmutes their limited reality, accepts the results of what is presently thought of as a mystery, or miracle and reality becomes applied knowledge. One must be able to deal with unknown outcomes. It is actually detrimental to your path to get hung up on the outcome of events.

What is going to happen is outside of your present sphere of awareness; therefore, it is unknown to you. It is a science and you are the apprentice scientist. The experiment is to journey into and know the Self within......to take that knowledge and through applied experience, understand your true relationship to the whole of the Universe.

What is it that makes a flower? What is the true nature of physical matter? What is Creation, and what is the nature of the God that creates? What is my relationship to all of it? Why are there causes and effects? Why do things happen the way they do?

To answer these and the other questions occurring along the journey, you must alter your present level of Consciousness. Expanding your Awareness enables you to accept more than is presently acknowledged as your reality. You must go beyond limited Mind. Anyone can learn.

The rudimentary requirement is your desire to know, combined with your commitment to completion. You are going to go beyond your present limitations. You cannot create something new from the same consciousness that conceived it. In order for creation to occur, the manifestation must be the result of an expanded consciousness. In other words, a consciousness that is greater than the original thought. A new thought!

So, the first step involves the understanding of how to transmute your present state of Consciousness. You need to identify what is keeping you locked in limited reality. Then you must come to understand the principles that are involved. So, let us begin with four basic elements, **Mind, Consciousness, Awareness, and the Soul.**

MIND: Is like a computer waiting to be programmed by Consciousness. Of itself, Mind is a no thing. It is strictly mechanical, possessing no heart, no emotion, no reason. It is not capable of grasping the abstract. The Mind is simply a tool that we program. It responds likewise. Its abilities are severely limited to its user, which is activated Consciousness.

CONSCIOUSNESS: Exists in the great void, it is the Source. Here is where all things potentially lie...... yet no thing materially exists. This is the realm of Creator, yet not the completeness of Creator. Consciousness of itself is likened unto a dream state, constantly flowing like a river full of ideas and possibilities.

It is ever changing, yet remains the same to our primal perception. Asleep Consciousness is waiting for the user to tap its unending knowledge, much like the empty canvas of the artist waiting to be given life.

AWARENESS: Is an energy; it is the flow of the river realizing itself. It is powered by desire. Awareness is the recognition of a self-purpose, the elemental essence that distinguishes the difference between the rose and the dandelion. It is personality. It is the individual essence that makes us unique.

In its self-fulfillment, it merges with Consciousness and becomes the ultimate desire. In its commitment to fulfill itself, its only desire is **To BE**. As it expands it becomes the cause and is realized. It is that which consumes the darkness, making the unknown the known. From our thoughts, all things materialize into reality.

THE SOUL: Is the embodiment of our memory Awareness. Your **Soul** holds the emotional memory of every experience that the Awareness has explored since the beginning of creation. The **Soul** is unemotional in its function and totally impartial. It is the program holding the knowledge of Consciousness, programmed intuitively with the knowledge of the **Kryah**.

The **Soul** is used by Awareness to fulfill desire. It is the program, the computer chip of the Mind. Herein lies our every experience since the beginning of time. The Soul possesses the individual memory, as well as the collective memory. It is the God of your embodiment.

The Mystery aligning these four elements together is the **Kryah**. It enables us to recognize and read the frequencies of the Universal Life Force and Universal Laws. The Egyptians called it **Ska**, as do the Lakota people here in North America. Some would call it magic. Some call it God.

However you define it, **Kryah** is the Mystery Intelligence that makes up the embodiment of all things. It is the very nature of existence...... The Master Dreamer.......Spider Woman weaving her web.

It is time to become the dreamer again as we weave the new reality. In the process we get to put in the qualities we choose rather than what was handed down to us and accepted without question. We will no longer be living someone else's dream but truly we will be living our own. As we become step by step the Masters of our destiny once again.

THE EQUATION

Gen-ISIS & the Dawn Star

It has been said that the Coptics of Egypt received from Yeshua the sign of eight. A cross with an X layed upon it making eight lines. At the end of the eight lines were eight small circles.

So we look for the sign with eight planets upon the Cross of the House of Stewart, symbol for the royal bloodline, the lineage of Yeshua ben Yoseph, whom the world, after the Roman Emperor Justinian, would come to be called Jesus of Nazareth, Jesus the Christ.

MYSTERIES OF THE EIGHT POINTED STAR

The mysteries of the eight-pointed star can be found woven throughout the cultures of the world. There are references to this star, or eight-pointed cell of perfection in the theosophical libraries where extremely enlightened people such as Helen Blavatsky and Alice Bailey deal with the subject with scientific reverence.

Again we see many references to the octahedron in Sacred Geometry. This subject has been heavily researched by contemporary figures such as Drunvalo Melchizedek and others.

There are extensive referrals to the eight-pointed star in the indigenous cultures of both North and South America. We have the eight-pointed Sioux Star and again similar references are to be found in the Celtics, English, and Nigerian people of Africa. We are told that Yeshua referred to this form repeatedly in his teachings and demonstrated its importance to the Coptics in Egypt.

In the rubbings of the stone writings of the Micmac people clearly shows it very clearly. Also in these photos you will notice that the Micmac's also have a star map to the upper- right of the Eight-pointed Star.

The Vela Supernova
THE DANCING FIRE

"In our galaxy, 12,300 years ago, and about 1,300 light years away, a supernova exploded in the constellation Vela, forming the Gum Nebula. People on earth saw the explosion about 11,000 years ago as a star of magnitude -10, as bright as a 7-day old Moon. Now we on earth see the remnants as a shell with radius about 1,000 light years, covering 30 to 60 degrees in the sky. (The sun and moon each cover about half a degree.)"

From the ...Kaufmann - Universe (4th ed) - Freeman 1994

Contemporary astronomers say Vela supernova most likely occurred 6,000 years ago (although other estimates based upon the deciphering of ancient texts and recently discovered artifacts would indicate that in fact the Vela supernova was seen by the people of Atlantis some 11,000 to 14,000 years).

At an approximate distance of 1,300 light years from earth, the Vela X pulsar is three to four times closer than the Crab Nebula. The Vela supernova would have hung low on the horizon over the Atlantic Ocean and the Mediterranean, a brilliant star shining as bright as the moon (-12.5 losing brightness at 4.5% per day).

Due to defects in the cornea of the eye, a person viewing the supernova would see "spikes" a quarter to a third the diameter of the full moon (7.5 to 9 minutes of arc). Vela would have appeared as bouncing or endlessly dancing, a varying mass of fire and could have even appeared as color rays or shooting spears of intense color looking much like a fountain.

Here on Earth both the landscape as well as the observer would have been flooded with this pulsing illumination from Vela. Tossed flocks of shadow bands would animate the landscape, moving eerily through forest and town appearing very psychedelic.

A wall-sized mural uncovered at Tell Ghassul, which was occupied from before 4000 BC to circa 2000 BC, "depicted a row of people - the first two of whom were seated on thrones — facing towards (or greeting) another person who had apparently stepped out of ***an object*** emitting rays.

"The archaeologists who had discovered these murals during the 1931-32 and 1932-33 excavations theorized that the rayed object might have been similar to a most unusual rayed 'star' found painted in another building. It was an eight-pointed 'star' within a larger eight-pointed 'star,' culminating in a burst of eight rays.

The precise design, employing a variety of geometric shapes, was artistically executed in black, red, white, gray, and combinations thereof; a chemical analysis of the paints used showed that they were not natural substances but sophisticated compounds of twelve to eighteen minerals.

"The mural's discoverers assumed that the eight-rayed 'star' had some 'religious significance,' pointing out that the eight-pointed star, standing for the planet Venus, was the celestial symbol of Ishtar. However, the fact is that no evidence of any religious worship whatsoever, no 'cult objects,' statuettes of gods, etc. had been found at Tell Ghassul, yet another anomaly of the place."

"This, we suggest, indicates that it was inhabited not by worshipers but by those who were the subject of worshipping: the 'gods' of antiquity, the Anunaki."

Zecharia Sitchin,... "The Wars of gods and men"

Some relative established historical data from Sir Laurence Gardner:

"Many books talk about the hermetic schools of Tuthmosis III of Egypt, who reigned about 1450 BC. But it is not generally known that the school he originally inherited was the Royal Court of the Dragon. This had been founded by the priests of Mendes in about 2200 BC and was subsequently ratified by the 12th dynasty Queen Sobeknefru.

"This sovereign and priestly Order passed from Egypt to the Kings of Jerusalem; to the Black Sea Princes of Scythia and into the Balkans - notably to the Royal House of Hungary, whose King Sigismund reconstituted the Court just 600 years ago. Today it exists as the Imperial and Royal Court of the Dragon Sovereignty, and after some 4,000 years it is the oldest sovereign Court in the world.

"But what were the earliest aims and ambitions of the Order back in Pharaonic times? They were to perpetuate and advance the alchemical strength of the Royal Bloodline from Lord Enki, the Archetype. The kings of the early succession (who reigned in Sumeria and Egypt before becoming Kings of Israel) were anointed upon coronation with the fat of the Dragon (the sacred crocodile). This noble beast was referred to in Egypt as the Messeh (from which derived the Hebrew verb 'to anoint'), and the kings of this dynastic succession were always referred to as 'Dragons', or 'Messiahs' (meaning 'Anointed Ones').

"In times of battle, when the armies of different kingdoms were conjoined, an overall leader was chosen and he was called the 'Great Dragon' (the 'King of Kings') - or, as we better know the name in its old Celtic form, the 'Pendragon'.

"One of the interesting items from the archives of the Dragon Court is the origin of the word 'king-

ship'. It derives from the very earliest of Sumerian culture, wherein 'kingship' was identical with 'kinship' - and 'kin' means 'blood relative'. In its original form, 'kinship' was 'kainship'. And the first King of the Messianic Dragon succession was the biblical Cain (Kain), head of the Sumerian House of Kish.

"On recognizing this, one can immediately see the first anomaly in the traditional Genesis story, for the historical line to David and Jesus was not from Adam and Eve's son Seth at all. It was from Eve's son Cain, whose recorded successors (although given little space in the Old Testament) were the first great Kings (or Kains) of Mesopotamia and Egypt.

"Two more important features then come to light when reading the Bible again, with this knowledge in mind. We all tend to think of Cain as being the first son of Adam and Eve, but he was not. Even the Book of Genesis tells us that he was not, and it confirms how Eve told Adam that Cain's father was the Lord. Who was 'the Lord'? The Lord was Adon, (Adoni/Adam/Aton)) and Adon was Enki. Even outside the Bible, the writings of the Hebrew Talmud and Midrash make it quite plain that Cain was not the son of Adam."

(* *Sir Lawrence Gardner, <u>Genesis of the Grail Kings</u>*)

CORRELATIONS BETWEEN THE HOPI AND THE SUMERIAN CULTURE

Information shared by the Hopi elders at a meeting near Oriabi where I was present. This information has been shared in parts through other forums and I thought it appropriate

The Hopi believe the Creator of Man is a woman. The Sumerians believed the Creator of Man was a woman.

The Hopi believe the Father Creator is KA. The Sumerians believed the Father Essence was KA.

The Hopi believe Taiowa, the Sun God, is the Creator of the Earth. The Sumerians believe TA.EA was the Creator.

The Hopi believe two brothers had guardianship of the Earth. The Sumerians believed two brothers had dominion over the Earth.

The Hopi believe Alo to be spiritual guides. The Sumerians believed AL.U to be beings of Heaven.

The Hopi believe Kachinas (Kat'sinas) are the spirits of nature and the messengers and teachers sent by the Great Spirit. The Sumerians believed KAT.SI.NA were righteous ones sent of God.

The Hopi believe Eototo is the Father of Katsinas. The Sumerians believed EA.TA was the Father of all beings.

The Hopi believe Chakwaina is the Chief of Warriors. The Sumerians believed TAK.AN.U was the Heavenly Destroyer.

The Hopi believe Nan-ga-Sohu is the Chasing Star Katsina. The Sumerians believed NIN.GIR.SU to be the Master of Starships.

The Hopi believe Akush to be the Dawn Katsina. The Sumerians believed AK.U to be Beings of light.

The Hopi believe Danik to be Guardians in the Clouds. The Sumerians believed DAK.AN to be Sky Warriors.

The Hopi believe Sotunangu is a Sky Katchina. The Sumerians believed TAK.AN.IKU were Sky Warriors.

The Hopi name for the Pleaides is ChooChookam. The Sumerians believed SHU.SHU.KHEM were the supreme Stars.

The Hopi believe Tapuat is the name of Earth. The Sumerians believed Tiamat was the name of Earth.

The Hopi call a snake Chu'a. The Sumerians called a snake SHU.

The Hopi word for "dead" is Mokee. The Sumerians used KI. MAH to mean "dead."

The Hopi use Omiq to mean above, up. The Sumerians used AM.IK to mean looking to Heaven.

The Hopi believe Tuawta is One Who Sees Magic. The Sumerians believed TUAT.U was One from the Other World.

The Hopi believe Pahana was the Lost Brother who would one day return to assist the Hopi and humankind. The Sumerians would recognize PA.HA.NA as an Ancestor from heaven who would return.

The Hopi not unlike the Mayan and the Inca await the return of our Ancestors from the stars..... The Hopis call these beings as Kachina's

A Hopi Chiefs'. Last Cry

*I am often asked the question…"What are the living Indigenous elders and spiritual teachers telling us about this time?"…. The late Chief Dan Evehema, eldest Hopi Elder, before his passing in 1999 left this **Message to Mankind**; it was Chief Dan who worked with me and gave sanction to my writing of Last Cry which was also to include a documentary film… But life happens. The film was made but the Hopi elected not to release it…*

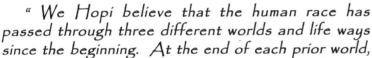

Chief Dan: *in an open letter….. Hotevilla, Arizona, Hopi Sovereign Nation*

"I am very glad to have this time to send a message to you. We are celebrating a time in our history, which is both filled with joy and sadness we know many of you are having the same troubles.

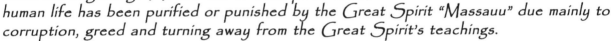

" We Hopi believe that the human race has passed through three different worlds and life ways since the beginning. At the end of each prior world, 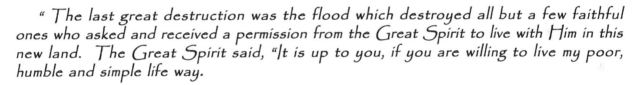 human life has been purified or punished by the Great Spirit "Massauu" due mainly to corruption, greed and turning away from the Great Spirit's teachings.

" The last great destruction was the flood which destroyed all but a few faithful ones who asked and received a permission from the Great Spirit to live with Him in this new land. The Great Spirit said, "It is up to you, if you are willing to live my poor, humble and simple life way.

" It is hard but if you agree to live according to my teachings and instructions, if you never lose faith in the life I shall give you, you may come and live with me."

" The Hopi and all who were saved from the great flood made a sacred covenant with the Great Spirit at that time. We Hopi made an oath that we will never turn away from Him. For us the Creators laws never change or break down.

" To the Hopi the Great Spirit is all powerful. He appeared to the first people as a man and talked with them in the beginning of this creation world. He taught us how to live, to worship, where to go and what food to carry, gave us seeds to plant and harvest. He gave us a set of sacred stone tablets into which He breathed all teachings in order to safeguard his land and life.

" In these stone tablets were made, instructions and prophecies and warnings. This was done with the help of a Spider woman and Her two grandsons They were wise and powerful helpers of the Great Spirit.

" Before the Great Spirit went into hiding, He and Spider woman put before the leaders of the different groups of people many colors and sized of corn for them to choose their food in this world.

" The Hopi was the last to pick and then choose their food in this world. The Hopi then choose the smallest ear of corn.

" Then Massauu said, "You have shown me you are wise and humble for this reason you will be called Hopi (people of peace) and I will place in your authority all land and life to guard, protect and hold trust for Me until I return to you in later days for I am the First and the Last."

"This is why when a Hopi is ordained into the higher religious order, the earth and all living things are placed upon his hands. He becomes a parent to all life on earth. He is entitled to advise and correct his children in whatever peaceful way he can. So we can never give up knowing that our message of peace will reach our children.

" Then it is together with the other spiritual leaders the destiny of our future children is placed. We are instructed to hold this world in balance within the land and the many universes with special prayers and ritual which continue to this day.

" It was to the Spider woman's two grandsons the sacred stone tablets were given. These two brothers were then instructed to carry them to a place the Great Spirit had instructed them.

" The older brother was to go immediately to the east, to the rising sun and upon reaching his destination was instructed to immediately start to look for his younger brother who shall remain in the land of the Great Spirit.

" The Older brother's mission when he returned was to help his younger brother (Hopi) bring about peace, brotherhood and everlasting life on his return.

" Hopi, the younger brother, was instructed to cover all land and mark it well with footprints and sacred markings to claim this land for the Creator and peace on earth. We established our ceremonials and sacred shrines to hold this world in balance in accordance with our first promise to the Creator.

" This is how our migration story goes, until we meet the Creator at Old Oribe (place that solidifies) over 1000 years ago.

" It was at that meeting when he gave to us these prophecies to give to you now at this closing of the Fourth World of destruction and the beginning of the Fifth World of peace.

" He gave us many prophecies to pass on to you and all have come to pass. This is how we know the timing is now to reveal the last warnings and instructions to mankind.

" We were told to settle permanently here in Hopi land where we met the Great Spirit and wait for Older Brother who went east to return to us.

126

" When he returns to this land he will place his stone tablets side by side to show all the world that they are our true brothers.

" When the road in the sky has been fulfilled and when the inventing of something, in Hopi means, gourd of ashes, a gourd that when drops upon the earth will boil everything within a large space and nothing will grow for a very long time.

" When the leaders turned to evil ways instead of the Great Spirit we were told there would be many ways this life may be destroyed.

" Great Spirit Said that if human kind does not heed our prophecies and returns to the original spiritual instructions our world would be no more.

" We were told of three helpers who were being sent by the Great Spirit to help the Hopi bring about a peaceful life on this Earth.

" We were told not to change our ceremonies, or our ways, or even our hair, because the true helpers might not recognize us as the true Hopi. So we have been waiting all these years.

" It is known that our True White Brother, when he comes, will be all powerful and will wear a red cap or red cloak.

" He will be large in population, belong to no religion but his very own. He will bring with him the sacred stone tablets.

" With him there will be two great ones both very wise and powerful. One will have a symbol or sign of swastika which represents purity and is Female, a producer of life.

" The third one or the second one of the two helpers to our True White Brother will have a sign of a symbol of the sun. He, too, will be many people and very wise and powerful.

" We have in our sacred Kachina ceremonies a gourd rattle which is still in use today with these symbols of these powerful helpers of our True Brother.

" It is also prophesied that if these three fail to fulfill their mission then the one from the west will come like a big storm. He will be many, in numbers and unmerciful.

" When he comes he will cover the land like the red ants and over take this land in one day. If the three helpers chosen by the Creator fulfill their sacred mission and even if there are only one, two or three of the true Hopi remaining holding fast to the last ancient teaching and instructions the Great Spirit, Massauu will appear before all and our would will be saved.

" The three will lay out a new life plan which leads to everlasting life and peace.

" The earth will become new as it was from the beginning. Flowers will bloom again, wild games will return to barren lands and there will be abundance of food for all. Those who are saved will share everything equally and they all will recognize Great Spirit and *speak one language.*

" *We are now faced with great problems, not only here but throughout the land. Ancient cultures are being annihilated.*

" *Our people's lands are being taken from them, leaving them no place to call their own.*

" *Why is this happening? It is happening because many have given up or manipulated their original spiritual teachings.*

" *The way of life which the Great Spirit has given to all its people of the world, whatever your original instructions are not being honored. It is because of this great sickness-called greed, which infects every land and country that simple people are losing what they have kept for thousands of years.*

" *Now we are at the very end of our trail. Many people no longer recognize the true path of the Great Spirit. They have, in fact, no respect for the Great Spirit or for our precious Mother Earth, who gives us all life.*

" *We are instructed in our ancient prophecy that this would occur. We were told that someone would try to go up to the moon: that they would bring something back from the moon; and that after that, nature would show signs of losing its balance.*

" *Now we see that coming about. All over the world there are now many signs that nature is no longer in balance. Floods, drought, earthquakes, and great storms are occurring and causing much suffering.*

" *We do not want this to occur in our country and we pray to the Great Spirit to save us from such things. But there are now signs that this very same thing might happen very soon on our own land.*

" *Now we must look upon each other as brothers and sisters. There is no more time for divisions between people. Today I call upon all of us, from right here at home, Hotevilla, where we too are guilty of gossiping and causing divisions even among our own families; out to the entire world where thievery, war and lying goes on every day. These divisions will not be our salvation. Wars only bring more wars, never peace.*

" *Only by joining together in a Spiritual Peace with love in our hearts for one another, love in our hearts for the Great Spirit and Mother Earth, shall we be saved from the terrible Purification Day which is just ahead.*

" *There are many of you in this world who are honest people.*

" *We know you spiritually for we are the "Men's Society Grandfathers" who have been charged to pray for you and all life on earth never forgetting anything or any one in our ceremonials.*

' *Our prayer is to have a good happy life, plenty of soft gentle rain for abundant crops.*

" We pray for balance on earth to live in peace and leave a beautiful world to the children yet to come.

" We know you have good hearts but good hearts are not enough to help us out with these great problems. In the past some of you have tried to help us Hopis, and we will always be thankful for you efforts.

" But now we need your help in the worst way. We want the people of the world to know the truth of our situation.

" This land which people call the Land of the Freedom celebrates many days reminding people of the world of these things.

" Yet in well over 200 years the original Americans have not seen a free day. We are suffering the final insult. Our people are now losing the one thing which give life and meaning of life—our ceremonial land, which is being taken away from us.

" Hotevilla is the last holy consecrated, undisturbed traditional Native American sacred shrine to the Creator.

" As the prophecy says, this sacred shrine must keep its spiritual pathways open. This village is the spiritual vortex for the Hopi to guide the many awakening Native Americans and other true hearts home to their own unique culture.

" Hotevilla was established by the last remaining spiritual elders to maintain peace and balance on this continent from the tip of South America up to Alaska.

" Many of our friends say Hotevilla is a sacred shrine, a national and world treasure and must be preserved. We need your help.

" Where is the freedom which you all fight for and sacrifice your children for? Is it only the Indian people who have lost or are all Americans losing the very thing, which you original came here to find?

" We don't share the freedom of the press because what gets into the papers is what the government wants people to believe, not what is really happening.

' We have no freedom of speech, because we are persecuted by our own people for speaking our beliefs.

" We are at the final stages now and there is a last force that is about to take away our remaining homeland.

" We are still being denied many things including the rite to be Hopis and to make our living in accordance with our religious teachings.

" The Hopi leaders have warned leaders in the White House and the leaders in the Glass House but they do not listen.

' So as our prophecy says then it must be up to the people with good pure hearts that will not be afraid to help us to fulfill our destiny in peace for this world.

" We now stand at a cross road whether to lead ourselves in everlasting life or total destruction.

" We believe that human beings spiritual power through prayer is so strong it decides life on earth.

" So many people have come to Hopiland to meet with us. Some of you we have met on your lands. Many times people have asked how they can help us. Now I hope and pray that your help will come.

' If you have a way to spread the truth, through the newspapers, radio, books, thought meeting with powerful people, tell the truth! Tell them what you know to be true.

" Tell them what you have seen here; what you have heard us say; what you have seen with your own eyes. In this way, if we do fall, let it be said that we tried, right up to the end, to hold fast to the path of peace as we were originally instructed to do by the Great Spirit.

" Should you really succeed, we will all realize our mistakes of the past and return to the true path-living in harmony as brothers and sisters, sharing our mother, the earth with all other living creatures.

" In this way we could bring about a new world, a world which would be led by the great Spirit and our mother will provide plenty and happiness for all.

" God bless you, each one of you and know our prayers for peace meet yours as the Sun rises and sets.

" May the Great Spirit guide you safely into the path of love, peace freedom and God on this Earth Mother.

" May the holy ancestors of love and light keep you safe in your land and homes. Pray for God to give you something important to do in this great work which lies ahead of us all to bring peace on earth.

" We the Hopi still hold the sacred stone tablets and now await the coming of our True White Brother and others seriously ready to work for the Creator's peace on earth.

" Be well, my children, and think good thoughts of peace and togetherness. Peace for all life on earth and peace with one another in our homes, families and countries.

"   We are not so different in the Creator's eyes. The same great Father Sun shines his love on each of us daily just as Mother Earth prepares the sustenance for our table, do they not? We are one after all.

Thank you Grandfather Dan. May you finally be able to walk softly and find those happy days you talked to me about....

Chief Dan Evehema, from what we can estimate was at least 105 years of age at his passing. He was a Spiritual leader, Hopi Sinom and Eldest Elder Greeswood / Roadrunner Clan Society Father / Snake Priest / Kachina Father

The Last Hopi Prophecies

"...While we can still see the twins, the comet up there with the two tails (Hale-Bopp) in the sky we will still have time to change our patterns and change our ways. When we no longer see it in the sky it will be the sign that we have very little time left. .....Perhaps 18 months or less before the purifier returns.

" The purifier will appear as the Red Kachina. Maybe that means it will appear red in the telescopes that the scientists use. It will remain almost in one place for a long time... Like an eye watching us. ....

"That is when Saquasohuh, the one that is called the Blue Star Kachina will also return. Saquasohuh is benevolent, but the others will not be so. When the others come...there will begin the war in the heavens as we have been told...."

Dan Evehema Eldest Hopi Elder, February 1997

Note: There is a vast difference between the Hopi Sinom, and a Hopi Elder...By the time many of you read this their may not be any Hopi Sinom left. They are the traditional Elders from Old Oriabi who have held to their ways for thousands of years... It will be a pity because along with their passing goes a body of ancient knowledge that cannot be replaced.... We are witness ... watching an entire way of life dissolve before my eyes..

HOPI...Prophecies Yet to be Fulfilled

From various Interviews...and meetings in the desert...Livin on Hopi time

Chief Dan Evehema, and members of the Hopi Sinom, were at these meetings I attended and was allowed to record, near Hotevilla. There simply are no more messages coming from the Hopi at this time. The time of magical sharing is now passed, another part of the Great American West has gone down that long road.. to the memory place, the blue world..

As we look ahead at the transpiring of events in our cities, around the globe and in our heavens we can have little doubt that we have entered the War of Valued life. Some of Chief Dan's last words to me...." We are now in the End Times... see you on the other side Phanna"

? The time will come when from the earth will arise a mystic fog which will dilute the minds and hearts of all people. Their guidelines of wisdom and knowledge will falter; the Great Laws of our Creator will dissolve in the minds of people. Children will be out of control and will no longer obey the leaders; immorality and the competitive war of greed will flourish.

When the end is near, we will see a halo of mist around the heavenly bodies. Four times it will appear around the sun as a warning that we must reform, telling us that people of all colors must unite and arise for survival, and that we must uncover the causes of our dilemmas. We will see those from the stars returning. Unless man-made weapons are used to strike first, peace will then come.

So the time will come when we will experience late springs and early frosts, this will be the sign of the returning Ice Age.

We Hopi believe militarism is born out of the injustices of poverty and ignorance where absolute governments refuse to hear the grievances of minorities. So the people resort to violence, demonstrations and even terrorism when they see no other way to be heard. What can we do when our world leaders and the people are acting like fools in attempts to solve the problems confronting us? According to prophecy, the day will come when people in high places will be hunted down. This will get out of control. The hunting will gather strength and spread. They will be going after the spiritual elders, like shooting eagles. This situation might even erupt on our land of the Hopi. Finally, this will lead us to the Biblical version of Armageddon... The End Times.

Our Hopi story of the End Times is very similar about some things that can be found Christian Bible.

There will be a final decisive battle between good and evil. This will occur under one God or Chief. The prophets say in that time we will speak one language and that this will happen in Hopi land, in the village of Oraibi, where the new life plan will be drawn, in the pattern and cycle of religion. We will make choices in this time; some will follow their hearts and survive, others will not and die in awful manner when they realize it is too late for them to change.

Here also a final decision will be made for the wicked. They will be beheaded and speak no more. A great Star Warrior, a Kachina, who will come in those times, will do this. Many Kachinas will return in the time of the purification.

For the Kachinas will know that if this does not materialize, and the evil ones, the two hearts, are not stopped, then there will be a total destruction through the acts of man or nature.

Then new life will begin again from a girl and a boy. This is a frightening prophecy and will not be supported by many. But it has been foretold as one of the possibilities. Some will choose this path.

It is in the prophecies of the Hopi that in a case like this the Navajo may help our cause. Also the Bahannas (White People) or the Paiute Tribe may come to help. We doubt that the U.S. Government will easily concede to our sovereignty.

There are two water serpents, one at each pole with a warrior sitting on his head and tail. These are those who we call the Twins. They will return when we see the comet with two tales in the heavens.

These twins command nature to warn us by her activities that time is getting short, and we must correct ourselves. They will change the weather, and things will happen at the wrong time. It will snow in summer and the rains will not come with regularity, or they will come all at once. Crops will die, and many will go hungry. If we refuse to heed these warnings, the warriors will let go of the serpents; they will rise up, and all will perish.

We should be much concerned about the climate. No one seems to be able to predict the weather accurately from day to day anymore. However, we know according to our time markers when it is past due for certain seeds to be planted and when it is their proper time.

In recent springs, we were reluctant to plant due to the late snow and cold weather. Once more maybe our ancient prophecy is right, that one day we will plant wearing finger sacks (gloves) clearing away snow with our feet before planting.

The summers will become shorter for maturing the corn for harvest. The result is anybody's guess.

The question is, will this occur the world over? This would depend on the geographical areas. In the regions with different climates, things will happen in different ways. For instance, tropical land could become a land of ice, and the Arctic regions could become tropical.

This need not happen if we, the people, get our leaders to do something about the harmful things being done to the environment. We see the planes, and we hear the sounds of their machines, we can feel them moving the Earth...

It is said that, if the future generations find out that we did nothing to preserve the good ways, they might throw us from our houses into the streets. This suffering will be of our own making.

The lack of peace in our own spiritual being could trigger the revolution. Our True White Brother might come and find we have forsaken the sacred instructions. Then he will whip us without mercy.

Let us take a look into the future through the eyes of our prophets. We Hopi were instructed to tell of the Great Purification just ahead of a time when Humankind would once again become highly civilized, tending to become careless and leading us to self-destruction.

They said (Our Ancestors) that, along the way, the industrialized world will have certain problems. People will be uncomfortable because of the changing times and they will have to make adjustments to find new life styles.

Many will come to the Hopi in these times for everything will be dying and they will not know what to do. But many will come too late and have weak hearts.

The Industrialized nations will become careless in getting more resources out of the Earth. Believing all these things will last forever, soon natural resources will be depleted. Fuel shortages will occur; industrial machinery will come to a standstill.

The machinery used for planting, harvesting and transport will become useless. Supermarket shelves will become empty of farm produce. The farmers and those who grow their own food will not sell their produce.

Money will become worthless. The white man with all his intelligence and technology will not be able to repair the damage.

We will see extraordinary events in Nature and Earth, including humans who will come as messengers.

And in the heavens the Kachinas will be making their presence known hoping that we turn things around here even in the last minute. For there are those coming who will not be friendly towards us. We have always known of these beings. Some of them live beneath the Earth.

Modern man looks upon old wisdom and knowledge as dead, useless and it is no longer respected. Modern man thinks that much of what we say are just stories like little children. They will find out we are not making these things up.

Modern man depends on the money system and no longer on Mother Earth for food. According to prophecies, when this happens, when he forgets the Earth, then Mother Earth will hide her nourishment because of the view that ancient food is poor man's food.

When all food disappears, modern man will try to correct his mistake, the conditions he caused upon the Earth through his inventions and carelessness. He will try to achieve some kind of method to heal the wound, but this will not be possible when we reach the point of no return.

This prophecy is similar to the Biblical versions of that which may yet come to pass. It goes on to say that common people will become concerned and frustrated because of their hectic world.

They will be particularly angry about the bloodthirsty policies and the deceitfulness of the world leaders. The common people the world over will begin to band together to fight for world peace. They will realize that their leaders have failed.

People in high places will be hunted down like animals, perhaps through terrorism. In turn, leaders will retaliate and begin hunting each other. This condition will gather strength and spread far and wide. It will get out of control the world over. Revolution could erupt on our land here in Hotevilla.

The liberators will come in from the west with great force. They will drop down from the skies like rain.. They will have no mercy.

They will light up the heavens. We must not get on the housetops to watch. They will shake us by our ears, like children who have been bad.

This will be the final decisive battle between good and evil. This battle will cleanse the heart of people and restore our Mother Earth from illness, and the wicked will be gotten rid of.

If this event fails to materialize, it will be because our Great Creator elected to do this thing another way and then the forces of nature will do the task. It could be total destruction in many forms then. Very few people would survive.

Eventually, a gourd full of ashes would be invented, which, if dropped from the sky, would boil the oceans and burn the land causing nothing to grow for many years.

This would be the sign for a certain Hopi to bring out the teachings in order to warn the world that the third and final event would happen soon and could bring an end to all life unless people correct themselves and their leaders in time. We have tried to do this but the Bahannas do not listen well.

The final stages, called The Great Purification, have been described as a Mystery Egg (Tinsel Bubble of time... the hologram) in which the forces of the Swastika and the Sun will rise again,.

We will not be able to travel. There will be borders between states then. It will be very dangerous to go from one place to another as we do now. We take everything for granted. Everyone will have to have a mark if they are allowed to travel.

Plus, a third force will rise, this one will be symbolized by the color red, will appear to bring back the spiritual ways and stop the dark ones. This culminates either in total rebirth or total annihilation; we don't know which. But the choice is yours; war and natural catastrophe may be involved.

The degree of violence will be determined by the degree of inequity caused among the peoples of the world and in the balance of nature. In this crisis rich and poor will be forced to struggle as equals in order to survive.

The reality that it (the future conditions) will be very violent is now almost taken for granted among Traditional Hopi, but man still may lessen the violence by correcting his treatment of nature and their fellow man. Ancient spiritually based societies, such as the Hopi, must especially be preserved and the people not forced to abandon their wise way of life and understand the natural resources they have vowed to protect.

The man-made systems (the matrix) are now destroying the Hopi. The are deeply involved in similar violations throughout the world; it is an artificial way of living it is not natural ad all that exists within it gets distorted. It ignores all of nature's laws.

The devastating events predicted in the prophecies is only a part of the natural order.

If those who thrive from that system, its money and its laws, can manage to stop destroying the Hopi and others like us, then many may be able to survive the Days of Purification and enter a new age of peace. But if no one is left to continue the Hopi way, the hope for such an age is in vain.

Since mankind has lost peace with one another through conflict due to the new ways, the Great Spirit, the Great Creator, has punished the people in many ways. Through all of this there was always a small group who survived to keep the original ways of life alive.

These small groups are comprised of those who adhere to the laws of the Creator, who keep the spiritual path open, out from the circle of evil. According to our knowledge we are not quite out of the circle.

Now we enter the time of testing that only the Great Creator can confirm. We will know the time by the alignment of the planets, we were so kindly informed about by the star watchers and has been awaited by the Hopi The stars are our clock, and they can not be altered.

We were told that when the end is near, we will see a halo of mist beginning to appear around the heavenly bodies. Four times this mist will appear around the sun as a warning that we MUST reform.

During the Days of Purification ambitious minds will decrease, while the people of good hearts, who live in harmony with the earth and each other will increase until the earth is rid of evil.

If the Hopi are right, this will be accomplished and the earth will bloom again. The spiritual door is open it is our choice to go through or stay asleep. Why not join the righteous people?

The Horny Toad Woman gave Massau'u a promise that she would help him in time of need, saying she too had a metal helmet. After the Hopi have fulfilled their pattern of life, Massau'u will be the leader, but not before, for He is the First and He shall be the Last.......

The Final Hopi Message from the Hopi Sinom...

The Hopi Sinom are the legacy of over ten thousand years of succession, a lineage that placed the emphasis upon spiritual understanding and human compassion..that went back along very ancient footsteps...The Elders pictured here were my friends, my teachers, and my family...and my friends

Grandfather David   **Grandfather Titus**

I wonder if one day after this book is written, people will never know the old chiefs as I have... The new breed I see coming down the path simply is not the same. At the time of the writing of this work only Grandfather Martin survives...after 11,000 years it's down to one.

Grandfather Dan

Grandfather Martin

Dungeons and Dragons

The Sounding of the Final Thunders

The Final Thunders the indigenous Grandfathers told us, in 1982, will last for over forty years, as it is now seen. Humanity is presently experiencing the throws of the greatest initiation it has ever endured. This are the final steps before we begin to ascend into a higher light order, taking on the true nature of an evolved solar species, and enter a multidimensional galactic reality.

As the Spring Equinox 2000 approaches and throughout the first decade of the New Century, Great Solar Forces of Father Sun will continue to increase in velocity. As they build up, the Solar Winds of Change are altering forever the subtle balances of Mother Earth's energy, and humanity itself will enter a climactic juncture. We have suddenly found ourselves at the end of a long-forgotten cycle and it is harvest time. As you look around, you will notice we are not unlike the ants, who, just before a storm, slip into a state of hyper-dimensional transition and scurry about in a robotic frenzy.

Caught in the currents of change, humanity desperately stumbles — with our limited abilities and technology — through the fragments of debris left behind by our ancestors who once communicated with those from beyond the Sun. Yes, they were star voyagers and we are their Star Seed descendants. Against all odds and competing with the ticking of the clock, we seek to piece together the truths of our origins and what happened to them…Wondering occasionally, were they us?

What was it that caused such utter and complete devastation in certain areas of our Earth? What happened to our ancestors who once could build such magnificent structures by means and technology we can, at best, only theorize about how it was accomplished, knowing we ourselves are rendered inept at being able to duplicate what they left behind.

Energies are shifting, and the physics of cause and effect seem to no longer apply. The mystical essences composing the geometry of our holographic reality vaporize as they transcend into other realities. It is time now to prepare for what once seemed to be fairy tales of the future. Stories told by Shaman of the days to come and the Wars of the Heavens have been recorded upon the cliffs and caves where some took shelter for a time.

Remember how we sat around in circles waiting in anxious anticipation for the next word to come forth from **Zardar**, (**demonstration only**), who was some entity from another time and another world, channeling through the innocence of one of our Sisters or Brothers telling us how we became divine children of a mythical race. We would take breaks and eat sprout sandwiches while we camped out for days in tents. We endured all sorts of inclement weather just to hear the words that affirmed within us some fantasy that justified why we were not content here in our present dream.

Remember leaving everything behind, selling all that you owned to find the new dream? You friends thought you were crazy and your children prayed for your salvation from the dark forces that possessed you and stole you away. Remember sleeping in vans and calling the children to tell them you were OK?

Well, welcome to the Alchemical Garden! You have made it this far through the labyrinth. Those of us who were adventurous and dared to break away from the mold to explore the new frontiers of consciousness will not be disappointed with what is about to occur. The Seventh Thunder is about **Change**, complete change…Paradigm shift, utter and complete Alchemical change. When all warnings have been exhausted and the web of life can no longer hold the essence of the life force any longer, Grandfather will declare a new dream to be woven and call the Spider Woman…to spin her magic.

Grandmother Spider

Grandmother Spider will spin herself a new web, for Makakaan, the Goddess of Emerald, is a dreaming Goddess. Her children are dreamers and they will be born anew. Slowly her children fall into cosmic slumber. Like the caterpillar inside its chrysalis they came trusting their divine calling, knowing that when they awoke they would no longer be what they once were. The new strands of consciousness are in place, and tomorrow when you awaken from your slumber, you will remember the words of this book and everything from this moment forward will be different.

Old ways of doing things will no longer apply. Yet, many new and amazing doorways will be opened at the same time as you enter into a era of new choices, accelerated spiritual and personal growth, and you are taught by the forces of the Sacred Mother Herself to own your spiritual self and take personal responsibility for your thoughts, words, and actions. You will rise to meet the challenge of the new day, which will be to find the balance in the chaos.

The first year of this new century is the year of the Labyrinth. Humanity will find itself living in a self-created paradox as it realizes, even to the simplest of peasants, that we are indeed walking between two worlds, walking between our past and our future. Earth and her children are entering the great cycle of Solar Storms that will bring the long-awaited renewal and purification we have heard so much about.

Most of us by now are quite aware of the strange and intense energies that seem to be affecting every waking minute of our daily lives... peaks and valleys of weird energy drains, emotional highs and lows, as well as the confusion of thought and personal direction.

The upsetting of our physical bodies as well as our emotional ones has taken its cost on our personal relationships. A lot of this is due to the activity of our Sun at this time. The amorphic energy that is moving through our universe at this time is the amorphic energy that activates the Christ consciousness; it not only affects two-legged human types, it affects the whole of the universe.

The positive side to this occurrence is that many are being freed from relationships they never would have gotten out of otherwise. We are finding out first-hand and rather dramatically, the false reasons upon which we have based our life paths. And the new energy of the Christos with which we are merging will not allow for this compromise to exist any longer.

Primal Screams

I know as you read this, there are many of you who are silently and some perhaps not so silently screaming, "*I WANT OUT OF HERE*!". Well, as a friend once said, "No one gets out of here alive" almost encapsulates what is currently going on, and he was almost right.

Know the turmoil is far from over and in our present form, stuck in our limitation and rigidity of principles, which are only 'mythical laws' we are nearing a destiny from which we cannot escape. Sorry, but that is no longer an option. We have one direction if we hope to actually **break on through to the other side**, and that is to move straight ahead and deal with our imbalances on a moment-to-moment basis. Each opportunity will make itself known to you along the way, as you need to know it.

Holistically, as humanity, we can expect even greater acceleration and change in every aspect of our reality. Yes, every aspect — physically, mentally, materially and spiritually. The days to come are now the days that are; this experience is what our ancestors have prophesied as the shift of the ages.

When the Shift hits the fan

The next 5 years is when **the Shift hits the fan**… We will go through a temporary nightmare, dealing with the Anti-Christ scenario, while on the same scope of reality the Masters themselves will be appearing in many places around the world, as ancient cities and truths as to our real heritage and origins continue to emerge. So you might as well buckle up and get ready for the ride. We are in the cosmic birthing cycle and the only pathway is through the process.

Change is the order of the day, and lots of it! At times it may feel that you have lost touch with the Creator. You may feel betrayed, abandoned or apart from life around you. You might even get angry cause you will be trying everything in your power, but things will not seem to work the way they once worked. It is time now for you to learn to take responsibility for being here; this is a weaning process. Humanity has been spoon-fed long enough. It is a gift to be here on Mother Earth, especially at this time.

So you'd best go and prepare for shift. Make your choices as to what is most important to you and those you love with great reverence and reflection. Remembering that what radiates from your heart this very moment, your true inner desires will be the foundations for your future experiences. And remember how does the saying go, "Don't get discouraged, **Shift Happens.**"

Learning to stand on moving ground

We are, as I have spoken of for so long to those desiring to understand the path of the initiate, learning to stand on moving ground. Many paradigms will shift, and the laws of cause and effect may not always work out the way you are accustomed to seeing in the past. At times it may feel that you have has lost touch with the Creator.

You may feel betrayed, abandoned, or as if you were caught in a separate reality. When that happens try to reach out, touch someone, expand your horizons. Human existence is predicated upon exchange, not isolationism. We move through life because of the connections we make, one hand reaching out to assist the other. Judge not less you be judged, for in the moment of judging you call to you the experience you have judged.

That does not mean not to draw borders. There is a saying amongst native people. "**When I know you for three winters...I will know who you are and I will see all your faces.**" So don't be too eager to give away your inner sanctuary too easily and then respond with the attitude of a victim after you have been violated.

This is, after all, a predatory world and experience is still the best of teachers. For the most part, humanity has forgotten the rules of the giveaway, and the old adage, "One good turn deserves another." Now it is time for us to commit to being here, on this planet, at this time, and wipe away the haze of indecision. Take charge.

Humanity is in training. We are being tempered to become supreme warriors of Light. Remember the term Rainbow Warrior? Well, when did you forget that you signed up for the adventure...? For from here many of us will elect to move on to other worlds, and experience the true expanse of our reality potentials. Yes, there are many hurdles and many sand traps. Always expect the unknown to happen and know that life will turn on a dime.... Have you got the game plan yet? Are you ready to give up the struggle and 'go with the flow', or at least find out what the term means? The question to ponder is whether we can relearn to be Hu-man once again.. can we learn what it means and what it takes?

Dragons, Gods and Suns of the gods
A Sumerian story of Gen-ISIS

The brief history of the human race"

A prelude to the Mayan Teachings for the Days of Destiny

What you are about to read is taken from an understanding of many historical accountings bridging both hemispheres of the Earth. For each story existing in the Bible there are even more existing in the ancient records of the Americas. I am certain there are others, as well. I have spoken to Aboriginal elders from Australia and Africans who have told me of their records. Also, there are some very interesting legends in the Pyrenes of Spain and Ireland, England and Greece. The accountings of the Mayan, Inca, Kogi and Hopi speak of the migrations of people originating from here after the demise of Atlantis.

What we must realize in this revealing of our true history is that during the time of Atlantis, the Pleiadians had control of the Atlantean Empire. The historical records herein-described occurred after the demise of Atlantis, when Earth had been abandoned for lost. There were, however, those who survived taking shelters in the caverns and passageways beneath the surface world. Upon the arrival of the Gods, the Nephelim, Enlil and Enki and others, unexpected groups of Cro-Magnon and previous Hybrid races were already beginning to develop upon the Surface-world after the destruction.

What is interesting is that in the tablets I have found in North America the reference to Egyptian, Hebrew, Celtic and the Old Language, as it is called, refer to the same gods and goddesses that are named in Sumeria by the Celts and Norsemen from Northern Europe and the British Islands. Apparently there was a time here in North America when the splendor that was Egypt as well as Maya existed here simultaneously. As fantastic as this might sound, very shortly my colleagues and I will present this information to the world as hard evidence to these words. Some of the findings you have seen in this publication.

It appears there were forces on both Hemispheres who tampered with human life and the natural order of evolution, as well as with other life forms existing here on Terra. They tampered with them environmentally as well as biologically. Genetically, we were altered so extensively that, for the most part, we have no genetic memory link to our past. There is a break-off point where the information in every culture simply ends leaving no trail.

The War of the Gods... The War of Angels (Part 1)

We present here a very abridged version of what seems to have occurred to the Earth, beginning some 35,000 years ago. This information comes from indigenous records and is not necessarily in agreement with contemporary Judeo-Christian records. The stories may be familiar, and then, again, a lot is borrowed from the indigenous people of this Earth and edited to suit the times…………..

This is a story about the Star Nations and the War of the Heavens. It is a story not yet over, for we are now moving into the final chapter, if you will, as the **Seventh Thunder** unfolds. It is a war between brothers…the worst kind of war.

Enki's half-brother and rival, Enlil, was the commander-in-chief of the ET Earth Operation. They were a scientific exploration group from Orion. They came to Earth on a regular basis, for it was a mining stop and a layover for supplies. They had no opposition, as Earth beings were, for the most part, a giving and friendly people. There were some who opposed the visits from the Gods, but the technical superiority of the Lords of the Heavens was no match for anything being generated on Earth.

After the demise of Atlantis, small oases of civilized life had survived the holocaust. Most of what our Orion explorers wanted from Earth were minerals and crystals; these were found outside the sparsely populated areas anyway. The Orions were more interested in the mineral wealth of this very unusual planet that, after Atlantis, came under the protection of the Sirians and Andromedans. They were responsible for the restructuring of the " Light Grid", after the Grid was destroyed by the Atlanteans. Prior to that, the main source of planetary galactic overseeing during the time-experience of Atlantis was the domain of the Pleiadians.

When opposition afforded itself, the offenders were easily thwarted and the **Star-gods** took control of the younger, (in the evolutionary sense), gentler and non-warlike Sons of God, who were at the time mainly Cro-Magnon 9 Yet very tall in stature. Possibly hybrids. Yes, the answer to your question I can hear even as you read these pages is that, in fact, Homo-Sapiens as a species are a hybrid…of a different kind, being a genetically engineered race; Homo-sapien-sapien was the result of genetic alteration in the laboratory and not through the cross-breeding of the species through natural means. The evidence to the fact is overwhelming and understood within almost every high indigenous culture.

Essentially, the territory we are speaking of, meaning after the "War of the Gods" took place here in the Americas, is the land remaining under the influence of the Draconian or Enlilian forces. According to the Sumerians, this area was the Mesopotamian region between the Tigris and Euphrates rivers. This was the condition so to speak after the Wars of the Gods and the near total annihilation occurring here to the then-civilized world. As you read on, this fact becomes very clear.

There exist many, many similar stories amongst the Maya, Inca, Kogi and Hopi in the Americas, a Continent much more populated in ancient times than we have been led to understand. Most of the lands here survived better the effects of the Atlantean holocausts, the Great Flood and the nuclear devastation that also occurred. The Hopi legend has it that the 'ant people' led us to the inner Earth and therein dwelt for some 580 some odd years, escaping the devastation above. Would you go underground to escape floods? Unlikely. But you would go underground to escape nuclear devastation. Yes…"Logical, Spock."

The main mission here upon the Earth was one of mining, for their home planet had run out of many required minerals, primarily gold and crystals, for use in the their hyper-dimensional spacecraft and some unclear or undefined Alchemical needs of the Orion Queens.

On a lonely mission far from their home planet of Orion, we have the Hebaru priesthood who were under the command of Enlil. Enlil is Enki's brother and not a very nice fellow. They arrive on a strange vessel called by the Mayan "Nibaru", not Nibiru. The Hebaru are the working drones of Nibaru, hence their name proper.

To the Egyptians, Enlil was Ra/Jehovah, while Enki was Ra/Osiris. Both are Sun gods, as they come from beyond the Sun.

" We can trace the Sumerian written records back to about 3700 BC, and they tell us that the gods in question were brothers. In Sumeria, the storm god who eventually became known as Jehovah, was called 'Enlil' or 'Ilu-kur-gal' (meaning 'Ruler of the Mountain'), and his brother, who became Adon, the Lord, was called 'Enki'. This name is really important to our story because 'Enki' means 'Archetype'" This same god was to the Maya known as Chuac…the Elephant god.

Recently Zechariah Sitchin has changed his original thoughts saying that " perhaps the origins of civilization might be older then we originally thought, considerably older, perhaps even hundreds of thousands of years."

In his words

"The texts inform us that it was Enlil who brought the Flood; it was Enlil who destroyed Ur and Babylon, and it was Enlil who constantly opposed the education and enlightenment of humankind. Indeed, the early Syrian texts tell us that it was Enlil who obliterated the cities of Sodom and Gomorrah on the Dead Sea - not because they were dens of wickedness, as we are taught, but because they were great centers of wisdom and learning. (*Sir Lawrence Gardner, Genesis of the Grail Kings)

Interesting to note here is that the Mayan god, Cauac, (CHAK) is also referred to as the god of storms and water god, the God of Thunder and storms.

CAUAC - (*Chak*)- Storm God, controls the water and the rains - Cauac is a very powerful male God, who is depicted in Mayan culture as the Elephant.

During the reign of Kukulkan we are told of many inter-marriages between the Toltec-Mayan and the other gods from the stars. Whole centers or great universities were established to accommodate the education of the children of these gods in both the Inca "Empire of the Sun" such as Machu Pichu and the Mayan Empire such as Chezan Itza, Palenque and Uxmal, which were all grand ancient Mystery Schools.

Today these structures still command reverence, and tremendous energies are being awakened from these centers of power; you could call them the fingerprints of the gods — evidence that something grand once existed upon this plane. There are many testimonies clearly showing our direct connection to these gods of old, although the true unclouded tener of our interrelatinships with them have been forgotten. We cannot understand these relationship that were in existence for tens of thousands of years prior to this present reality state of consciousness, a state of reality which is very young and as yet undeveloped…

An interesting note is that the Nazarene himself was an initiate in nine of these ancient schools of knowledge, and he never denied them…He mastered each one, and in fact he embraced them and incorporated them into his original teachings. These original teachings themselves are just now being uncovered and revealed to us after thousands of years of deliberate manipulation and in some cases the actual removal of his teachings from the scriptures that were to end up as the modern day Bible.

So as you press forward student of the light… proceed with an open mind let your heart be your guide and keep in your thoughts along the way that you have not been told all there is to know, from which you now draw your conclusions and make your stand. The story of the Nazarene Master is much larger than most presently perceive, or could possibly imagine. His was the greatest of dramas. He touched many souls, bringing his teachings to every corner of the globe, and presently is bringing his humanity back unto to fold of galactic realization and acceptance even as you read these pages. Moreover, know this is part of the destiny that lies ahead for all the sons and daughters of God. For thisis not the only reality that *IS.*

Just ponder for a moment this piece (right) that was found in the late 1970's in a deep cave in what is today Bolivia, and explain the existance of this artifact which is thousands of years old, found residing in a geographical area where history tells us it cannot possibly be?
There is more much more.. are you inclined to take a field trip with me?

Or this piece that was found along with it?

Or Perhaps this one found in the Rocky Mountains U.S.A. (below left) The one on the right may be easier it comes from the British Museum (circa 800 BCE).

More Dungeons and Dragons

Whining will do you no good.   You are the only one that can hear. **Or haven't you noticed lately?** We as a species are in training for the biggest quantum jump humanity has ever experienced in its entire history as a species in progress.

Earth's holographic fields and the way we relate in consciousness to everything around us is radically changing, and it is happening at an accelerated rate, as well. This is the advanced **Dungeons and Dragons,** the adult version of virtual reality, folks. Our spiritual and physical lives are merging into one just as the Earth herself is merging into the Fifth Elemental reality.

Life is becoming a very up-front matter, as it gets more and more personal. In fact, it is going to reach out and touch you, and rest assured there are no secrets; and, by the way, watch those fingerprints. Welcome to the labyrinth; here we dance that gauntlet of consequence.

We must unravel every thread of thought we have ever spun. And the web is layered, is it not? We are being asked to apply the great spiritual teachings that we have enjoyed playing with so casually, as the teachers who presented them to us tried to tell us, "This is serious stuff, and not a leisure time activity"... and so many of us did not heed their words. We took for granted that we would get by, that something always comes along. And now the voice in your head is saying to you. **"So you really did not believe it was coming now, did you...."**? Well, it's here! The future has arrived.

This first year of the new century is the final hour to prepare, but we will have to pick it up as we move along the path, for the march into forever has already begun. It is time to let go of all that no longer serves our higher universal plan. We had best learn to let the weight go. It is of no further use anyway. The first few weeks or months of this process may be painful, as we learn to let the pride of ego ... go a little, as we adjust to new patterns.

Also, it might get down right uncomfortable and frustrating, as things keep not working out for you. Just a little nudge from Spirit letting you know that you have to keep going, and the old plan doesn't apply any more. But if we can, remember.... Stop every once in awhile and smell the flowers.   When we look out at the world around us it won't be hard to see the effects of the change manifesting upon those who don't exercise the effort.

Do you like roller coaster rides? Well, a barrage of new frequencies from the cosmos are affecting us, and we are still feeling the effects of old ones. Some frequencies we have known are simply disappearing. Remember the rule: Nothing can die. It can only transmute and change into another form... Well, that applies to frequencies, also. And when you think of it we are just a frequency aren't we!

Frequencies manifested from our careless thought forms will attract like to like. Those resonating in the lower magnetic will transform your deepest darkest secrets. Many who have not consciously worked on cleaning up their act will experience the dark night of the soul, as long forgotten issues will suddenly rise up like nasty dragons to greet us head on.

Also I might as well warn you — these energies will be free of any restrictions relating to time lines and belief patterns that do not resonate with the divine source. The ownership of self, and who we truly are is our ground upon which we stand. And the heart is our shield, tempered by the knowing of our truth of origin. For faith and love will and can overcome all things.

Habitual and mindless thoughts and memories, as well as our robotic programming will get even more confused than they have been. It will appear at times as though we are in a dream that is dissolving, and this is precisely what is going on. You will have to jump over to the alternative current in order to make things work.

It is time to lighten the load and let go. Only that which is in harmony with the higher octave will be able to be carried through the veil now. All our academically installed programs which do not serve the higher purpose will seem to go up in smoke as the intensity of the solar waves pick up. Do watch the Sun. Watch it closely, and feel it emotionally; in that way you will understand it and come to know its consciousness

Watch closely to see how it interacts with you; learn the secret of the matrix of the cosmic laws of cause and effect; it is the best game in town.... and the only one that will be useful to you if you want out of the old corrupted matrix of the dream that is passing.

So, now, I can already hear the questions… What about the evil ones? What about the Anti-Christ? What about? What about? You didn't get it yet. That is not about you. It has nothing to do with you..... It never has. We are talking about the dream. You are the dancer in the dream.

Yes, you are having the dream but what do you really understand about the nature of the dream? You can see the corruption but you let it consume you and take your emotions over? You can see it because you are not it. That is why you can see it, while others do not. You never see the color red in the rainbow if you are the red. Remember that one?

Those who are dancing this dance of self-destruction are part of the old corrupted program, and they are playing out that dream. When that dream has its conclusion they will pass along with it. But you, you are one of God's kids. You have a different dream, you always have.

That is why you never quite fit into the picture. Why, others seemed to get away with murder …sometimes literally, while you, for the slightest imperfection, would get bounced out of the game. See, you are part of a different game. You are part of the bigger, grander game. You get to have a chance at coming home. You can leave Pleasure Island and all the temporary gratification of the material reality that are being polarized now so that they can be done with once and for all.

It's only a game?

Come on, now. Cheer up!!! It's a game. You love games! You are making games up all the time. Life in your world is a grand game — I think they call it role-playing, or is it virtual reality? It is hard to tell… You are always jumping back and forth on both sides of the fence, never sure who you really want to be. It is a labyrinth game. Very realistic isn't it? One could almost think it was real, couldn't they?

Oh, yea... The way out!! You simply need to remember to take '***The road less often traveled***'. ***(Wasn't that a book title in your last life ?.)***

There will be some new elements we are going to implement in the nature of the game. I know I have been going in and out of style, but I am sort of a classi-traditionlistic and I have a lot of experience at this game of life, you know. I mean it was a good game, but these newcomers? Well, they tried to take short cuts and lost quality control over the outcome. They tried to jury-rig everything and some even forgot there was a master program that overrides anything that is not in harmony with it.

Some things are best left to God, but some people think it is not fashionable these days to bring up that topic. It's not cool. Your friends might think you were co-dependent. The game was intended so that everyone could play and everyone had a chance to live their dream. Everyone was a winner. Now the program is corrupted. The ones who manipulated the game are so confused, wondering whom to blame, that some of them are even blaming God. Imagine that.

Oh, yes! I almost forgot—the new elements. You can expect the veils between 4-D and 3-D reality will become very thin. So thin that at times you may not know if you are dreaming or are awake. If you are making it up or it is making you up. The reality of your dreams will bridge over to your waking lives. It will be like sometimes you can see, actually see the screens, and the picture may slip now and again, cause you are not yet fully aware that you are making the movie...

At other times you will actually be able to see the connecting fibers connecting things together. Meanwhile in your inner visions you will be able to see these fiber as they flow like a spider's web between all our experiences, past, present and future, awake and dreaming. The realization that time is collapsing will become very obvious.

Now, there is this old issue of Karma. Well, Michael broke those chains back in the year 1995, but some of you still are not aware of that I guess, and have gotten stuck in old outdated programming. It is when the new grid took hold, the one that I am communicating to you through now.

You will be aware as you embrace your truth that Karma will appear to dissolve as quickly as you drop your altered-ego, which keeps you tied to the hip by your image of yourself. The image is not real... it is a contrived reflection. That's why it is distorted. If you are a reflection of the Light you cannot be the Light. So desire to be the Source and you will be the Light itself.

And in case you need a little push along the way, know that your thoughts will begin to manifest instantly, as well as the reaction to your thoughts. Now are your thoughts complete? Did you really mean what you just thought? Can you remember what you just thought? Ever think about how many of those thoughts you have a day?

Remember that the old program is used up. It is the end of the show, 'curtain time', as they say in show business. It is only the tyrant and their 'puppet sheeple' that are staying for the bows… So you are going to have to take the responsibility to get your self home in the dark. The trumpets have sounded — you were called but you were busy and didn't hear the message, as usual. And where you are going… Well, tyranny and fear cannot pass into the Fifth World, the new world. All that will be washed away. All will be purified. ALL! So there is no where to run.. just get real and own who and what you are.

You will of course be challenged every inch of this journey to evolve into your divine HU-manness. This is the ultimate fairytale, and you are very experienced at roleplaying. You can play any role you choose, even the Angel if you choose. But remember the Angel next to you has the same right as well.

You will be tested constantly to be true to your feelings, true to your path, your actions and to speak and live your truth, no matter what the oppositions or evidence to the contrary may appear to be. Remember the secret has always been "Cycles of Truth, Pathways of Peace". What is not serving the higher frequencies will blow away in the Solar winds that are about to bluster.

In the first three years of the new Century, you will have the opportunity to define your position in the great universal game. It is highly important that your choices are clear and we discern your true motivations thoroughly because with absolute certainty you will manifest the pathway to your heart's desires in physical reality by the end of this first year of the ninth Toltec Era. For here is where dark and light either separate forever or through the secrets of alchemy they join into the Divine oneness in which they were created, mirror aspects of each other creating the perfect hologram, through which you project your dreams………....

During the next 40 to 50 years of Earthly Experience, Humanity is being honed through the process of survival to come into harmony. Through the process, however we will experience a lot of soul shaking due to the frequency fluctuations and our innate resistance to change. Language will change as well. We will develop sort of a universal Earth language that will be layered over English, yet will include words from the global culture, making the speaking of simple truth quite vogue in the new paradigm.

We will find, if we haven't already, that life is going to afford us many instances where we will be urged to employ a policy of "tough love" to many situations, not out of reprisal but out of the necessity to preserve honor and respect and a degree of human dignity. If you realize the divinity in yourself, then you empathically feel and see it in all things. But here's the hitch... you can't fake it.

Before we can reach this realization, however, there is a wild strain in us all... the escape artist... *must* and *is* working its way out of our psyche. We are finding many instances where we are playing out our fears and age makes not the barrier for these actions.

Because of stress which is being heightened by our naturally short fuses, displays of violent actions both on the part of those protesting controls and those employing them upon the populations of the world, are due to a natural shifting of energies as we merge into the higher octaves of the emerging Fifth World.

People will be given to displays of momentary insanity quite frequently. Remember to always place yourself in the Light of Divine Love before taking actions when you are confronted with energy that causes you to respond with strong emotion. We are learning our emotions are extremely powerful tools, and even our words are capable of crippling someone for a very long time. So during the learning cycle it would be best to adopt an attitude of allowance... allow, allow, allow...............

The Star Seed Journals

The Truth is, we are Star Seed

During this period of intergalactic marriages and divine promiscuity, many of those who were with these explorers from Orion began to take the daughters of the humans as wives and began to have **hybrid children...** "Starseed"...

Enlil saw this as an abomination of his race and wanted the human race destroyed. Enlil tried on many occasions. He withheld information regarding about the coming of Nibaru negating any possible recourse for the Earthly Empires and the possible catastrophic events that might and did result causing almost the entire devastation of the original Earth races by floods, earthquakes, plagues and finally nuclear blasts.... probably coming from the destruction of underground complexes.

However, we had friends amongst the Angels, and Enki thwarted Enlil's plans at every possible opportunity. The price to the Children of the Sun in this war between these brothers was devastating, especially in the lands of what is now the Americas and in Central China. . That is correct ......The **War of the Gods** was not just occurring in the Euphrates, but here in the Mother Land as well, amongst the Inca and Mayan peoples and up North in the Land of the Puans (U.S.). We have some hard evidence of that, too.

The Enlilian forces were separatists (supremacists for the pure race) who decided to eliminate these very bright Children of the Sun. This situation began to heat up, leading to further divisions. You might say we have now the unilateral consequence told about in almost every high culture we will refer to as the War of the Gods or the War of the Heavens erupting as a battle of power between extraterrestrial forces possessing amazing technology, for the purpose of determining the Fate of the Earth (Terra) and her natural children, which included the children of mixed blood, the Annunaki.

Enki's first-born son was, as it turns out to be, Osiris, who believed that he, rather than Enlil's first-born son Ninurta or Marduk, was destined to rule the Earth from the Enlilian city of Babylon, the "Gateway of the Gods". Osiris wars against Marduk and brings his forces right up to the very gates of Marduk's fortress city. Osiris began in 3114 BC and sets forth an edict exiling his own half-brother, Marduk. Osiris, along with Thoth from Egypt (he was Kulkulkan to the Maya) began the first Egyptian pharaonic dynasty with permanent military forces to guard the royal bloodline. He also establishes the first Mystery Schools, or temples of learning.

The following millennia would be a time of war between these competing extraterrestrial Gods and their armies in the Persian Gulf. It was a war between the Enlilian gods Marduk/Amen Ra, who had, by his warmongering and power-hungry actions, also alienated himself from four of his five brothers, which included Thoth/Kukulkan.

While the war of the heavens was raging in the Persian Gulf, Thoth\Kukulkan left Egypt and we discover he could be found helping mankind evolve by teaching the earth-based sciences, pyramid building, astronomy, calendar sciences, the arts and herbal remedies and healing to different cultural tribes around the world.

It was Thoth who established the Temples of Divinity (Edgar Cayce called them Temples of Beauty) that became the Schools of Isis/Osiris (Ti and TiÁ). Menoin Carthagenians, Greece, Glastonbury, Thoth then continued west to the motherlands of the Andes mountains, Peru, and even unto the lands of the Puan (the Mound Builders) in what is now America, thus founding the Mayan temples of old.

Osiris meanwhile holding position in the Empire to the East is himself the victim of assassination, and his body being immortal in nature, is cut up into 14 pieces and distributed throughout the land. This is mainly so that his Priestess Isis could not use her knowledge of alchemical science to revive him. But, as legend has it, she manages to find most of the pieces of Osiris' earthly embodiment and manages to revive him long enough to become impregnated with their Royal Son...Horus.

This land we now know as America was often called by the Egyptians "the Land of the Dead" because of the Enlilian wars which were particularly devastating in the western hemisphere, where the Forces of Enlil/Jehovah had to deal with the cities of the Star-Seed Atlantean settlements which were well established. Most all Cities in North America fell, save for a few outposts in Chaco Canyon and the Urintha Mountains in Utah, leaving only the ones in the South such as Teotihuacan, Palenque, Tikal, Cahokia, Chetza nitza of the Maya, and Macchu Piccu of the Inca, in Peru.

Horus is kept from avenging his fathers murder for a period of time. We are told 480 years, by Thoth, who is busy completing the plans he and Osiris had initiated here in the West, and reestablishing the temples of learning and the education of the Star Seed of their true heritage and being, as god/men god/women. Also, Thoth himself is busy routing out the remaining forces of Marduk and his influences in the lands of Sumer.

Clarity Point : America A Miracle ... consisting of both North and South American continents, in the Master's teaching, was often referred to as the "lands of the dead" in new Egypt, which rose along the banks of the Nile River. Old Egypt was in fact here in the Americas, and you may expect very shortly archeological evidence to rise to substantiate this as a grand truth.

The Masters teachings also tell us that America is the land of the phoenix, where the legend of the phoenix rising was born. In the Phoenix Prophecies we are told. " From the ashes of the destroyed civilizations of the Sons of God it is prophesized that the New Annu, (a new Race) shall rise once again and lift humanity to new heights and enter a new consciousness that will bring about a golden age."

By the recovered Sumerian records it is established that Marduk-Ra/Jehovah had conquered and ruled the Enlilian Empire from Babylon to the Balkans and all of Persia. From the vantage point of the Western Empires, they were held at bay by Thoth and the remaining forces of Osiris.

However, history tells us that in 1595 BCE, (it was actually more like 3500BCE), the Enki/Yaweh-influenced Hittites regained control Babylon, the Enlilian forces of Marduk-Ra/Jehovah, themselves escaping back into space only after some very devastating attacks on the newly established settlements of Horus in the west. This final series of battles, it seems, destroyed the Great temples of learning, the forces of Thoth in hot pursuit leaving a small contingency here on Earth to prevent the return of Murduk-Ra/Jehova forces. (Perhaps this is were we get the story over and over again through the countless cultures of the world of the promise of the return of the gods...)

The Royal Lineage now flowed through new kingdoms of the Earth, mainly Celts, as the old rings of civilization and the Ring Lords were vanquished by Ra/Jehovah's forces. New Egypt is the only remaining expression of the once glorious global power it once was, and it falls into a gradual state of degeneration as a result of the Enlilian Wars. Old Egypt is no more. The Temples of Learning in the Western Empire to the south were also devastated by the Forces of Ra/Jehovah and humanity became destined, for a time at least, to survive with the memory of the grandeur once existing upon this plan of physical expression of copulating gods.

For as the Age of Man came upon us, the Sons of God were for the most part diminished in numbers, their cohesive strength making them little more than wandering refugees upon the land. Their cities reduced to mostly ashes, their technology vanquished along with their culture, they were reduced to warring amongst each other.

They lived in constant fear of the ever-growing number of primitive warlike Homo-Sapien-Sapiens that constantly descended upon them as they tried time and time again to rebuild their lost empires of old in remote mountain areas.

There were many more elements involved in the story, and perhaps I will bring those forth in future works as the Mystery and the evidence to support the Myth makes itself available.

The war continues: A War of Angels...

It is evident as more information becomes available from the many surviving records, and more unearthing of ancient artifacts occurs, these Children of the Sun, these hybrids who were the creations of Enki and his kind, were more than the Enlilian forces had anticipated.

Their fear was that being such a young race (Anu), given time to mature, these hybrids might surely become more powerful than even their creators. It became apparent that the Enlilian forces needed to change their previous apocalyptic plans.

The human species had populated over the entire Earth and in some instances had use of similar technology with which to defend themselves. It was now too difficult to wipe out humanity with tactical military maneuvers, and the use of Star Wars tactics proved too destructive and might render the planet useless even to Enlil and his followers. Even their use of technology to create natural disasters, earthquakes and volcanic eruptions, was not having the effect they had anticipated.

Attempts at shifting the magnetic poles were too dangerous and the potential for creating another ice age without rendering the Earth herself becoming lifeless was too risky.

The Enlilian gods then began their alternative plan for the ultimate destruction and crippling of the human species. There were enough of their kind on Earth to initiate not only political conflict, but to employ genetic and biological warfare upon the humans who populated Earth. As a result of these actions whole animal species perished and died out, as well as plant life, and the entire bio-structure was altered abruptly and cataclysmically.

Entire races of people have often without explanation simply vanished, quickly and forever from our planet without a trace. Eventually, through being able to breed on their own, new species of hybridized hominoids appeared. which was never part of the original plans, but for reasons we can only guess, the ability to procreate was afforded us by Enki the Benevolent one; who may well be one and the same as the god Yahweh (YHWH). it was hoped and preferred by his brother by Enlil / Jehovah, that the gene pools would be destroyed and the potential for a united human race would never be a threat to their **Pure Nibaruian Kingdom.** ruled by their offsprong the Raphiam, and the Anunnaki.

A safety mechanism was installed within the genetic coding whereby the brain itself was split and most of the DNA strands would become inoperable after a few generations. Humans were reduced by this action to two strands of functioning DNA so they would never have full brain potential. Basically, humans were destined through this process of their own natural need to breed, rendered to become a slave race.

The tenacity of the Hybrid races as well as their ability to rejuvenate and regroup was again a surprise to the Enlilian forces, one that they did not anticipate. Further, the work being done by other entities under the guidance of Thoth/Kukulkan in the Mystery Schools in the Motherland (South America) was not anticipated. The war against the centers of learning, the schools of Isis, (what would later become known as the Mystery Schools), began. And the preoccupation with the searching out and ordained annihilation of the Royal bloodlines, as well as any reference to the goddess, became the edict of all organized religions. Sad, but non-the-less true.

We, the conglomerate that we are, I call it "Cosmic Soup" are nonethe less the Children of the Sun, have an uncanny ability and are considered masters of survival. NephilimEnlil forces were not entirely able to manipulate the earthly elements. Thoth/Enki/ Kukulkcan and the Children of the Sun survived dispite the attempts oof the dark side to remove all traces of memory from ourconsciousness. If we don't think we are, we aren't .

There was intervention by Sirian forces and Andromedans and the travesty was turned around, in a manner of speaking. The effects of the devastation, however, would have long-range effects. Only in the frontier regions of the Euphrates were there survivors whom the Enlilian forces could dominate. Without the technology of the old world, only the sea remained as a means of communication and a barrier against the onslaught from the survivors of the Ra./Jehovah races. This was true until recent times.

Thus, the subtle wars of genetically manipulated races and the purging of the surviving schools of ISIS would lead, even into the present day, to each side attempting to match the other in consciousness abilities and prowess of the species to survive. One has the focus on Compassion and Nurturing, while the other is constantly recreating the superior warrior and is engaged in the thirst for blood and destruction. The cycles of the serpentine and the serpent would commence through the struggle of the DNA and we entered the cycles of destruction that would result.

ABOUT THOSE ANGELS... OPHANIM AND THE SERAPHIM ... AND THEIR STAR SEED

Following a linear story in the telling of this tale is difficult with so many pieces to the puzzle coming into view at different points, so allow me to try to simplify the issue of the original split of the races. Earth, about 100,00 years ago, was essentially inhabited by many races from many parts of the galaxy. Some of those on Earth were from other galaxies, mainly the Pleiadians, Andromedans, Sirians and Orions who were a composite group of mainly reptilian beings.

They (all of them) interbred with the natural, or earth people, and had hybrid children. Understand there were close to 72 original Star Races here, so this could be a book in itself. Some of the physical species inhabiting the Earth were in fact hybrid from the stars, and some natural or indigenous peoples. (Remember the two Adams?) The main indigenous species making up Man-kind who seemed to populate earth were the **Neanderthal**, or primitives, and the **Cro-Magnon,** or progressives**.**

Homo Sapiens came later. They are not natural to this planet and were created from the hybridization of the Orion Seed from the royal lineages of the Orion Queens, being the **Ophanim** and the **Seraphim**. The Orion Queens interbred with Cro-Magnon, and from the Womb of the Orion Queens were born Sons of God, and from the Womb of Man (woman) later were born Sons of Man ... In both lineages did this occur, being Ophanim and that of the Seraphim, and thus the knowledge was genetically encoded within the human genetics forevermore.

Thus began what seems to be the endless battle of the Light and the Dark (the War within), which was our imposed destiny until one side won over the other or a balance was reached, or until the artificial time grid would no longer function and the natural changes based upon celestial cycles would reach the point is has today.

For the great plan and the suffering of the Children of the Gods was not to be an eternal condition. When the "**end of time**" came, in that experience, would come the separating of the wheat from the tares, and the Sons of Man.... would join once again with the Sons of God.

We are fast coming to the universal understanding that the Bible, at best, is little more than a watered down collection of grossly mistranslated accountings of the Sumerian tablets, and by the way, did you know that the word **Summaire (Sumer)** translates to **Drac - as in Dragon**-Draconian in the ancient Celtic language?

The original Orion dialect was what we call ancient Aryan (meaning of Orion), the word ori-gin means linked to Orion, specifically to the 'crossing over' of the blood lines of the NIB.. (Nib-elung) as human - bird (as in Birdtribes) DNA with the URU, which was the Draco or Dragon-Reptilian (winged beings). Those who possessed the blood (genetics) of the Dragon Kings were the Messah, Messiahs.

MESSIAH translates quite literally to *'...one fed by Reptilian Blood. One born of the royal Lineage of the Court of the Dragon.'*

OPHANIM: Annunaki, Birdtribes, adawi , the Golden Ones, Yeshua from: Star- seed born of the Orion Queens.

SERAPHIM: Sera Phi, SaraPhic reptilian bloodline of the Orion Queens, as in Magdalene, priestess of Isis

Yeshua + Magdalene = Royal bloodline - the Blue Bloods

Matthew, Ch. 13

36   Then Jesus sent the multitude away, and went into the house: and his disciples came unto him, saying, Declare unto us the parable of the tares of the field.

3": He answered and said unto them, He that soweth the good seed is the Son of man;

38: The field is the world; the good seed are the children of the kingdom; but the tares are the children of the wicked one;

39: The enemy that sowed them is the devil; the harvest is the end of the world; and the reapers are the angels.

40: As therefore the tares are gathered and burned in the fire; so shall it be in the end of this world....."

Earth Chronicles: ...   Quoting Zecariah Sitchin:

Excerpted from his work *Earth Chronicles*

"ARY-AN Gods were listed with their parents and grandparents, the "Olden Gods", Anu & Antu, Enlil & Ninlil, Ea & Damkina.. ..". Then p 80-81 War of Gods & Men"...

"For Enki was the first born son of Anu by Id, one of his concubines, and could have been expected to follow Anu on Nibaru's throne... but then- as in the biblical tale

of Abraham- his concubine Haggar and his half sister Sara - Anu's half sister wife Antum, bore him a son Enlil, and by the Nibaruan rules of succession - so faithfully adopted by the biblical patriarch, Enlil became the legal heir instead of Enki.

"And now this rival, this robber of Enki's birthright came to Earth to take over the command" (& SO began the tirade of the angry interventionist between Enlil and Yahweh and the war of the brothers in Edin..) .... The War of the Heavens...

OK you are still a non believer?... the images below represent some from the Sumerian Civilization (Cicrca 800 BCE The very symbols that Zechariah is talking about. they represent the 'Watchers' they talk about in the Bible

Below right we have a photo of a crop circle in England that appeared at the turn of the century . Is someone trying to tell us something? ... I think they ae shouting at us.

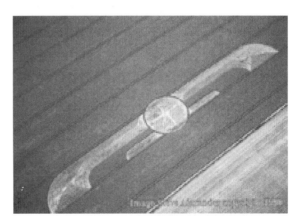

The Nephilim

In **Genesis 6**, the Bible describes the "Sons of God" (B'nai Elohim) (Elohim =ancient translation Angels) took wives of the "daughters of men," and spawned the "Nephilim.". (Mixed blood-hybrids) The B'nai Elohim is a term that directly refers to angels. The term "Nephilim", derives from the Hebrew "naphal" (to fall), and literally means "the fallen-down-ones" because the fathers were tall celestial beings who fell from the sky.

They and their descendants are mentioned often in the early books of the Old Testament. They were known by the following terms: Rephaim, Emim, Anakim, Horim, Avim, Annunaki, and Zamzummim. In Babylonian, they were known as the Annunaki. These beings were by the Hebrew descriptions virtual giants.

The ancient religions often referred to the parents and their half-breed offspring interchangeably and usually they were referred to again as the Giants. Likewise, the term Nephilim was interchanged often with the term Annunaki. Both terminologies usually denoted the half-breed offspring resulting from the union of human females and their astral fathers, referred to as non-other than the fallen angels themselves.

Regarding the Annunaki, it must be understood that there were some gross misinterpretations regarding the Annunaki — some deliberate and some out of ignorance. There is a difference in the translations lost to over two millennia of translations and misunderstanding of language. In this author's humble opinion, the Annunaki were not reptilians, although I concur, from first hand experience and exploration into the matter that they were giants in those times by normal standards.

There exists a degree of discrepancy here, for according to the altered texts, the "old ones", the Annunaki, were not flesh eaters nor were they debauchers. They were the ancient ones who initiated the ancient Temples of Learning many thousands of years BCE. Perhaps this is due to misunderstandings as to those who were the Nephilim and those who were Annunaki. As my circle of influence see the matter, the Nephilim were the Gods themselves, where the Annunaki on the other hand were the offspring of the Gods.

Also, in all fairness, with specific regard to references to Reptilian DNA and the bloodlines, the term Reptilians is generally grossly shrouded with fear, fairytale and misconception due to our general lack of knowledge on the subject. Not everyone has access to ancient records, nor is every one a student of ancient mythology, so the tendency to take some one else's word for how things were, is usually the case.

We had best become familiar with the term Reptilian, as well as the lineage, for the time of '**this present illusion'** is nearly over. Reptilian does not translate to "**all are evil**", for the reptilian gene is quite common within our composite genetic makeup. Our understanding of the 'term' Reptilian has been, for 2000 years at least, a problem of misinterpretation layered over misinterpretation. Other people's **dogma**…again.... we find it is always a matter of **His-story** Vs. **My-story**…or Mythology.

The Dragon throughout history has always represented Great Knowledge and Spiritual powers, Magic if you will. As it has already been explained in this work, the very term 'Messiah' is derived from the ancient Egyptian term 'Messah' meaning " One who is descent of the Royal Court of the Dragon.." This can be a problem if you hold to "watered down" dogmatic Nuevo Christian understandings of the ancient texts.

One who cares enough to read up on the subject will soon find that in fact the Dragon was a very important symbol to the Early Christian Movement prior to the Justinian Roman version of Sanctioned Christianity, which alters considerably from the original text and teachings. Argue the fact after you read up on it please, for ironically it is a matter of recorded historical fact.

From the Bible

The outcome of the demonic corruption was violence, perversion and a brood of monstrous beings. Compare:

GENESIS 6:4.

"The Sons of God saw the daughters of men that they were fair; and they took to them wives of all which they chose.

GENESIS 6:2 "There were giants in the earth in those days; and also after that, when the sons of God came in unto the daughters of men, and they; bare children unto them, the same became mighty men which were of old, men of renown.

GENESIS 6:4 " The Nephilim were upon the Earth in those days and thereafter too. Those sons of the gods who cohabited with the daughters of the Adam, and they bore children into them. They were the Mighty Ones of Eternity, the People of the Shem.

THE SHEM ?

URU is the aboriginal name for the EL place of the URU. This place of El or inter-dimensional phase shift is called Shem. Shem is a place where often we will find megaliths, usually made of Granite. They act like antennae projecting into the Earth energy and the grid lines.

The monolith (Pyramid, Ziggurat, Stonehenge, etc.) creates a sort of acupuncture needle to connect that vortex energy spot to another one inter-dimensionally. It is therefore called a **Shem**, a place where the "Els" (Quezalcoatl, El-ohim) could make their 'EL' or phase-shift thru a portal at light speed from circle to line in their DNA, were 'ported'.

The Shem also refers to a place where Shaman could use the folding foci of the 'Eye of the Shaman' to see thru the heart of the Sun to any place literally that consciousness could conceive with focused intent, regardless of time or distance, for the Shem is in the NOW, and not effected by the time space continuum or inter-dimensional circumstance.

And then there were giants

We are told the giants remained throughout the early times of King David.

SAMUEL 21:18-22 *records the following glimpse of the giants still living in Israel:*

SAMUEL 21:18-22

"After this there was again war with the Philistines at Gob; then Sibbecai the Hushathite slew Saph, who was one of the descendants of the giants. And there was again war with the Philistines at Gob; and Elhanan the son of Jaareoregim, the Bethlehemite, slew Goliath the Gittite, the shaft of whose spear was like a weaver's beam.

" And there was again war at Gath, where there was a man of great stature, who had six fingers on each hand, and six toes on each foot, twenty-four in number; and he also was descended from the giants. And when he taunted Israel, Jonathan the son of Shimei, David's brother, slew him. These four were descended from the giants in Gath; and they fell by the hand of David and by the hand of his servants."

An important difference to note between the accountings of the Nephilim in the Bible and the Book of Enoch, occurs in the titles these creatures have. Genesis refers to them as "**Sons of God**" while the Book of Enoch most often calls them the "Watchers". In the Bible this term is only found in the Book of Daniel .

This is important because it gives us a key to understanding that there was a distinct difference between those who were Nephilim and those who were Annunaki.

DANIEL:4:17: **"This matter is by the decree of the watchers, and the demand by the word of the holy ones: to the intent that the living may know that the most High ruleth in the kingdom of men, and giveth it to whomsoever he will, and setteth up over it the basest of men."**

The text of the Book of Enoch alleges that two hundred of these 'Watchers' descended to Earth in the days of Jared, an event that can be corresponded with the text in GENESIS 5:18. *Some are identified by name.*

The worst of this group is called Azazel. Other Jewish manuscripts also identify an entity called Azazel who "scattered over the earth the secrets of heaven and rebelled against the Mighty One". He is also mentioned in LEVITICUS 16 *as a demon who inhabited a region in the Judean wilderness.*

Book of Enoch: 6_1-6 (excerpt)

1. And it came to pass when the children of men had multiplied that in those days were born unto them beautiful and comely daughters.

2 And the angels, the children of the heaven, saw and lusted after them, and said to one another: 'Come, let us choose us wives from among the children of men

3 and beget us children.' And Semjaza, who was their leader, said unto them: 'I fear ye will not

4 indeed agree to do this deed, and I alone shall have to pay the penalty of a great sin.' And they all answered him and said: 'Let us all swear an oath, and all bind ourselves by mutual imprecations

5 not to abandon this plan but to do this thing.' Then sware they all together and bound themselves

6 by mutual imprecations upon it. And they were in all two hundred; who descended in the days of Jared on the summit of Mount Hermon,

Enoch further says:

"I saw Watchers in my vision, the dream-vision. Two (men) were fighting over me, saying...and holding great contest over me. I asked them, 'Who are you, that you are thus empowered over me?' They answered me, 'We have been empowered and rule over all mankind'. They said to me, 'Which of us do you choose to rule (you)?"

" I raised my eyes and looked. One of them was terrifying in his appearance, like a serpent, his cloak was many-colored yet very dark... And I looked again, and...in his appearance, his visage like a viper, and wearing...exceedingly, his serpent eyes I replied to him, 'This Watcher, so is he?

"He answered me, 'This Watcher...and his three names are Belial (**as in the Edgar Cayce readings**) and Prince of Darkness and the King of Evil.'"

"Testament of Amram"

(Dead Sea Scroll Fragment 4Q535, Manuscript B.B.O.E.)

Let us look once more at the artifact found in Bolivia. Beyond it's obvious historical importance to the placement of cultures around the globe thinking about the Bible regarding the Nephilim. what might we be really looking at here..?   Buried for centuries under 3 feet of Guana

Mayan Elder, Day Keeper
Hunbatz Men

Shares with us a little about the Prophesized rebirthing of the Mayan Mystery Schools

This is the time that we have known that the reincarnated Masters would be returning to these lands of the Mayan to communicate with the great spirits of their ancestors.

According to High Initiation, it is written that the wisdom of the cosmic light will return.- When the human race begins to slip into the darkness of ignorance, oblivion, and despair, it will be the wisdom of the seven brothers of our Father Sun that will shed the great light of wisdom in order to awaken the powers that have remained dormant in human beings due to an erroneous form of education.- In this New Age, the Mysteries Schools have the responsibility of reclaiming a confused mankind and leading it through the path of the multicolored light of cosmic education.

According to High Initiation, it is written that the wisdom of the cosmic light will return.- When the human race begins to slip into the darkness of ignorance, oblivion, and despair, it will be the wisdom of the seven brothers of our Father Sun that will shed the great light of wisdom in order to awaken the powers that have remained dormant in human beings due to an erroneous form of education.- In this New Age, the Mysteries Schools have the responsibility of reclaiming a confused mankind and leading it through the path of the multicolored light of cosmic education.

Again the time of the Mayan cosmic education has come.- Thousands of years ago, the sacred teachings from the cosmos were deposited in many magnetic centers throughout the world: Chan Chan (Peru), Huete (Spain), Tulle (France), Hu-nan (China), Bethlehem (Israel), Tih (Egypt), Mississippi (United States), Humac (Brazil), Nagasaki (Japan), Mul (England), Maya (Russia, Naga (India), and Chukotz (Bering Strait).- The names of all these places are of Maya origin, which confirms that, in different periods of times, the Maya were present in these sacred magnetic centers.

For many moons and suns, mankind has been disoriented.- In these modern times, it is with sadness that we see how ordinary human beings are manipulated and consistently forced into the abyss of physical and spiritual destruction, or simply used as experiments, by a few groups that control the majority of mankind.

Hunab K"u, who can see and understand everything, knows that the time for the great change has come.- The word for us to return to the ancient temples has been received from the cosmos.- It is here and now that the great Spirit is beginning to call us back to the magnetic sites.- The incarnated Masters are beginning to raise their voices of knowledge in the ancient sites that the cosmic word to attain wisdom in a gradual manner has been received.

The Mayan prophecies are being fulfilled even now; others will be fulfilled on the coming of the morrow. But that it is happening is known, and that gives us courage.

The Mayan prophecies are very respected and known to be accurate. This is because the Mayas knew the nature of cosmic time. They knew that in certain times it would be necessary to keep this cosmic wisdom secret. This was the purpose of the prophecy so that they might be able to communicate their secrets to the initiates of the future.

It is prophesied that initiates shall return to the sacred land of the Mayas to continue the work of the Great Spirit. Here in the lands of the Maya, in the cycle of light, there surged a great wisdom, which would illuminate humanity for many millennia. This wisdom was given to the Mayan-Atlantis Itzaes, the ones Western civilization calls the Toltec-Mayan.

These reincarnated Mayan-Itzaes are coming to the Sacred land of the Mayas so that together they may understand what shall be the new initiations which will be put into practice; so that humanity, the reincarnated masters and the great spirits of the Itzaes may fuse into one. Then they will be able to travel like the wind, descend like the rain, give warmth like fire and teach compassion like our Mother Earth and Father Sun.

These Masters will come from many places. They will be of many colors. Some will speak of things difficult to understand. Others will be aged. Some less so. Some will dance while others will remain silent as rocks. Their eyes will communicate the initiatic message, which is to continue through the cycles of the next millennium.

It is also prophesied that this initiation of cosmic wisdom is for future initiates. They will be young and old, men and women who will have the understanding that this modern civilization is not meeting its educational responsibilities. It is well known that this so-called modern civilization has caused a regressive effect in spiritual development.

The Mayan ceremonial centers begin to emanate the light of the new millenium, which is much needed today. Many Mayan cosmic ceremonial centers begin to beckon, with their solar reflection, to the many initiates who will come to continue the work of the Great Spirit. In many Mayan ceremonial centers, Solar Priests will begin to walk among the multitude of tourists. They will be touched by the Solar Priests to be initiated with the cosmic wisdom. It will be then that the initiates of the second level shall begin to work among the new initiates.

The Mayan masters will begin to manifest in the trees, in the sun, in the moon and in the stars. They will appear also in homes to inform families that the new time to begin the initiatic cosmic work has commenced. Many will not understand because this will happen when people are asleep, or when they are sleepy or when people will have lost the notion of time, if only for a few seconds. Everything shall be moved to the new time, including human genetics which will be moved by the sacred energy of Father Sun and the 7 cosmic brothers who will help elevate human consciousness.

When the sacred energy of the masters and students is begun at the ceremonial centers of the sacred Mayans of Ek Balam, Uxmal, Paenque,Oxkintok, Mayapan and Chichen Itza, and many others, then shall the gods who are in the stars look upon us and bless the sons and daughters who have returned once again to continue the cosmic spiritual work of the new millenium. These gods of the stars will announce to the four cardinal points, the good news of the new beginnings of the human race. They are already in our heavens and have given us many affirmations of their returning, as they had promised.

These gods of the stars will call the lords of the day, and of the night, and of the inner world and also of the exterior world and they will say to them to look again upon humanity and to assist them to awaken into the solar light. The gods will also look into the bodies of the humans and they will ask the heart to beat newly in rhythm to the universe; to the stomach they will ask us to accept only natural foods. In this way will they be able to speak to many parts of the inner body. To the head it will ask that it should not let itself be deceived by the false modern society.

Then when the Masters and the students are in one accord, the manifestations of the spirits will come. The eagle will teach us what it knows about our ancestors. The serpent and the jaguar will do the same. Then the sacred tree of our genetics will illumine us with its wisdom. They will all then begin to see us in the same manner as the ancient Mayas. This will be the moment to begin the grand ritual of the cosmic conjugation within every living being.

In the beginning of this millennium, we will begin our rituals and ceremonies in some of 4,000 Mayan ceremonial centers we have in Mexico in those sacred lands of the Maya. Today there are a few million initiates doing this work. But tomorrow, the Mayan prophecies indicate that humanity will return to the ancient ceremonial centers to fulfill their obligation, which was interrupted by colonialism.

There exist four Mayan ceremonial centers of extreme importance where the energy must be activated so that their energy of light may serve to illuminate the steps humanity must take in this new millennium. Each sacred center will give its message as will be explained:

OXK INTOK will be the sacred Mayan center where the solar light will illuminate the law of the trinity. Here humanity will understand who is its father. He will know who is his mother and he will understand where he will go when he leaves his physical body. Here humanity will know the importance of who is his own physical parentage and also his spiritual parentage. Here in Oxkintok man will understand this cosmic law.

Here they will also understand why they are a solar sons and daughters. They will understand that their spirit is a Solar Energy, which comes from the Sun, and when life is transcended it returns to the Great Father Sun. He will understand that all existing being is a product of the solar energy and that without this energy, which sustains life he would not exist in the third dimension.

Oxkintok is the center where rests the purity of the divided energy; divided in its three manifestations which govern all life principles. It will be understood that this solar energy light can be wrongly used. It can also destroy the body. The unlimited wrongful use of this energy can actually cause forest fires, which debilitate our Mother Earth.

Here also, at this ceremonial center of Oxkintok exists the Labyrinth Temple where many are initiated into the knowledge of the eight senses (not seven) so that they might know how to orient themselves in darkness. The initiate should know that one-day he/she will enter the fourth dimension with their physical body. They should be able to enter and leave in full consciousness, or memory. It will be the awakened senses that will help he/she do this initiatic work they have come back to do.

We shall also learn at this sacred sight about the statues, which are found in a place called 'of the devil'. One of these statues has two holes on top of the head. In ancient times, this Mayan statue had two flints on the head that resembled two horns. These flints served like antennas to capture Line energy. There are other symbols on this particular statue and it is good to stand before symbols that have not yet been deciphered by investigators.

CHI CHEN ITZA, remains that largest Mayan ceremonial center was considered by the ancients as the cosmic University of Meso-America and the world. Many persons will come here to study all manner of science. In its pyramids and temples reside (still exists) the knowledge of the human race our purpose and our origins. Here was deposited the great knowledge of the Mayan-Atlantis Itzaes when they arrived in these Maya lands after the great destruction of the red land.

The Kukulcan pyramid records the sacred Mayan calendars. At first glance the initiate will observe the calendars of the sun, the moon and the Pleiades. After learning these he may begin to understand the other 14 calendars in order to comprehend the 26,000-year Pleiadians cyclic calendar, which in reality is the one, which affects the great changes upon Mother Earth.

At the astronomic observatory of the sacred center of Chi Chen Itza we can understand how the ancients made their observations of the planets, stares and galaxies. Here you will observe all the solar movements. Through the tiny windows of this observatory the ancients calculated the movements of Venus, Mars, Jupiter and the other planets in our solar system. Through this line knowledge they were able to predict the future of our Mother Earth.

In what is called the 'church' at this sacred Mayan ceremonial center, we will observe how the ancient Mayas enacted the water initiation. You can see the mouth of the Grand Chauac where the initiates entered to understand how this watery liquid is converted into blood, perspiration and the liquid of the bone. This sacred teaching was given at this ancient temple by the SOVEREIGN SOLAR COMMAND OF THE CHICAN ITZAAB for the initiates of the future who would come to the sacred lands of the Maya.

In **EK BALAM**, sacred Mayan center, we will understand why the ancient Balam (Priests of a special order, initiates of Kate Zahl) did rituals to the cosmic stars. Through meditation we will enter the dimension of the Balams. We will learn more about the sacred work of these Mayan Priests. We will understand how they made their predictions by reading the stars. We will apply this knowledge to the new millennium that is about to begin. Understanding the cosmic knowledge in this way will show us what destiny lies ahead for Mother Earth and her children.

We will be witnesses to many recent discoveries by anthropologists. We will be the first initiates of the new millennium to see these new findings. We will see recently discovered figurines made of stone, which have no relation to the Mayan culture. However it is important that we the masters and initiates of the New Time be here to see and observe. Perhaps these pieces hold the knowledge needed to understand that missing link of humanity.

It is important to also visit the small temples where the Aluxes (guardians) do their spiritual work. The Aluxes, (pronounced **A- loo- shas**) to the Maya, are the spirits of things that exist. Generally they manifest as children. They are the essence of all manifested life. They are the purity that is responsible for the continuity of life. The ancient Maya knew how to live in harmony with these etheric beings. When the Mayan masters left the ceremonial centers, they left them in the care of the Aluxes.

In **MAYAPAN**, sacred ceremonial Mayan Center we will visit the observatory. Like in Chichen Itza and many thousand others that we have here in the land of the Mayan, we will learn about the knowledge of the cosmos and how through this observatory the movements of the constellation Castor and

Canopus were calculated. This is done through the doors of the observatory. Through meditation we will understand more about the mathematical calculations of the cosmos.

At the principal pyramid we will learn how the ancient Maya recorded their sacred calendar Tzolk' in. They wisely recorded this wisdom on the staircase. This is the only pyramid to this day discovered, from which the knowledge of the sacred calendar may be acquired by the initiate in just 21 minutes. This calendar synchronizes the other 16 calendars that demonstrate the Mayan mathematical understanding of the universe.

The greatest gift we, the masters and initiates, can receive is to be able to observe a stucco figure 2 X meters. This giant relief confirms the great understanding the Mayas had of the sacred lands of this American continent and of other continents on this earth. For once the wisdom of the Mayas was in each of these places.

On one side of the principal pyramid can be found this great figure that according to my understanding represents the union of the continents. To better understand this I will try to describe it. This future of a man stands with both arms outstretched holding in the right hand the Condor of the Andes and in the left hand the figure of the eagle. The man appears to be levitated. Beneath him there appear to be waves of the sea. His rib cage seems to protrude and where they meet at the front we can see three double circles. Where the rib cage meets at the central part there is a finger coming forth from the joint of the last row. It is important to observe that much importance was given to the umbilical area.

It is of utmost importance to observe that this statue is headless. Where the head would be there is only a hole. Remember beloved initiates that in order to understand the Mayan culture it is very important to understand everything about this figure in its entirety. It is also important to realize that one of the ways to understand the Mayan culture is to understand the complexity of symbolism.

The Mayan language is one of the most complex advanced languages that still existwith its original understandings intact in the world today and has survived many civilizations that followed it whose languages are now considered dead languages.. but the language of the Maya is living.

Hunbatz: *..I will give a brief description as to how I understand this figure*
(following page)

The Condor represents the South American Continent.

The Eagle represents the North American Continent.

The man levitating over the sea represents the human man of North and South of this continent of America. It can also represent other humans from other continents.

The protruding rib cage is symbolic of the spirit breaking outside of the body. It can also symbolize the spiritual union of all human beings from whatever latitude or longitude of the world.

The symbolic finger speaks of the root of our ancestors of millions of years ago.

Any esoteric knows that the umbilical area represents the union, firstly between a person and his other, whether terrestrial or physical and both represent the union of the cosmos. This can symbolize many other things.

The most important is to be able to enter into the dimension of Mayan thought so that we may understand why the Maya did not place a head on this figure. He who enters into high initiation and who belongs to the Mystery Schools can understand what the Mayas represented in this mural made of relief. It is difficult for the 'experts' to understand the high symbolism, which was shaped into this ancient figure of Mayapan.

For us, the traditional Mayas, this figure represents beings of the American continent and of other continents in both the physical and the spiritual aspect. It also represents a memory to the ancestors of their physical aspect. It speaks of its connection, as a seed from the Pleiades. It also represents other things that we will explain in another study. The most important is that this symbol can represent the union of the human being with his religious and physical aspect as well as the mental. We can now use this cosmic symbol as an identifier of the new millennium..

SHALL WE SAY, IN THE NEW MILLENNIUM MANKIND MUST LEARN TO BE MORE SPIRITUAL AND GAIN CONTROL OVER THEIR NATURE.

MANKIND MUST BECOME MORE ALIGNED TO THE GRAND LAWS OF THE UNIVERSE IF THEY HOPE TO CONTINUE ALONG THE FORWARD EVOLUTIONARY THRUST OF LIFE SEEKING ITSELF...

Pictured above, is a depiction of the iniation of a priest into the circle that holds the knowledge of time travel Hunbatz talks about.

The Return of Our Ancestors

A TOLTEC_MAYA TALE

A little over 520 years ago when the Spanish **Conquistadores** came to the New World from Spain they discovered a great civilization of the Aztecs. Although they constantly waged war to take captives for bloody sacrifices, Hernando Cortez was impressed that their way of life was as orderly and convenient, and their "standard of living" was nearly the same as in Spain.

They had, according to Cortez, received much of their cultural knowledge from the Toltec Indians, whom they had conquered a few centuries before and from the ancient prophet-ruler of the Toltecs, Quetzalcoatl (the Feathered Serpent, as he was called). Just as the Spaniards made a slaughter of the Indians in the name of Christ, whose Message was of love, the Aztecs had also fallen away from the similar teachings of Quetzalcoatl....Quetzalcoatl's message of love and wisdom is reflected in the following advice of an Aztec noble to his sons:

"Take great pains to make yourselves friends of God who is in all parts, and is invisible and impalpable, and it is meant that you give Him all your heart and body, and look that you be not proud in your heart, nor yet despair, nor be cowardly of spirit; but that you be humble in your heart and have hope in God. Be at peace with all, shame yourselves before none and to none be disrespectful; respect all, esteem all, defy no one, for no reason affront any person."

Toltec- Mayan Prophecy

The Promised Return of Quetzalcoatl

There are many tales of the god Quetzalcoatl that are told throughout Central and South America and its various cultures...as many as there are differences in languages between regions, each with its own particular flavor and identity like the spices available in the Mercado in Merida. Quetzalcoatl is described in nine out of ten instances, as a white man, a Pale Prophet with a beard, who wore long robes and who gave a message of love and compassion. His teachings were of the One Supreme God, and giving, forbidding the blood sacrifices, putting the emphasis on the divine Hu-man rather than the subjective human.

Quetzalcoatl is credited with giving the Toltec-Mayan civilizations many understandings that have become the wealth of their culture, such as the calendar, understanding the cosmos, and the mysteries of the DNA and the keys to life and death, much like **Thoth** of Egypt.

The far-reaching effects of Quetzalcoatl's teachings and his influence are even spoken of as far north as the Canadian woodlands and to the land of the Iriquois. We are told he left the Toltecs after many, many years, because of the enmity and persecution of powerful religious leaders who were fearful of his teachings and true laws of **Hunab Ku** but promised one day to return, as he had left, from the East, over the ocean.

Author's note : Some stories indicate that Quetzalcoatl may have lived as long as 800 to 1200 years. This accounting confuses many; however, if we ponder that Quetzalcoatl, the Pale Prophet, Yeshua, Sananda may well be one and the same entity, then as an ascended being this individual would have been in our understanding at least immortal. So the argument lies in whether or not the legend is factual or not. My friend, only you can answer that my friend… Live, learn and Grow in your understandings and personal knowledge.. I know there is a Creator, I can't prove the tangible existence; however I can prove that there is not, not a Creator...Understand..?

Quetzalcoatl (Kukulkan) in his flying Machine. (right)

Notice the Serpent, delineating his royal blood lineage and status as a Dragon King....

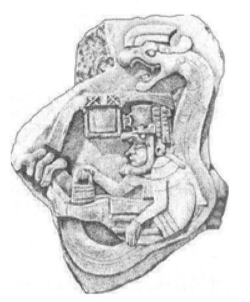

Quetzalcoatl "our Prince of Peace"
As told by a Daughter of Meso-America:
anonymous by request….

"It is difficult to please everyone when speaking of these things. You must understand that today many of the Native people in Mexico have an understanding of their heritage that is a composite of different religions and cultures. In many instances they are saying the same thing. It is just that different people have different names for the same. Also this can be true of each individual region, but we know that we are speaking of the same God, even when it is a different name, understand?

In the case of the God Quetzalcoatl, it becomes even more confusing if you do not understand this, for he is both man and god. In Christianity it is called the Son of God and each new place he went and taught he was called by a different name, but the same meaning. Also in each location these Temples that were actually universities, were always built with the roads coming into the city in the form of a cross, which he wore upon his Robe. It was his sign. The Cross within the Circle.

There is no difference to us between the Jesus of the Christian faith and the one we call the Prophet or Quetzalcoatl; he was Our Prince of Peace Quetzalcoatl. He was a powerful holy person accredited with performing many miracles. His teachings brought big religious change to Tula. His way was very different, but the people followed him for they saw all the miracles he did, and his knowledge was even more advanced than our priests, and even the secret orders in the Mountains, where he always would go.

Quetzalcoatl believed that human sacrifice had to be stopped and so it was done. But others were not pleased with this; those who had followed Tezcatlipoca were angry. Their god had demanded the nectar of human blood as his tribute. Thus those who followed Tezcatlipoca believed in blood sacrifice and was himself a shape shifter. He plotted to do away with Our Prince. Death, unfortunately, was not an answer.. For in death, they believed that Quetzalcoatl would gain even more followers and that his teachings could never be silenced. No, they sought to destroy him in such a manner as to discredit his person and place doubt of the people who believed in his message, for this would be more painful than death.

Hence they set out to trick Our Prince. They held before him, one day, a mirror and to his astonishment Quetzalcoatl had seen how old he had become; his hair was silver and his skin translucent. He had forgotten how long a time he was here with the people. Some of our stories say he was here for many centuries; that he was thought to be immortal. There are stories about this pale God that are over a long time, perhaps 1,000 years. Some of the stories tell of a red-haired man coming upon a Dragon ship with those like him, and other stories tell of a silver-haired man who left to continue his work in another place, in the Red Land, leaving upon a Dragon Ship, as well.

Falling into despair, he wondered what to do. Seeing how much he had aged he was shocked, and became confused. There were those who were close to him who were really with the other priests, and they acted like friends saying they could help him.

They said to him that they could make him young again, and produced for him a cure. Believing this was his salvation, Quetzalcoatl had taken this offering. But this cure was induced by the *pulque* (hallucinogenic), which his lips had never before touched. The *pulque* racing in his blood caused Quetzalcoatl to act not like himself at all. It is even said that he had relations with strange women. This is something he would have never committed otherwise.

When word spread about these things throughout Tula, the people were shocked and ashamed. Many withdrew. And the old priests who were still practicing human sacrifice took advantage of the situation and returned to their old ways. They formed armies and threatened harm to the people if Quetzalcoatl did not leave. Seeing his people's faces and hearts, Quetzalcoatl, decided it was best to flee, for he remembered his visions of war and blood upon the temple steps and did not want to be the cause of this..

So, arrangements were made for him by his priests (who also wore the long robes), and a Great Dragon ship came and took Our Prince to the Red Land to the East. We are now nearingthe prophecized time of his return...

A Meso-American Messiah

Quetzacoatl: The Prince of Peace

Quetzalcoatl is to the New World what Christ is to Europe: the center of a religious cosmology and the pre-eminent symbol of the civilized nations of Meso-America. Both were considered to be men who ascended into heaven upon their death; Christ to sit at the right hand of God, Quetzalcoatl to become the Dawn Star. Both were tempted by evil powers; Christ by Satan, Quetzalcoatl by the wizard-god Tezcatlipoca. And both were prophesied to return one day to earth, Christ as the Prince of the Kingdom of Heaven, Quetzalcoatl as a god-king returned to claim his kingdom of peace in Central Mexico.

To understand the life and teachings of Jesus Christ is to understand Christianity, the root religion of what we refer to as Western Civilization. To understand the life and mystery of Quetzalcoatl is to understand the religious thought of what we call Meso-America. We cannot read only half the book and assume we know the whole story.

The Feathered Serpent

The figure of the Feathered Serpent predates Topiltzin by at least 500 years, with an archaeological history stretching from the Temple of Quetzalcoatl (100-200AD) at Teotihuacan until the founding of Tula Tollan (c. 700AD). It has a written history extending from the beginnings of the Toltec State to the end of the Aztec Empire (1520).

Quetzalcoatl is the best known of the Meso-American gods who appear throughout pre-Columbian archaeology. In the days after the fall of the Toltecs, Quetzalcoatl as the Feathered Serpent became the symbol of legitimate authority, a kind of coat of arms for many rulers and houses of the royal bloodlines. The Aztecs considered themselves the descendents of this political tradition, even if Huitzilopochtli (a later version of Tezcatlipoca) had become their primary tribal god.

Quetzalcoatl, according to Mayan Myth is attributed with having established the following:

Named all of the landmarks of the Earth (mountains, seas, etc.).

Brought Maize to the People.

Established codes of human hygiene.

Created a religion based upon compassion and the loving creation of one supreme God who was formless and unlimited in nature. Hunab Ku, the God with no image... I Am that I Am.....

Created fire (in the guise of Mixcoatl).

Established the maguey culture—octli brewing and ceremonial drunkenness.

Gave instruction of music and dance.

Forbid any kind of sacrificing of life, human or animal in ceremony; created a standard of sacred offerings - food, flowers, scents from the flora and sacred herbs, music and chanting of the OM.

Prophesied the future through the 21st Century and created the records upon the Mayan Calendar Stone.

Cured eye ailments, blindness, coughs, skin afflictions; healed those possessed by demons, commanded the weather, Lord of Wind And Water.

Gave the priests the practice of curandero, the diagnostic casting of lots (a sort of medical divination) Naturopathic healing.

Helped with fertility problems.

Sired his own Royal lineage.

Established the priesthood—gave proper instruction of sacrifice and created the Tonalmatal (Book of the Destiny Days).

Began the practice of domesticating the animals.

The Prophecies of Quetzalcoatl
A new and expanded view

Now, what I propose based upon a clearer understanding of the prophecies of Quetzalcoatl is that there were two, not one, appearances of the Prophet, with two manifesting in the 13th Toltec-Mayan Era, which is indicated by the prophecies of the Itzaes-Maya. And, that indeed The Prophet, by indications of recent discoveries in North America, was the very same Yeshua Ben Joseph, the Nazarene, who came to reunite the tribes of Israel and was a priest in the order of Aaron. (See the Arc of the Covenant in the Hall of Records at the end of this Manuscript).

We know that during the latter part of the 15th Century there appeared among the Itzaes-Maya a famous seer or prophet by the name of Chilam Balam, who is said to be fair of complexion and coming from the region of the Mayan lands known today as Guatemala. We are told that he prophesied many things about the future apocalyptic events, laying them out in the calendar wheel of the Mayans, according to his knowledge of the calendars.

He foretold the returning of the younger brother (white man), the irreverent ones who were sent away, and he described the times in which they would arrive. He even went so far as to give details of the diseases and methods of war they would bring, and gave the dates of great disasters that actually came true according to his calculations through the Mayan calendar.

The Venus calendar proves to be an excellent tool for time computation. It has been used for this purpose since ancient times and continues to be the vehicle for cyclic predictions according to any reliable time line concerning natural events and phenomena. Venus circles the sun on an inside orbit, and makes thirteen revolutions to eight of the Earth's.

Therefore, in cycles of 8 thirteen-year cycles, or 104 years, they are back in the originating position of their cycles. It appears that many Native Americans use the half cycle of 52 years when predicting cycles, as in the thirteen Lords of Light and the 9 Lords of Darkness. This understanding was spread throughout the Americas by the Pale Prophet, as he taught and traveled.

Dark Times.. in the latter days

Keep in mind, we are following the Mayan premise here that Quetzacoatl and Chilam Balam by all indications were one in the same.

The Prophet Quetzalcoatl foresaw the coming of this present reign of darkness and destruction, where mankind would be going through their rage as the final days grew closer and closer. About those coming times, which are these times at the turning of this millennium, the Prophet said this:

- " For five full cycles of the Dawn Star, the rule of the war-like strangers will grow unto greater and greater orgies of death and destruction. Remember well all that I have taught you, return not to the serpent and the sacrificers. Their path will lead only to the last destruction.

- Know that the end will come in five full cycles of the Dawn Star. Five is the difference between the Earth's number being 8 (Meaning Frequency) and that of the Dawn Star, which is the number of these children of destruction."

There exists a book of his prophecies, referred to today as the "Book of the Jaguar Priest". I have seen two versions, one newer and one older of the book, although I have never been able to locate one in print and available for purchase across the counter. The 'Book of the Jaguar Priest', according to the story surrounding it was created by Spanish-educated Mayans and rendered not into Latin script, but into the Mayan Language we see commonly used today.

The oldest and apparently most authentic of these translations is called the **Book of Chilam Balam of Tizimin** and it has the extraordinary prophecies we are going to quote here. It is quite evident that Chilam Balam foretold the People that they would fall into decadence and their great knowledge would be lost to them for a while.

He told them of the destruction of their great empire. He as well told them about the terrible days that would follow, where the Mayan people themselves would have to suffer and endure the rule of the returning younger brother from across the oceans where he had been sent long ago.

The Mayans say in their legends that the younger brother, 'the irreverent one', was sent away because he did not respect the Earth nor take responsibility for the guardianship and duties were inherited by mankind in its care taking. . The younger was prone to emotional outburst and was a war-loving creature. He was sent away from the 'Motherland' that he might learn through playing out his destructive energies elsewhere. (Yes, this sounds much like the Kogi Story from Columbia.)

Chilam Balam, although delivering some rather severe prophecies, also gives the Mayan hope, telling them that one day their ancient glory would return, that many of the initiates under his instruction were being sent into the future to help restore this ancient knowledge and in a distant time would be successful; that the beauty and grace of their empire would return along with him in a distant time, after the destructive tendencies of mankind and their misuse of their dreaming abilities had been corrected.

This was all a process emphasized by certain acts of genetic manipulation committed by dissident factions of the Star Brothers, who were not necessarily friendly to our species. Their leader and most of his forces had been driven off and moved to the below world. This, along with references to what amounts to be a ' War of the Heavens', god pitted against god. There were terrible battles leaving most of the 'Old World' completely destroyed, with the exception of the few remaining Temples of Learning in the area we know today as Mayaland, being Southern Mexico, Guatemala, Belize and parts of Ecuador.

Mankind, as a result of these wars and the genetic manipulation, was destined to go through several cycles of the negative destructive energies, as well as periods of great growth and enlightenment. The destructive energies would not be easily overcome. At the time of the culmination of these cycles the Lords of Light, those from beyond the Sun, would return.

In this future time, which would be after a time of complete tyranny when all seemed lost and beyond repair, there would be the emergence of a new Spiritual understanding that would come about mysteriously to all upon the Earth. After a period of great struggle the former grandeur of the Mayan Culture and its true teachings would be restored... 'As if all that happened in between were but a dream.'

There are legends perpetuating through contemporary times about those special 'Priests and Initiates' who were sent into the future to correct the things resulting from the age of destruction and who would bring this New Spirituality forth. In this new time Chilam-Balam would also be returning with a host from the heavens after the fourteen days of light.

This New Spirituality would be very different from the 'Dead Religions of the Past', yet it would feel strangely familiar by all it touched and all who came to embrace it. The Civilization of the Mayan, as well as their great knowledge and splendor of living would be restored by the future priests of this new religion. Once again, through their great temples of learning, this new understanding would bring the entire world into harmony and they would see a Golden Age emerge upon this Earth like has never before been known. For at this time mankind would take their rightful place amongst the many nations of the cosmos. He himself would appear to a chosen few... 'those who kept the original teachings close to their hearts'... prior to the times of terrible destruction and decay.

The Chilam Balam

We find in the Chilam Balam (Quetzalcoatl) in one section of the book lamenting over the loss of the priests who keep the calendar and the ancient knowledge of the Maya and the loss of the incredible splendor that must have prevailed throughout the lands ..

" How can the generations of the sons of the Itzaes tell us the days of the prophecies and the days of the tun? How can we celebrate the rites of Lord 5 Ahau in the twelfth tun, when he comes in benign holiness. . . in Katun 5 Ahau, in the twelfth tun?"

from the Chilam Balam

Katun 5 Ahau next arrived in 1519 according to the book on September 30. The book also speaks of the indigenous people continuing to be oppressed by their conquerors after 1519.

It appears this coming of a Great Prophet must be considered to occur at the next turn of the Katun Wheel, which would mean in approximately another 260 years or late in 1779 A.D., just about the kick-off time of the American Revolution, the War for Independence. It is recorded history that both Washington as well as Jefferson had divine visions and influence regarding the formation of America.

Chilam Balam left calendar calculations of when certain events would take place, including his reappearances to those of 'One Heart'. He tells us that in the twelfth tun in part of both 1831 and 1883, which would be the date of the coming, there would appear a Great Prophet "in benevolent divinity". To clinch this prophecy Chilam Balam gives another sign by which the coming of **One or more** whose teachings will unite the world shall be known.

It was in or about September of 1827 that a young man was given information from some very ancient books, made from gold leaves. It was shortly after in1831 that Joseph Smith started the Mormon Church based upon almost identical information to that which I am tracking here through the Mayan Records and a site found in North America according to an ancient manuscript my Friend Speaking Wind and I spent many years working on attempting to put together pieces of a jigsaw puzzle. (Author's note: I am not Mormon)

Again it was about 1883 that the Paiute Prophet, Wovoka, began his teaching of Peace and Compassion from visions and understandings he received from a divine 5th dimensional being. This became the Ghost Dance Religion, which upon full understanding and dedicated research one will find out is all about the Pale Prophet, the Plumed Serpent, Quetzalcoatl. (Not to be confused with the event of Wounded Knee and the terrible devastation of hundreds of innocent Lakota women, elders and children who marched in the cold winter solstice to do the Dance of the Prophet only to be killed in massacre by the U.S Calvary.)

It is said that at the Ghost Dance of 1889 where tribes came from all over the Western territories (most weren't states at the time), to a place in the Nevada Desert... Strange lights appeared in the heavens and that there appeared to be one who walked down what seemed to be a stairway of light to those assembled, stepping forth from a large round orange cloud of that appeared in the sky... That must have been some optical illusion due to the winds and sand storms that appeared near the area. ? Testaments to this event can be researched in the Boston Globe Archives.

These occurrences would also agree in approximate time line with the Toltec prophecy of the return of Quetzalcoatl in the 13th Toltec Era. This is, as yet, only partially understood, as we must again look at the holistic picture. There is the implication in the Chilam-Balam indicating that there would be a coming of two great Prophets, one right after the other!

The Chilam Balam also refers to two bearded beings, one from the East: "**One goes forth as an emissary. Another awakens Itzamna Kauil.**" (God of the Heavens) in the West. Joseph Smith came from New York; which could be the East. Wavoka came from Nevada, which would have been the West. Both had profound and lasting effects on our western spiritual belief systems, did they not?

Also, on the same text it says:

"The temple receives its guests, the bearded ones from the lands of the Sun (the east) The Sun Kings. These you will know, for they will bring a sign; you will know the sign by their hand. (A handshake? As in "In Lak'esh...I Am, your other Self" in Maya). It shows they are remembering that they are from our Father Sun - Ahau: They bring blessings in abundance!" The sign is in the handshake itself. (Here's a clue. It is not a Masonic handshake.)

There will apparently be at least two important Lords who manifest themselves at this time, one as an ambassador, preparing the way, and the other appearing as the one who gives the world-uniting

Message. It speaks further of the sign, foretelling of the blessings of abundance:

"Yes, this sign is your assurance that they come from heaven. These sacramental objects of yours, O Itzaes, these holy things of yours, derive from Kukulkan. Find your holiness in truth and penitence.

"Find holiness with the people of the God . . (obliterated this is a very old book). . in the world of Hunab Ku, The One Supreme God. He comes to you from heaven in the drops of rain. It is good, what I say unto you assembled here, O Itzaes.

" Let the earth awaken when they tread upon it, and attend, in another katun later on. Sufficient unto themselves are my words, for I am Chilam Balam, the Jaguar Priest. I repeat my words of divine truth: 'I say that the divisions of the earth shall all be as one!'"

The Spiritual Son of Kukulkan/ Thoth ...Quetzalcoatl

The Mayans too wait for a second coming, which is what they tried to explain to the Black Robes, but often met with death instead of understanding.. The Mayans awaited the Second Coming of the Spiritual Son of Kululkan/Thoth...Quetzalcoatl.

Accounting of dates of Spanish arrival and conquests of Central America according to their own records:

On April 21, 1519, Cortez landed near the site of Veracruz. To prevent thought of retreat; he burned his ships. He left a small force on the coast and led the remainder into the interior.

On Nov. 8, 1519, Cortez reached Tenochtitlán (now Mexico City) and was welcomed by Montezuma, the Aztec emperor.   He found many of the natives to be worshiping large stone crosses a practice he thought strange.

Cortez besieges Tenochtitlán again the following May with a large fully armed legion, including heavy artillery. His cannons leveled the stone crosses and he then turned them upon the city of the Aztec Emperor and leveled their temples. His records indicate that on Aug. 13, 1521, Guatemoc, the new Aztec emperor, surrendered. This was the symbolic end of the Aztec Empire.

Cortez explored Lower California from 1534 to 1535 and served against the pirates of Algiers in 1541. He also led an expedition against the Mayas of Yucatán. He died near Seville on Dec. 2, 1547, still considering himself the Emperor of New Spain.

Depiction of Quetzalcoatl (Left)

Quetzalcoatls Prophecies

Now, what I propose based upon a clearer understanding of the prophecies of Quetzalcoatl is that there were two, not one, appearances of the Prophet, with two manifesting in the 13th Toltec-Mayan Era, which is indicated by the prophecies of the Itzaes-Maya. And, that indeed The Prophet, by indications of recent discoveries in North America, was the very same Yeshua Ben Joseph, the Nazarene, who came to reunite the tribes of Israel and was a priest in the order of Aaron. (See the Arc of the Covenant in the Hall of Records at the end of this Manuscript).

We know that during the latter part of the 15th Century there appeared among the Itzaes-Maya a famous seer or prophet by the name of Chilam Balam, who is said to be fair of complexion and coming from the region of the Mayan lands known today as Guatemala. We are told that he prophesied many things about the future apocalyptic events, laying them out in the calendar wheel of the Mayans, according to his knowledge of the calendars.

He foretold the returning of the younger brother (white man), the irreverent ones who were sent away, and he described the times in which they would arrive. He even went so far as to give details of the diseases and methods of war they would bring, and gave the dates of great disasters that actually came true according to his calculations through the Mayan calendar.

The Venus calendar proves to be an excellent tool for time computation. It has been used for this purpose since ancient times and continues to be the vehicle for cyclic predictions according to any reliable time line concerning natural events and phenomena. Venus circles the sun on an inside orbit, and makes thirteen revolutions to eight of the Earth's.

Therefore, in cycles of 8 thirteen-year cycles, or 104 years, they are back in the originating position of their cycles. It appears that many Native Americans use the half cycle of 52 years when predicting cycles, as in the thirteen Lords of Light and the 9 Lords of Darkness. This understanding was spread throughout the Americas by the Pale Prophet, as he taught and traveled throughout the Americas, where in each culture he was given his own name (as is the custom and character of the indigenous people)

The name given to someone is a descriptive matter. i.e. The Green Grass, the Red Road, the greasy Grass, where three Rivers flow.. it described his gifts and attributes. In the case of the Pale Prophet most terms infer he was the Lord of the Wind and Water, Lord of the Wind, the Plumed Serpent ….throughout al the cultures and his travels were vast ranging from Washington state where he is first said to have come to the Land of the Turtle Island, where he was known as **Tacoma**. To the lands of the Maya in the South, where he is known as **Quetzacoatl** the plumed Serpent, and also **Gogogatz,** and **Kulkulkan.**

We know that he reached as far north as Canada, and the lands of the Six Nations. here he is called **Degana Weda** meaning the Peacemaker. He is spoken of by the natives of Southern Illinois, and again with the Mound builders in the Ohio River region. To even the hardened Lakota who knew him as **wa coma tete,** meaning the Lord of the Wind. Where as the term ***Hu' nab ku*** is the term for **the Maother-Father of all, the Source, the Creator**...

Quetzalcoatl... the Bearded god

... warnings about the days to come and the cycle of self destruction

Keep in mind, we are following the Mayan premise here that Quetzacoatl and Chilam Balam by all indications were one in the same.

The Prophet Quetzalcoatl foresaw the coming of this present reign of darkness and destruction, where mankind would be going through their rage as the final days grew closer and closer. About those coming times, which are these times at the turning of this millennium, the Prophet said this:

- " For five full cycles of the Dawn Star, the rule of the war-like strangers will grow unto greater and greater orgies of death and destruction. Remember well all that I have taught you, return not to the serpent and the sacrificers. Their path will lead only to the last destruction.

- " Know that the end will come in five full cycles of the Dawn Star. Five is the difference between the Earth's number being 8 (Meaning Frequency) and that of the Dawn Star, which is the number of these children of destruction."

There exists a book of his prophecies, referred to today as the "Book of the Jaguar Priest". I have seen two versions, one newer and one older of the book, although I have never been able to locate one in print and available for purchase across the counter. The 'Book of the Jaguar Priest', according to the story surrounding it was created by Spanish-educated Mayans and rendered not into Latin script, but into the Mayan Language we see commonly used today.

The oldest and apparently most authentic of these translations is called the **Book of Chilam Balam of Tizimin** and it has the extraordinary prophecies we are going to quote here. It is quite evident that Chilam Balam foretold the People that they would fall into decadence and their great knowledge would be lost to them for a while.

He told them of the destruction of their great empire. He as well told them about the terrible days that would follow, where the Mayan people themselves would have to suffer and endure the rule of the returning younger brother from across the oceans where he had been sent long ago.

The Mayans say in their legends that the younger brother, 'the irreverent one', was sent away because he did not respect the Earth nor take responsibility for the guardianship and duties were inherited by mankind in its care taking. . The younger was prone to emotional outburst and was a war-loving creature. He was sent away from the 'Motherland' that he might learn through playing out his destructive energies elsewhere. (Yes, this sounds much like the Kogi Story from Columbia.)

The Chilam Balam, although delivering some rather severe prophecies, also gives the Mayan hope, telling them that one day their ancient glory would return, that many of the initiates under his instruction were being sent into the future to help restore this ancient knowledge and in a distant time would be successful; that the beauty and grace of their empire would return along with him in a distant time, after the destructive tendencies of mankind and their misuse of their dreaming abilities had been corrected.

This was all a process emphasized by certain acts of genetic manipulation committed by dissident factions of the Star Brothers, who were not necessarily friendly to our species. Their leader and most of his forces had

been driven off and moved to the below world. This, along with references to what amounts to be a 'War of the Heavens', god pitted against god. There were terrible battles leaving most of the 'Old World' completely destroyed, with the exception of the few remaining Temples of Learning in the area we know today as Maya land, being Southern Mexico, Guatemala, Belize and parts of Ecuador.

Mankind, as a result of these wars and the genetic manipulation, was destined to go through several cycles of the negative destructive energies, as well as periods of great growth and enlightenment. The destructive energies would not be easily overcome. At the time of the culmination of these cycles the Lords of Light, those from beyond the Sun, would return.

In this future time, which would be after a time of complete tyranny when all seemed lost and beyond repair, there would be the emergence of a new Spiritual understanding that would come about mysteriously to all upon the Earth. After a period of great struggle the former grandeur of the Mayan Culture and its true teachings would be restored… 'As if all that happened in between were but a dream.'

There are legends perpetuating through contemporary times about those special '**Priests and Initiates' who were sent into the future** to correct the things resulting from the age of destruction and who would bring this New Spirituality forth. In this new time Chilam-Balam would also be returning with a host from the heavens after the fourteen days of light.

This New Spirituality would be very different from the 'Dead Religions of the Past', yet it would feel strangely familiar by all it touched and all who came to embrace it. The Civilization of the Mayan, as well as their great knowledge and splendor of living would be restored by the future priests of this new religion. Once again, through their great temples of learning, this new understanding would bring the entire world into harmony and they would see a Golden Age emerge upon this Earth like has never before been known. For at this time mankind would take their rightful place amongst the many nations of the cosmos. He himself would appear to a chosen few... 'those who kept the original teachings close to their hearts'... prior to the times of terrible destruction and decay.

We find Chilam Balam (Mayan Sacred Book) in one section of the book lamenting over the loss of the priests who keep the calendar and the ancient knowledge of the Maya and the loss of the incredible splendor that must have prevailed throughout the lands ..

" How can the generations of the sons of the Itzaes tell us the days of the prophecies and the days of the tun? How can we celebrate the rites of Lord 5 Ahau in the twelfth tun, when he comes in benign holiness. . . in Katun 5 Ahau, in the twelfth tun?"

Katun 5 Ahau next arrived in 1519 according to the book on September 30. The book also speaks of the indigenous people continuing to be oppressed by their conquerors after 1519.

It appears this coming of a Great Prophet must be considered to occur at the next turn of the Katun Wheel, which would mean in approximately another 260 years or late in 1779 A.D., just about the kick-off time of the American Revolution, the War for Independence. It is recorded history that both Washington as well as Jefferson had divine visions and influence regarding the formation of America.

The Chilam Balam

The Chilam Balam left calendar calculations of when certain events would take place, including his reappearances to those of 'One Heart'. He tells us that in the twelfth tun in part of both 1831 and 1883, which would be the date of the coming, there would appear a Great Prophet "in benevolent divinity". To clinch this prophecy Chilam Balam gives another sign by which the coming of **One or more** whose teachings will unite the world shall be known.

It was in or about September of 1827 that a young man was given information from some very ancient books, made from gold leaves. It was shortly after in 1831 that Joseph Smith started the Mormon Church based upon almost identical information to that which I am tracking here through the Mayan Records and a site found in North America according to an ancient manuscript my Friend Speaking Wind and I spent many years working on attempting to put together pieces of a jigsaw puzzle. (Author's note: I am not Mormon)

Again it was about 1883 that the Paiute Prophet, Wovoka, began his teaching of Peace and Compassion from visions and understandings he received from a divine 5th dimensional being. Who the Paute called **Kanechi ta Kaneci wa** or the Great White Chief. These visions of Wavoka later evolved into the Ghost Dance Religion, which upon full understanding and dedicated research one will find out is all about the Pale Prophet, the Plumed Serpent, Quetzalcoatl.

Author's note: *Not to be confused with the event of Wounded Knee and the terrible devastation of hundreds of innocent Lakota women, elders and children from Big Foots Band, who marched in the cold winter solstice to do the Dance of the Prophet only to be killed in massacre by the U.S Calvary before they ever arrived.*

It is said that at the Ghost Dance of 1889 where tribes came from all over the Western territories (most weren't states at the time), to a place in the Nevada Desert... Strange lights appeared in the heavens and that there appeared to be one who walked down what seemed to be a stairway of light to those assembled, stepping forth from a large round orange cloud of that appeared in the sky… That must have been some optical illusion due to the winds and sand storms that appeared near the area ? Testaments to this event can be researched in the Boston Globe Archives.

These occurrences would also agree in approximate time line with the Toltec prophecy of the return of Quetzalcoatl in the 13th Toltec Era. This is, as yet, only partially understood, as we must again look at the holistic picture. There is the implication in the Chilam-Balam indicating that there would be a coming of two great Prophets, one right after the other!

The Chilam Balam also refers to two bearded beings, one from the East: "***One goes forth as an emissary. Another awakens Itzamna Kauil.***" (God of the Heavens) in the West. Joseph Smith came from New York; which could be the East. Wavoka came from Nevada, which would have been the West. Both had profound and lasting effects on our western spiritual belief systems, did they not?

Also, on the same text it says:

"The temple receives its guests, the bearded ones from the lands of the Sun (the east) The Sun Kings. These you will know, for they will bring a sign; you will know the sign by their hand. (A handshake? As in "In Lak'esh...I Am, your other Self" in Maya). It shows they are remembering that they are from our Father Sun - Ahau: They bring blessings in abundance!" The sign is in the handshake itself. (Here's a clue. It is not a Masonic handshake.)

There will apparently be at least two important Lords who manifest themselves at this time, one as an ambassador, preparing the way, and the other appearing as the one who gives the world-uniting Message. It speaks further of the sign, foretelling of the blessings of abundance:

"Yes, this sign is your assurance that they come from heaven. These sacramental objects of yours, O Itzaes, these holy things of yours, derive from Kukulkan. Find your holiness in truth and penitence.

"Find holiness with the people of the God . (obliterated -this is a very old book). . in the world of Hunab Ku, The One Supreme God. He comes to you from heaven in the drops of rain. It is good, what I say unto you assembled here, O Itzaes.

" Let the earth awaken when they tread upon it, and attend, in another katun later on. Sufficient unto themselves are my words, for I am Chilam Balam, the Jaguar Priest. I repeat my words of divine truth: 'I say that the divisions of the earth shall all be as one! "

The Spiritual Son of Kukulkan/ Thoth ...Quetzalcoatl

Mayan codice depicting the cycles of destruction
BELOW

The Mayans as well as the Inca, we come to find, also wait for a second coming, of their prophet which is what they tried in vain to explain to the Black Robes, but often met with death instead of understanding.. The Mayans awaited the Second Coming of the Spiritual Son of Kululkan/Thoth...Quetzalcoatl. To the Inca Veracocha, the red haired pale skinned bearded god.

Accounting of dates of Spanish arrival and conquests of Central America according to their own records:

On April 21, 1519, Cortez landed near the site of Veracruz. To prevent thought of retreat from his men, he burned his ships. He left a small force on the coast and led the remainder into the interior.

On Nov. 8, 1519, Cortez reached Tenochtitlán (now Mexico City) and was welcomed by Montezuma, the Aztec emperor. He found many of the natives to be worshiping large stone crosses, a practice he thought strange.

Cortez besieges Tenochtitlán again the following May with a large fully armed legion, including heavy artillery. His cannons leveled the stone crosses and he then turned them upon the city of the Aztec Emperor and leveled their temples. His records indicate that on Aug. 13, 1521, Guatemoc, the new Aztec emperor, surrendered. This was the symbolic end of the Aztec Empire.

Cortez explored Lower California from 1534 to 1535 and served against the pirates of Algiers in 1541. He also led an expedition against the Mayas of Yucatán. He died near Seville on Dec. 2, 1547, still considering himself the Emperor of New Spain. The natives of the Americas looked with sadness and despair for they knew that the Cycles of self destruction had commenced and would last for Five full cycles of the Dawn star, for Quetzalcoatl .. had forewarned them...

Quetzalcoatl's Calendar Stone

As a meditation tool

In Mayan the Great Creator is called Hunab K'u and Father Ahau (SUN)

The Solar calendar of the Quetzalcoatl is called the Tzolk'in's. In general terms, it is composed of cycles of approximately 260 years. This is a Mayan year. It is composed of 13 months of 20 days each composing a solar year that is 360 days long; one Solar Cycle is approximately equal to 260 Gregorian years. In Mayan the year is a "tun" and 20 years make a "Katun". A Katun is named after the last day in it, which would be a day "Ahau", preceded by a number. A particular Katun, like "Katun 5 Ahau" would reoccur every 260 years. This is the same as the calendar of the old Empire and the teachings of Kukulkan.

13x20=260 is a frequency of universal creative force through which we manifest our conscious reality, the 13 (numbers) being the spirit, and the 20 (glyphs) being the body of the calendar. The 13 and the 20 together represent Hunab Ku, the creator of all there is. This frequency can exist in larger or smaller sized cycles of time, space and dimension as long as they do not lose their symmetry of 13x20=260. As an example of the cosmic perception, the Mayan understand that the cells in our body contain a universe in proportion to the one in our Milky Way.

260 solar years could be equal to 260 breaths during a meditation, where we come into alignment with our universe and in sync with cosmic time. We can determine what time is in relation to space and dimension on our planet, by relating to the most powerful influence of cosmic time we have had since the creation of our race, the Sun.

Our 'timing frequencies' come to us through the Sun. The Sun is responsible for the character of time on our Earth through the Great Pyramids that exist all over the world. These pyramids act as cosmic activators or Pezio electric circuits that send impulses to the central core of the Earth.

We have currently a problem on our planet, which is slightly complex. One situation is that we are moving into a new cycle. This is allowing new energies to effect our planet and all life upon it, including human beings. This new energy is causing us to be very hyper.

Our planet also is becoming hyper and a quickening of sorts is occurring; we are all feeling as though time is going faster. We cannot escape from the feeling we are running out of time; we can't keep up. If this is not placed under control within us we can suffer from extreme stress to our systems. *(Therefore, doing a Solar Breath meditation can be very beneficial in removing stress.)*

Also, our planet itself is slightly out of sync with the cosmos at this time, as is our Sun. Something is askew with our Sun. The Hopi talked about this back in 1994, along with me on the radio. It is missing the beat, so to speak and 'ticking when it should be tocking...' Think of it like a heart murmur. We can, however, bring this back into alignment if we get back into sync ourselves.

The circuits between our Sun and us have been "played with" by someone or something, here on earth. It would appear that something is also playing with the pyramids and sacred sites along the grid

This is throwing the planet off balance. So the planet is having difficulty reading the signals form the sun. As a result, there is a wobbling going on, in a manner of speaking, much like a corrupted computer program.

The energy is bouncing and is not as smooth as it should be. This is a temporary problem and will eventually correct itself as we merge into this new cycle. This wobbling is part of this merging of the cycles. We have forgotten our teachings and most have no way of understand what is actually going on at this time. Once we were causal as beings but with the absence of 'knowledge of' the inhabitants of this planet are now reduced to being merely reactionary embodiments.

The Sun, in what can be assimilated from fragmented ancient writings, is following a cycle wherein it is rebirthing itself, and it is presently going through its labor process. Anyone who has not witnessed a natural birth will be a little thrown when this process is first experienced. There is much contortion and there are labor pains. An amazing amount of energy is being displaced. As we enter this new Century the Sun is releasing its plasma, like a woman when she breaks water, indicating that the birthing process has begun. The period of pregnancy is about over and 'something' is about to occur, though no one is certain as to exactly what.

This changing of cycles is part of what Quetzalcoatl was speaking about in his prophecies of the future. He was telling us what to expect from the cosmos, as well as telling us how to read the signals from the cosmos telling us that he and those like him would be returning. Our bodies are of almost no use to us any longer as they presently are configured.

We, ourselves, are also transforming into something new. The whole experience right now is an incredible process affecting the entire Earth to the very core of our planet, as well as *the Milky Way* itself, and my guess is probably the entire universe. At this time I have not the full capacity to reach out that far with my own consciousness and come back, but I believe that is what is going on.

QUETZALCOATL'S RETURN _ A SECOND COMING

Quetzalcoatl was driven out of the land of Mexico by the Enlilian war god, Huitzilopochtli. Huitzilopochtli would later reinstate the religions of war and human sacrifice, even unto the Lands of the Toltec-Maya.

It is safe to assume that Quetzalcoatl was feared by many priests of political position, because of his ways which were mysterious to the Indigenous Maya. Quetzalcoatl you see was not a native indigenous Mayan, he was of the bearded ones, the pale ones. He constantly referred to those who were as he was and lived in a land to the East. In his prophecies he spoke about this 'Younger Brother" and his return to the lands of the Maya, and the Cycles of Destruction they would bring with them…

Quetzalcoatl was a man of peace and science, and from what we can tell extremely metaphysical and given to mystical ways. His reign according to legend was very long, lasting perhaps several hundred years. During which he became a white bearded god to the Maya, after many years of political opposition regressive and warlike factions finally drove him out of power. Because of his being so revered by the people and his magical powers Quetzalcoatl himself could not be killed. Rather than see the sensless killing of the Mayan people he had come to so loved by these waring Serpent Factions,, he left; continuing upon his own journey; promising to return…

Upon his departure from Cosmul to the land of Tia Pallan,(the Redland), Quetzalcoatl promises to return. We know that he gave us mathematical calculations for this arrival. These are encrypted in the Mayan Calendar Stone and in at least one of the Mayan Codex. There also exist many writings and Mayan records about this event. The Maya knew that if Quetzalcoatl returned on the appointed day it would signal the fact that mankind had evolved and a new era of peace upon earth was at hand.

If, however, a false Quetzalcoatl returned, prior to his actual return. and it was not at the predicted time, it would signal that the war gods had prevailed and a period of nine 52-year "cycles of destruction" under the 9 Lords of Darkness would begin.

The false Quetzalcoatl of the Babylonian Vatican stepped upon the soil of the Toltec-Maya in the form of Hernando Cortes. From 1519 adding 9 cycles of 52 years we arrive at the year 1987, the year of the Harmonic convergence. **Remember?**

We also refer to his own prophecy: " For five full cycles of the Dawn Star, the rule of the war-like strangers will grow unto greater and greater orgies of death and destruction.

If we count from 1519, the year Cortex landed in Central America and began his conquest of the People, for the five full cycles of the Dawn Star (104 yrs. X 5= 520years) we arrive at the year 2039…(See the calendar calculation following this segment.)

It has already been predestined by Quetzalcoatl's own calculations that he couldn't return until the time of the sixth sun - This is the Jaguar Sun, the Sun of Quetzalcoatl, the total eclipse of July 22nd, 2009.

He would be there to usher in the last Katun (approximately 20 years) of a Great 26,000 year in the 17 Calendar cycles understood by the ancient Mayan, which ends at the time of the winter solstice, December 21, 2012 on the Gregorian calendar. Again, we are referring to a dual occurrence here — the ending of one cycle and the birth of yet another cycle. It is that Kali energy again, the two-sided sword — life and death in the same blow.

This last Katun would be a time of great change, both in human consciousness and in physical Earth Changes. However, it is not the end of the world as we have been led to believe by those who have miscalculated the calendar based upon incomplete information.

For those of you who have been misled and misinformed by self -aggrandizing translators of the Mayan teachings what has been presented of the Mayan calendar is partially correct, but incorrect in its entirety. Therefore, the work must be continued, and continued with the Mayans, not the visitors.

We are dealing with a change of seasons, not apocalyptic occurrences. It is a time when our Earth Mother, Pachi Moma, returns to her garden state and humanity becomes a member of the **Galactic community**. It is a time of blessing, a time Quetzalcoatl spoke of in his prophecies. It is not a time of ending; it is not a time of the end of life. It is simply a changing of the seasons whereby we will enter a new energy and be able to merge with a new consciousness that is being born this very moment.

Like all birth processes there is an upheaval and a releasing of great energy. We must experience changes before the **Great Peace** of the new cycle is realized. And how we proceed from this moment until that time will determine the outcome. Where we are inside, with Creator, and within ourselves is where we will be. There will always be a choice. We have played with our gods and they have played with us. But now, this coming time is our time, for what we will be is already manifesting into the universe.

Man or Myth?
Some Historical Data

Quetzalcoatl is an amazing individual in Meso-American history. He established not only a religion, but as well established universities teaching the people all manner of arts, sciences and useful social customs. Not all histories can agree on exactly when Quetzalcoatl lived or even if he ever lived, though most tend to agree he did exist.

The name Quetzalcoatl translates to the Plumed Serpent, who is known as the Lord of the Wind and Sea. He is also known as the Prophet. As to when he lived, there is not much agreement either, some saying he lived in the 12th century, other evidence indicates that he was in the land of the Maya about the time of Christ.

One of the most important questions concerning the story of Quetzalcoatl we ask is how old and what are the timelines of his origins and proliferation; where does the fact and the myth begin and end?

Though archaeology tells us that Quetzalcoatl is old, they do not know if **old** means **ancient**. There are a group of archaeologists who believe Quetzalcoatl is a very ancient god and state that his origins can be seen forming within the Olmec era, which would place his birth so to speak at approximately 1200 BC, a considerably older date than 800 BC, which corresponds to the emergence of the Maya, if it was otherwise.

As we correlate the stories of the gods universally and find the links telling us people were talking about the same gods, the same occurrences, the same legends etc. as contemporary archeology is telling us, we would tend to lean towards the Ancient god Scenario.

Most stories indicate Quetzalcoatl, **the prophet**, said he would return from the East but before he returned the younger brother whom he described as being "bearded white man" would come to the lands of Pachi Moma. It was said they would conquer the People and enforce upon them a strange religion. However, he said when he returned all the ancient glory of the Toltec-Mayan would return.

There have been several attempts to try to reconstruct the various records surviving the holocaust of the Spanish destruction that speak of the Prophet Quetzalcoatl. It is very difficult to put these written remnants together due to the fact that Modern Mexico is a blend, or composite, of many cultures and faiths.

The destructuring of the cultures and the faiths was relentless until just recently in the last decade before the new century. I have sought another avenue to do this by going directly to the surviving artifacts and speaking with the Mayan Priests themselves to piece together the jigsaw puzzle. Currently the Mayan People are in a great struggle to rebirth their faith and heal the damage of many centuries of captivity.

The combination of artifacts and translations from the living Mayan records tell us the Prophet Quetzalcoatl spoke of a new religion coming to the Earth during the 21st era. In trying to reconstruct the timeline in accordance with the Prophets own Venus calendar- and based prophesies, I have come up with calculations coinciding with many spectacular events in modern history supporting the Mayan prophesies of Quetzalcoatl.

If we were to take as a starting point the twelfth century (1155) as the time most stories of the **Pale Prophet** tell us he left, promising to return, and we dealt with his own calculations and looked at events occurring, the prophecies of the Hopi, Nostradamus and what I wrote about in **_Last Cry_** and **_Winds of Change,_** a startling picture begins to emerge. The resulting datelines bring us to the occurrence of some very interesting events.

Further, if we tie these datelines in with the cycles of war and the rise and fall of empires we can begin to see the rhythmic patterns, creating cycles.....cycles of self-destructive behavior **the Prophet** spoke of continually with an emphasis dealing with the human experience of the Serpent and the Serpentine energies that were within mankind. He said…

"….**_the evil that man displays against himself is inherent in their very nature, for they suffer from their father's deeds_**…" (They are Hybrids.) The Prophet Chilam-Balam spoke of this internal battle causing us to fall blindly into cycles of greater and greater internal conflict, (the serpent eating its tail), and leading us ever deeper into the cycles of self-destruction. Could he have been talking about DNA? The eternal struggle of being born a mixed-blood hybrid brings to its proceeding lineage for generations? Curious is it not. 5 physical senses of man. 13 double helixes in our DNA.

The Prophet was very saddened about events he saw happening in the future and it was a major effort on his part to bury the records and holy teachings. .. " For a great period of destruction is coming and will be endured. There will be a time in the future when these things will be brought forth once again. When the season of mankind is in the final days, and they long for their memory. …"

Remember Quetzalcoatls' The Pale Prophet's warning once again…

(Research Popol Vuh, the sacred book of the Maya by Dennis Tedlock)

" For five full cycles of the dawn star, the rule of the war-like strangers will grow unto greater and greater orgies of destruction.

" Hark well to what I have taught you. Return not to the serpent and the sacrificers.

Their path will lead to the last destruction.

"Know that the end (of time?) will come in five full cycles of the dawn star, for 5 is the difference between the Earth's number of 5 (frequency) and that of the Dawn star which is 13, which is the number of these children of destruction....."

Venus, as I wrote about in **_Winds of Change,_** is on an inside orbit around our Sun in relation to the Earth, making 13 revolutions to Earth's 8. One full cycle of the dawn star is 104 years.

In the higher understanding amongst the cultures of Meso - America an era is calculated by half cycles, or 52 years. Five full cycles of the Dawn Star is 520 years. Looking at it from yet another perspective, we know that according to the European Calendar Cortez arrived in the western hemisphere in 1519.

If we add 520 years we arrive at the date 2039, approximately when it is prophesized the rule of the rising Anti-Christ will come to an end.

This is why Quetzalcoatl constructed the Great Mayan Calendar Wheel that can be seen in Mexico City today. (Until just recently it was called the Aztec Calendar wheel by western Archeologists but the truth is being revealed.

The records tell us he said he would return, and at that time there would be much purging and evil would be removed from this earth. And after the cleansing, there would be a reign of peace and the "advent of a new spiritual order". The Prophet was emphatic that he would return as he had left, from the East, across the sea. He would be bearded, Caucasian and wear long robes. He said he would return again in the time when the stars were in the same place as they were in the year of his birth, according to the Venus Calendar, "And you shall know me by the Morning Star, (Venus), for I am the Sun of the Morning Star."

Chart of Toltec Eras

Showing a time line for 21 Toltec Eras (21 eras each consisting of 52 years to complete a cycle). This section is going to take extensive research in order to complete the information as to occurrences during each era.

1st Toltec Era		1103 -1155 AD	
2nd Toltec Era	1207	12th Toltec Era	1727
3rd Toltec Era	1259	13th Toltec Era	1779
4th Toltec Era	1311	14th Toltec Era	1831

5th	Toltec Era	1363		15th	Toltec Era	1883
6th	Toltec Era	1415		16th	Toltec Era	1935
7th	Toltec Era	1467		17th	Toltec Era	1987
8th	Toltec Era	1519		18th	Toltec Era	2039
9th	Toltec Era	1571		19th	Toltec Era	2091
10th	Toltec Era	1623		20th	Toltec Era	2143
11th	Toltec Era	1675		21st	Toltec Era	2195

Remarkable timing on events of major import seems to go along with this system, which will be items of further study and presentation. It seems that whenever we are moving from a no-time zone, into a time specific zone there is always a three to five year variance in dates. This is due to some phenomena occurring with projected events in the time specific zone.

Angels live beyond time. There is no time specific for an immortal being. Dates and the thought of dates is absurd. A lot of seers do not give dates in prophecy in that events will occur if conditions remain unchanged, thus the events will occur on that time line.

With the occurrence of the various "Montauk Experiments" The German Vrill (WWII) and other even more insidious Experiemnts time lines are no longer accurate and cannot be relied upon. Further, there is a natural sway, or meander that occurs with a time line, much like water it flows in a serpentine manner. . (Is time fluid?)

It seems very little happened in the way of major events in the rest of the world (European history) since the fall of Rome until they came here in the 16th Century. However, from that period onward many dates are more than coincidence... American and French Revolutions and Joseph Smith and the rise of Mormonism.

The Cycles of Light _ Secrets of the Mayan Calendars

from Elder Hunbatz Men

"Now is the time in the cycles of the light which is called Ox Lahun Baktun, which means the cycle of the 13 heavens. It has a duration period of 13 times 52 years. This gives us a total of 672 years. This cycle began in 1991, and is the cycle of the 13 heavens. We Mayans realize that the cycle of light does not start right away; that everything begins gradually, not like a light where you can push the button and the light is on. It is going to take time. This cycle has nine years of gestation. These nine years are going to end in the year 2001.

"This period of gestation is like the period when a human being is created. In these years of gestation for the 13 heavens, it is going to be just like a period of the baby going through the growing process. The mother is going to feel the vomiting period and then the kicking period until the pain of the baby leaving the mother's womb comes about and then there will be another cycle."

"These changes are going to be at a planetary level. Then the planet will be restructured. There will be the union of two cycles. In another calendar called Ox Lahu Baktun is a calendar of 5200 years.

"Right now, we are in the fourth part of this cycle. This one began in 3114 BC, (remember the Kali Yuga) and it ends and changes from the fourth sun, to give way to the fifth sun. This happens of the 21st of December of 2012 in the Gregorian calendar. When we put together these two calendars, it gives us a period when a great destruction will take place for humanity."

"We are living the times of the prophecies and now in another calendar of Ox Lahu Baktun. It also talks about the cycle of the great changes. In this cycle of the 5085 years in the Mayan calendar there are still a few more years to go before this calendar can be completed, when this cycle is completed and another restoration of the planet will begin."

In La Kesh .....Hunbatz Men

Quetzalcoatl and the Universal Bird-Tribe Mythology
and the Dragon lineage of Royal Blood Lines

The Universal Myth of the Bird Tribes

The name *Quetzalcoatl* means Plumed Serpent. He is credited in Meso-American culture with the creation of humans and their instruction in the use of metals and the cultivation of the land and understanding of the cosmic cycles of the universe. He was fathered by ENKI, the "Lord of the Earth," an extraterrestrial master-geneticist, and one of the Creator Gods of the *Homo Sapien* species.

QUETZALCOATL
QUETZAL*COATAL (Remove the AL AL signifies Child Who Flys) ie. Elder Hunbatz Men

QUET Z COATQU
ET Z KO AT
QUKO Z ETAT (Remove the T* Tree/Bird of Life).
QUKO Z EA= Flying Child of Wisdom and Consciousness Master EA'S.

According to information from the Dead Sea Scrolls, as we are told in the decipherments of Zechariah Sitchin, En-Ki is the god/Extraterrestrial who is credited with creating the first *Homo Sapien-Sapien*, the A.DAM, (A DAM IC = MAN), by combining the egg of *Cro-Magnon* woman with the sperm of a male extraterrestrial,

(Origin unknown, thought by some scholars to be of Sirian origin, referred to in most translation including Zechariah Sitchin as being Anunnaki. *Suggested reading _ Sir Laurence Gardner, __Genesis of the Grail Kings__).

Enki thus encoded his new child with a double helix strand of DNA. The image of the double DNA strand thus became the symbol of Enki and his Annunaki descendants - the entwined double Serpent, known today as the Seal of Hermes (the Cartuses) to the West and the double dragon or eagle motif to the Meso-Americans.

In the Mayan teachings, Kukulkan, the Star god of the Maya, was known in the Sumerian Culture as the benevolent god NIN.GISH.ZID.DA, the "Lord of the Tree of Life," and the master architect and builder of the Sumerian stepped-pyramid, with which we most familiar as being astronomically aligned ziggurats. (Pyramids)

The other name for this god in the Sumerian Culture was Enki. The Dead Sea Scrolls tell us that it was Enki who held the knowledge to the genetic Tree of Knowledge or the Tree of Life, the same attributes given to the Mayan Star god Kukulkan and Thoth of the Egyptian Culture

Supposedly it was Enki who set up the escape from Sumeria for many of the priesthood who remained loyal to the original teachings during the period of the Great Flood, (the demise of Atlantis) and brought that knowledge to the Maya. The Maya were, according to Mayan teachings, the decedents of the original Earth race, who were thought to be giants.

Those who built the great Mayan temples and were the source of origin for the Mayan understandings of life and the cosmos, again according to Mayan teachings, were said to have originally come from the east upon great dragon ships.

The wars of the Heavens left most of the old world destroyed as we addressed in previous segments of this book, except for a few temples and places in the Southern hemisphere. The original knowledge from then, as well as the original descendents of the gods were, for the most part, annihilated in those experiences.

It was Enki, Kukulkan who passed over the time-honored Tables of Destiny to the Maya once again, and established a kingdom wherein we have the eventual emergence of Quetzalcoatl (through the Royal bloodlines) who is deemed Holy Emperor or Priest king descendent from the gods. Also, Enki or Kuklulkan/Thoth brings to them the 'tables of scientific law" which became the bedrock of the early mystery schools in Egypt as well as Mayaland.

The only other place or writings I have ever come across relating to anything similar to this 'Actual Mayan teaching' have been in the original texts of the Book of Mormon where it makes reference to the Paradise Lands, "Land Bountiful', and the culture which existed there, which also includes, I might add, stories of the Giants, the original descendants of the gods. In the Book of Mormon, this region, we are told, is thought to be near the Isthmus of Panama, which would have been at the time the geographical heart of the Mayan empire.

My being given this information and understanding by the Mayan priests with whom I worked was the initial reason and the basis for my writing this book.

There is much evidence of Egyptian-like symbols and writings discovered and unearthed here in the Western Hemisphere. Most have been under constant attack and alleged as fakes by academia Science who base their entire belief system upon the Judeo-Christian paradigm, essentially a take off of the Sumerian teachings, as evidenced by recent archeological realizations. In fact, for the most part, the Western European perception of the origins of man is a carbon copy.

The evidence can be found from the lands of Utah and the Urintha Mountains range all the way through the Grand Canyon. Many might well reference the discoveries of Kincaid in that region and the 'Lost Temple of Isis'. There are numerous books written about it and about those who dedicated their lives to this amazing real life discovery that some how mysteriously disappeared when given over to the Smithsonian Institute by Kincaid. There was a brief series of articles at the time (1909) and then all traces of this find vanished forever.

In the Mayan culture, Kukulkan was the god of science, mathematics, the arts, healing and the calendar using the sacred numeric cycles of 13, 20 and 52. He was the one entrusted with the knowledge of how to construct the Pyramids in the Sacred Lands of the Maya, and, as well, he instructed the priests in the understanding of Sacred Geometry and the mysteries of life.

The Mayan-Egyptian connections

From the Egyptian teachings, Thoth was said to have been given the special knowledge for building the great Pyramid in Egypt. Thoth is also associated with the magical number of 52, creating the basis for the 52-week calendar, which is also one of the most sacred number cycles of Mayan Time-Keeping and part of the key to understanding the Mayan mathematical calculations for the universe so precisely even NASA honors them for their accuracy.

The teachings of this knowledge and the obligation of holding the original knowledge of Kukkulkan/ Thoth have been handed down to Hunbatz Men, the Mayan Day Keeper of modern-day Mayan knowledge.

The correlations between the cultures of the western hemisphere and the Tigress Euphrates are amazing once ventured into in depth. Further, there exist many writings upon the living rock in the North American Rockies recently discovered and determined to be proto-Canaanite / proto-Egyptian with sophisticated alphabets that go back well over 3,500 years BCE. in origin. Once again showing clearly there existed a merging of trade and communications between global cultures and no doubt they also shared many common Spiritual understandings.

Both the Egyptian and the Maya possessed technology, such as the building of the pyramids, and means of electrical energy sources which understandings of the cosmos and how the cosmic clock works in harmony with the rhythms of a universe that is home to ten billion universes, and an undeterminable number of life forms species perhaps far in advance tyo humans. At least they were traveling the galactic highways long before man even had sunglasses and Velcro.

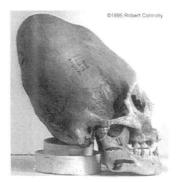

Yet the most undeniable evidence of the connections ofglobal cultures for the last ten thousand years and even earlier is in the species itself. Old bones tell great stories. We began in the stars, it is only likely that we will return to Source if we give ourselves the grace to continue to evolve. That this skull (right) and the continence of the Pharaoh Akenaten and his beautiful wife Nefertiti had genetic connections remains, at least to this scientist, an uncontestable fact.

Thoth.Kukulkan _ the Egyptian Maya Connection

In an ancient Mayan Temple of Palenque, in present day Mexico, there is to be found a wonderful depiction of the Mayan god Kukulkan. Kukulkan, according to historical Mayan accountings, came to Meso-America approximately 3000 B.C. A thousand years before Yeshua/Sananda. He was said to be the son of the god EA (Enki) and who in the Eastern perception was known as ISHTAR.

Kukulkan's other earthly name (as recognized by contemporary Maya) was Thoth, as he was known in the Egyptian culture. Kukulkan was also known as a "winged serpent", Quetzacoatl, who may have been his descendent actually, and by another earlier name of Asaru derived from the Aryan tongue. There are some very interesting correlations in the Norse Myths as well, which will be presented in future research work, I am certain. HERE!!!!

Ra/Osiris it is said was also known as Ningazidda, and was EA's second son. EA, we are told, was the genesis scientist on planet Earth... The story tells us that Thoth left Egypt, etc., when the prime directive after the fall of the Tower of Babel was to change languages. Humanity was getting it together to revolt against the ETs, but obviously they lost the battle, and Thoth would then come to the Yucatan and become known there as Kukulkan.

Over the millennia, the Enlilian war god religions of the Hebrew/ Christian/Islamic tribes would hunt down and destroy all believers and the true spiritual teachings of Enki and his benevolent son Kukulkan. As well, all references to Isis and the Temples of Beauty were systematically eradicated.

The same fate happened in the motherland to the Olmec, (who had originated from Northern Africa), and to the Aztec civilizations, constantly warring and destroying the more peaceful Toltec-Maya and Inca peoples. And in the North, The Great Puan, the Mound Builders who were the direct descendents of 'Egypta' and Atlantis, and known as the Sun Kings, Descendents of the **Ogwa Waha wi**, or the Bird Tribes, were warred upon as well.

Their God was called Yaweh, or Yah, he was the gentle God, and seems even to have the same nature described in the Hebrew texts. Remember there is a distinct difference in the various Hebrew gods, Yaweh, Jehovah, The Lord, etc.; they were different entitles with very different personalities and viewpoints about mankind.

Yes, in the first onslaughts of this War of the Heavens, Enlil and his forces were beaten. However, by the very laws of the hierarchy of Light, they could not destroy Enlil. Not too unlike the laws of the Native American culture today, which are carry-downs from the original understandings.

The main game plan it seems was to keep humanity divided amongst itself, one faction constantly fighting the other, for a united humanity with one faith would propose too much of a threat to the children of Enlil.

Here we get into a different kind of story, one that leads us to contemporary conditions. The fairy tale of the **Tower of Babbel** was just that — a fairy tale — placed as an imprint in the hearts and minds of men to create a pattern of fear should we ever again oppose the Gods. Guilt and shame work wonders on a young mind, and we are a young race, after all.

If there is any truth to the story of Babel, it is that the tower represents the Mystery Schools, and the knowledge of self and remembrance of origin when universally shared could unify us once again as an Earth People.

This premise if we think about it is very possible and perhaps the underlying subconscious reason, above all others, for the senseless genocide that has been waged against all indigenous people the world over. Keep them on the run, keep them in fear, pit them against each other and destroy all their sacred knowledge, for if there is even a chance that a shred of it will survive, they might remember who they really are.

It appears, if we take a good look at the world around us, as though we continually participate in these patterns where we relive the Enlilian **Warrior God** religions cycles of returning to sacrifice, (now possessing the abilities for wholesale slaughter). We are caught in the **Spell of Mortality,** the edict of the Enlilian wars**, "...and the number of years of man shall be 120."**

We are following the cycles of the last 2000 years fulfilling Enlil's systematic destruction of the human species and the destruction of the temples of wisdom established by Enki. It is as if it, too, has somehow been encoded in our DNA. There is a war of consciousness and both aspects are without a doubt occurring within us on a moment-to-moment basis.

We are at war with ourselves, caught in the current of the struggle - the endless friction that perpetuates the adrenal glands and shuts off the heart center. We are, for the most part it seems, helpless as we fall victim to Enlil's ultimate deception - the Armageddon. For the Armageddon, the **IT** already **IS**. *__Armageddon by the way is a place, not an event.__

The question Is this Kukulkans Space Ship or is it a Time Travel machine? The answer is in the Bible_ Ezekiel

Thoth on Reptilians.

Their departure and return...excerpted from an Ancient Text

Far in the past before Atlantis existed, men there were who delved into darkness, using dark magic, calling up beings from the great deep below us.
Then forth came they into this cycle.

Formless were they of another vibration, existing unseen by the children of earth-men.
Only through blood could they have formed being. Only through man could they live in the   world.

In ages past were they conquered by Masters, driven below to the place whence they came.

But some there were who remained, hidden in spaces and planes unknown to man.

Lived they in Atlantis as shadows, but at times they appeared among men. Aye, when the blood was offered, for they came they to dwell among men.

In the form of man they amongst us, but only to sight were they as are men.

Serpent-headed when the glamour was lifted but appearing to man as men among men.

Crept they into the Councils, taking forms that were like unto men.

Slaying by their arts the chiefs of the kingdoms, taking their form and ruling o'er man.

Only by magic could they be discovered. Only by sound could their faces be seen.

Sought they from the Kingdom of shadows to destroy man and rule in his place.

But, know ye, the Masters were mighty in magic, able to lift the Veil from the face of the serpent, able to send him back to his place.

Came they to man and taught him the secret, the WORD that only a man can pronounce. Swift then they lifted the Veil from the serpent and cast him forth from the place among men.

Yet, beware, the serpent still liveth in a place that is open at times to the world. Unseen they walk among thee in places where the rites have been said.

Again as time passes onward shall they take the semblance of men. when their seasons turn again.

Author's Note: This is from texts thousands of years Old....So the author could not have been influenced by present day Talk –Radio...or New Age trends. Now think about it for a moment and study what is being fed to us as well as our children on television, including the Disney Channel   ... So, this kind of subject matter is OK now. After all it's on Disney.

Dragons, reptilians, a world inside the Earth, the Land of the Smoky Sun, Thoth an Egyptian god here in the Americas, such foolish thoughts...perversions of reality.....Then again, how do we explain these artifacts found once again in Bolivia...placed in a cave many thousands of years ago...... **Notice the elongated skulls again.**

And all ths talk about the Hollow Earth, the Land of the Smoky Sun and the Halls of Almenti where the ancient initiates came to be rejuvenated and live another thousand years...An ancient temple built by the efforts of the Andromedan and Sirius beings, the Andromedan being the mind and the Sirian being the body for the new Anu...

The truth shall set you free...one day

Feeling our way through the Emergence

Within the early years of the new century many responsible people in the world governments will admit the presence of the extraterrestrials and their roles and involvements with the various world powers publicly. We can expect thisevent to occur clearly by 2006 or 2007. *(Meaning. being stated through the media with public knowledge\. Remember I see events not dates.)*

These people are already realizing it is no longer realistic, nor by the frequency of the appearances in our skies, is it feasible to keep **the UFO SECRET**. And as we approach the second and fifth year of the new century in rural areas, particularly those areas in the desert locations, the presence of these beings will become more and more frequently unshielded from public view. This merging process will be slow and staggered, allowing more time for the extraterrestrials to assimilate to earthly conditions. Humans are, after all, the more violent race...

Solar Cycles   the Galactic Seasons

As we discussed in the findings from Colorado and other sites where the ancient writings tell about the Solar cycles and the distractions that can result, we are in for some extraordinary experiences. Intense Solar flares upon our Sun, which is going through a birthing cycle, will have profound effects upon consciousness and its holographic patterns.

We are, after all, beings of Light. All intelligence is in light. The Sun, it will be admitted, is a living, feeling, thinking consciousness expressing in the form of solar ectoplasm, from which life forms as well as consciousness in this solar system manifests. As we awaken to our memory of the cosmic sciences, it will be discovered this is, indeed, a very old process.

Energy activated by solar flares will transform to obsolete foundations and programs and systems we have come to trust and rely upon.

Programs, systems, institutions, belief systems and dogmas based in illusion, lies, fear, ego, control and misuse of power will blow away with the solar winds and will be transformed within the burning fire of the SUN. Headstrong ways will lead to failure, and we will need to engage the heart in all our actions and decisions.

Politics based in power will give way to politics infused with wisdom and acknowledgment of human oneness, for the new Spirituality that will rise will be universal. We are already beginning to see an even sharing of power and position between genders as it was before the fall.

The Master learns to know when to let go and when to hold on. It becomes almost an art form. The artist's canvas is life. Timing is essential so that in the letting go we let go completely and flow with the cosmic current of Source. We are wind surfers and these are the Winds of Change. It is time to learn to surf these solar waves for we are the Suns of the Gods; we are the Angels of antiquity.

We came from the Sun and are a part of it. It feels what we feel and we feel what it is feeling, like the parent and the child... The Sun is In Lak'esh. Resistance to the emergence of this Fifth World will be ineffective in holding the inflowing cosmic energy at bay. It has its own commanding dynamics and is a raging river of Light.

The universe is constantly evolving and we are, after all, a part of the universe. When we finally realize that the divine law truly is "**as above, so below… so within, so it is without**" as a heart knowing, not just a mental understanding, we will have entered the temple of the living God that is within and without all things. We will have merged with source and we will radiate as the Light that we are.

This corporal body is merely a temporary projection of what we truly are. It represents a mere fraction of the true body we can and do express through and can be re-manifest in a moment.

Form always lets go; it disintegrates over time. The forms of our synthesized realities are in the process of degenerating; new forms are already being manifest to replace them. These forms are not made of clay but rather they are built upon an infrastructure of Light. Only that which holds the higher collective vision will survive.

In the face of chaos, which is the nature of the Kaliyuga, much good will arise from the ashes for the benefit of all humanity. Again, the coming of the Anti-Christ and the Solar Winds will leave no other options, as the only solution will be for previously conflicting peoples to work together as a cooperative to persevere and rebuild something that is based upon truth… something lasting.

Humanity and the love of the crowds can be fickle, inconsistent and uncertain. However, if we lose focus on the inside, the essence of what we are, we are then at the mercy of the strongest opposing force. Although we may appear to those around us to be alert and on top of things, inside many are struggling with confusion and uncertainty about a course of action. This energy can be paralytic and cause untold damage. All the opposing force has to do is cause this energy to manifest around us and our world can be brought to a standstill.

If we allow ourselves to succumb to doubt and prevailing emotional judgments we are then subject to believe in the myth being created ourselves. It is a trick of 'the image'; 'the image' knows best the game of imagery. We are of source, we have intrinsically no image and we are actually a composite of our feelings.

We know ourselves by our feelings; therefore, if negativity creeps in and manipulates those feelings, we perceive not only ourselves but the world around us through the lens of those feelings, or emotions. We then succumb to its power and truly become the sacrificial lamb. Remember the law "as above, so below… so within, so it is without".

If, however, we hold on to the knowing of who we are… If we understand the negative matrix which is tearing at us like a pack of mad dogs trying to tear down our self-esteem… If we realize, then the cause and the symptoms begin to dissipate. If we reinforce our thoughts, if we reinforce those around us and employ the tactics of "Tuff Love"… If we dare to reach out and ask for help, then the number of possibilities for solutions will increase dramatically and issues will now take deep contemplation to choose a correct path of action.

Humanity will feel driven to truly grasp and comprehend the reality in which they live and this will be an incredible challenge, as everything around us will be changing all at once. The energies will be convoluted and juxtaposed. It will be chaos. Just remember that chaos is OK, if we do not judge. And realize that chaos is part of the birthing cycle, as it is necessary for change. Through the process we will develop an amazing adaptability to change, which will also translate to a quickening of our mental processes.

Communication skills will become advanced and quite important. Remember this is part of the Aquarian energy. Also as part of the Aquarian energy we will inadvertently, by following the God Force within us, instinctively create in consciousness a true one-world order, not an imposed NWO. Watch how, through this struggle of the next few years, your Psychic abilities will expand and how quickly you will be able to grasp similarities between seemingly different perspectives. You are developing a new way of thinking, which will lead to a new way of being and expressing your humanity.

The new energies permeating this plane are going to help you develop a new kind of thinking process - an **Analogical** thinking process. (**Using both hemispheres of the brain at the same time.**) You will no longer be stuck in Binary mind, where you are caught in endless struggle with duality. Black-white, good-bad, higher and lower will slowly cease to be thoughts and feelings with which you will need to deal.

You will be in touch with a much more clarion vision and comprehension. You will, by desiring to come into alignment with these new energies, open doorways enabling you to access new thoughts, expanded thoughts, thoughts that can cause a paradigm to shift. That does not mean we would abandon values and the refinement we have developed. That is going backwards. There will be some that do — there always are. Analogical thought is about seeing the choices and finding the way through the labyrinth…. to the clearing.

With your newly realized abilities to grasp abstract thought, you will actualize solutions to many problems pressing our race in its struggle to survive as a thinking species… struggling through transition. If Karma has been released, then we are no longer bound to the sins of our fathers. We are responsible only to our present thoughts and actions.

Once this Earth was a home to those from other worlds, to whom we can, like some bushmen, only refer to as the gods. At best, we have remnants of written recordings of these beings, telling of events, a piece here and a piece there, from which we try to reassemble the geometry of that which once contained our consciousness. We are putting together a jigsaw puzzle and creating the missing pieces from sensory perception, pushing our empathic abilities every step of the way.

The entire population of Mother Earth, as a whole, will begin to follow a more defined spiritual path and will be inspired to live healthier lifestyles. Corporations will begin to see that without the players there is no game and they will come around out of necessity at first and join forces with like-minded groups to feed the hungry and house the homeless and sick of whom there will be many, many thousands.

The Corporations have those amongst them who are learning from those Masters who are present here upon the Earth at this time. They too know that something has gone awry in the plans for world dominance and the Matrix is corrupted. Not everyone whom we call the establishment is evil and dark. So do not give in to the tendency of turning away from your humanness, remembering always *In Lak'esh*.

As a result of experiencing the course of events occurring during the first 33 years of the new century there will be many more of these individuals rising to positions of prominence within the corporate structures. Many will not align themselves with the hordes of mindless individuals following the ways of the Anti-Christ. That is a cycle that completes the prophecies of the Prophet as we watch them grow ever more enmeshed in their orgies of destruction and debauchery of the Earth as well as her children.

Many Corporations will drop their materialistic madness again out of necessity to heal the pollution on Mother Earth. Remember those extended families? Well, they will begin to blossom into global communities, as the barriers between nationality, age, race, and gender are replaced with the consciousness of the human family and deepening community.

Remember always that what we are experiencing is truly a revolution, but a revolution of a different kind. Yes, it has all the makings of the Revolution for American Independence from the overbearing hands of the German Kings of England for liberty and justice. Yes....and it has all the passion of the French revolution, and the cry of injustices rendered to the common people that spurred the cause of the Russian revolution. God, how we love our wars, how we love our bloodletting and ritual sacrifice.

Know this is a revolution of a different kind. Our experiences of the past must be called upon in this time to raise the vibration of all mankind, for there is a different kind of enemy lurking about, one that is unseen, and stealth. Oh, yes, even those in the Black Forces of the Illuminati fear this shadow essence. For the darkness itself is not safe from it. We have tampered with divine law, and now the day of God is drawing ever closer.

The Splitting of Realities and the Silent Destroyer

There will be experienced a splitting of realities and like will be drawn to like. This Earth is in danger, as are her people. Something has been created that cannot merge into the new emerging consciousness... something demonic, twisted and unnatural. We have created our hells, and there are those, dear ones, who will not surrender them.

We, in our playing with biological techniques, and in greed for superiority over each other, always coming up with the best toy, have unleashed, in some instances, a life force that is beyond control. So once again we will have to rely upon our spiritual self to rescue us from the Murk and Mire.

AFTER THE WAR OF THE HEAVENS

...the re-establishment of the Temples of Divinity by Thoth..

There are several stories here in the western hemisphere regarding the Thoth myth. That give us at least a glimpse into the picture of the Egyptian/Mayan con-nection. As well there are several archaeological sites, and a myriad of ancient artifacts that give a certain degree of credence to the fact that the Egyptians were here, and had considerable impact upon the Americas. Like this artifact from a burial cave in Southern Illinois rendered possibly from as far back as 800 BCE. And there are many more which will be covered in detail in a future publication.

"There were great wars in the heavens in those days, the Mayans tell us. Almost all of the earth was destroyed in these wars as the gods fought each other and flew their flying machines. The Sun Kings, who were the children of those who came from the stars, were almost all destroyed. There was a truce after many years, and the feathered ones vowed to keep the knowledge alive and this is how they came to build the mystery schools here in the lands of the Maya.

All the great temples to the North were gone, and the children of these gods and the gods them-selves who were left were forced to live underground. The Inner Earth, the land of the Smoky Sun.

And these photos (Below) from the now sunken Tempel of Abydos which is beneath the the waters of Aswan Dam...How could the Egyptians have seen so clearly into the future? and

depict many present day events? (image right) is an enlargment of the freeze from Abydos prior page.. Take a close look...There is no way the Egyptians could have dreamed these images up. They had to see through a methodology that has been lost to us... Do you think they flooded the temple deliberatly ...?

"It was at the end of these wars that Kukulkan came to the Maya and began the building of many great cities, that were actually schools where the knowledge of the cosmos could once again be taught, for if they did not humanity would loose all memory of their heritage. Kukulkan would bring many of these children of the gods with him to assist in the teachings in these mystery schools..."

"After the wars of the heavens sometimes called the war of the Ra's in Egyptian myth, where Horus warred against his uncle who had murdered his father Osirus, there was a peace, perhaps because of the shock of the near total annihilation of life upon the Earth. The Mayan believe that those who created the original Egyptian civilization came from here in the deserts of North America...

"After these wars of the Heavens which are written about in petraglyphs from present day Mexico throughout America and Canada the climate was altered severely. There was much destruction and many areas were no longer fit for life. The sun began to put out energies that were destructive, and actually caused the gods and their offspring to become ill and die.. The gods returned and wondered where they would build their temple of knowledge, and the Lands of the Maya were the only place where it was favorable for living... without the sickness, although they carved out a great system of tunnels to connect them to those who were still in the North and could not come to the land of Maya.. There are many words in the ancient Egyptian language that come from the Mayan language, so this is proof that these stories are not just made up.." don Romirez Mayan Elder

Take a good look at the Crop Circle (above) which appeared in England at the turn of the century

Thoth/Kukulkan would be allowed to have his domains but only in the Motherlands, western Hemisphere) and he could not take the physical form as he once could. Enlil/Jehovah never had, but Thoth/Kukulkan did, as a result, have his involvement with humanness and produced his own secret lineage... **Anunnaki,** (Anu = the heavens, Naki = Earth (feminine gender) or as in Enki / Children of Enki) through which eventually Quetzalcoatl /Yeshua, the Peacemaker, ***Ogwa Wahanee,*** the Bird Tribes, would manifest.

"Enki the Wise, Guardian of the Tree of Knowledge, also had another name in the Hebrew tradition. They called him Samael (Sama-El) because he was the designated Lord of Sama in northern Mesopotamia. The teachings of the early mystery schools were specific about the Trees of Life and Knowledge and they emulated the very teachings of Enki himself. It was said: Nothing is obtained simply by wanting. And, nothing is achieved by relinquishing responsibility to a higher authority. Belief is the act of 'believing', for to 'be live' is to 'believe' - and Will is the ultimate medium of the Self. ***The image (above left) was uncoverd in Bolivia during the 1970's.***

To regain control in the Euphrates, Enlil elected to seek out the Kings of Jerusalem and the Black Sea Princes of Scythia himself. It was Enlil or 'Ilu-kur-gal' (meaning 'Ruler of the Mountain'), himself who appeared to the biblical Abraham, demanding to be worshipped as the one and only true god and declared the serpent gods as evil incarnate.

Image (right) is Mayan, an d represents (left) Hu-man or a Son of the gods and (right) a serpent-god actually / Quetzacoatl influening destiny through the power of the reptilian blood lines (DNA) the point where mankind went from Monkey -man to Hu-man..

So then, who are we...?

Many stories about our mysterious origins continue to show up over and over again amongst the ruins of the civilizations of ancient Meso-America. There are stories having undeniable correlations to the Judeo-Christian Bible, but with information that for some reason has been ignored by the faiths of the Judeo-Christian religions, or quite plainly, they are denied entirely... Why?

At a sacred cave at Lake Guatavita near Bogata, Colombia, we are told that the ancient Inca priests would drop offerings of gold and emeralds and other precious gems, into the water. Then at Sao Tome das Letras near Minas, Brazil, we can find caves associated with many mysterious indigenous legends, including stories of extraterrestrials and a tunnel system that connects with Machu Picchu and places in North America...like Hopi Land in Arizona. Once again in the Atacama Desert of Chile are hundreds of prehistoric carvings, similar to the Nazca lines.

Unexplained Mysteries

There is almost no other place on Earth that has left us with so many unanswered questions as Tiahaunaco and the Nazca Plains located some 430 miles to the West. Both locations are tied by a common bond and common relationship to the Star Nations and our ancestors from the heavens. "**Madness**" **some might no doubt venture to say**", ...Then explain this phrase *from THE BOOK OF JOB:*

Job: 9:9 " *...Which maketh the Arcturus, and Orion, Pleiades, and the chambers of the South..."*

There exist yet other stories of the Gen-Isis: One from the Meso-Americans again - this time from Bolivia and the Ancient Inca. It has to do with what may prove yet to be the oldest man-(?)-made city in South America and maybe even the world, the city of Tiahuanaco, the City of the Sun Kings. Where Angels an Mankind lived as one. The Inca's say these ruins are millions of years old. That they were constructed by Angels from the heavens and their hybrid children... By the size of them , it must have been the Rephiam, who are described in the Dead Sea Scrolls as being the children of the Nefilim, who it is said reached heights of over 200 meters....

Job 16:14) and rephaim when they reappear in a more limited fashion after the flood

Gabriel in Meso-America ?

The ancient city of Tiahuanaco is to be found on the southern shore of Lake Titicaca in the Andes of Bolivia. Although its altitude is now higher than 12,000 feet, more and more evidence is telling us that in fact the city of Tiahuanaco was once at sea level, and there is speculation that its ruins are at least 17,000 years old, pre-dating the great flood. Construction used enormous basalt stones quarried at least 40 km away, on the other side of the Lake. Ingapirca is the only Inca city in Eduador not demolished by Spanish invaders.

The Inca believe that the ancient inhabitants of Tiahuanaco still inhabit the ancient mountians and live in cities below... they alos hold firm that the ruins we see atop in the above world were constructed by Angels..

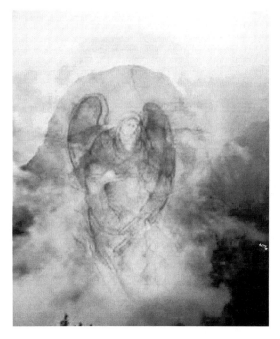

If you are of the Judeo -Christian or the Muslim faiths and I were to ask you if the Angel Gabriel existed, you would undoubtedly give an acknowledgement of "YES!" What if I were to ask you if, therefore, we are saying that the angel Gabriel existed, that he spoke of the ancient cities and people of Meso-America, what if he spoke of genetics and DNA, and the Children of the Sun, the Children of the Morning Star....

What would you reply?

Would it scare you?

Would it make you laugh at me and ask if I were a total lunatic who may have had one too many Shamanic journeys?

The Angel Gabriel addressing Job

Job: chapter 38

"1"Then the LORD answered Job out of the whirlwind, and said,

"2": Who is this that darkeneth counsel by words without knowledge?

"3": Gird up now thy loins like a man; for I will demand of thee, and answer thou me.

"4": Where were thou when I laid the foundations of the earth? declare, if thou hast understanding.

"5": Who hath laid the measures thereof, if thou knowest? or who hath stretched the line upon it?

"6": Where upon are the foundations thereof fastened? or who laid the corner stone thereof;

"7": When the morning stars sang together, and all the sons of God shouted for joy?

"8": Or who shut up the sea with doors, when it broke forth, as if it had issued out of the womb?

"9" Which maketh the Arcturus, and Orion, Pleiades, and the chambers of the South..."

It is totally possible that " the Chambers of the South.." spoken of in Job are a direct reference to the city of Tiahuanaco that lies upon the Southern shores of Lake Titicaca.

In the Bible: Job:38:

The angel Gabriel asks Job if he knows " who laid out the measures thereof and who stretched the lines upon the Nazca plains…and, who it was who laid the cornerstones and built the Ancient City there."

Again Gabriel asked Job ... if he knew...

"Where the Morning Stars sang together, and all the Sons of God shouted for joy?"

Now why would the Sons of God be shouting for joy? Would it be possible that this is a reference to the winning of the battle against the Giants that were killing the Sons of God and devouring them, quite literally, in the flesh? There is much reference to be found in the Bible and external texts that have been kept out or recently removed (mid 20th Century).

Some of the previously published works that were part of the Bible (King James Version) were unexplainably removed during the late 1930's and early 1940's during WWII and the brief but terrible reign of the Nazi's in Germany. Such as the book of Jasha, The Apocrypha, and the Book of Enoch, why? Let's leave that one up to your own investigations. There also exist among the surviving ancient records of Meso-America many stories about a War of the Gods occurring upon the Earth.

Who is Enoch:

By what authority does he issue forth his declarations… and prejudices.

It is fair to say the patriarch Enoch was as well known to the ancients as he is obscure to modern Bible readers. Besides giving his age (365 years), the book of Genesis says of him only that he "walked with God," and afterward "he was not, because God had taken him" **(GEN. 5:24).** This

exalted way of life and mysterious demise made Enoch into a figure of considerable fascination and a cycle of legends grew up around him.

Many of the legends about Enoch were collected in ancient times in several long anthologies. The most important such anthology, and the oldest, is known simply as The Book of Enoch, comprising over one hundred chapters. It still survives in its entirety (although only in the Ethiopian language) and forms an important source for the thought of Judaism in the last few centuries BCE.

Significantly, the remnants of several almost complete copies of The Book of Enoch in Aramaic were found among the Dead Sea Scrolls, and it is clear that whoever collected the scrolls considered it a vitally important text. All but one of the five

major components of the Ethiopic anthology has turned up among the scrolls. But even more intriguing, is the fact that additional, previously unknown or little-known texts about Enoch were discovered at Qumran. The most important of these is *The Book of Giants*. (*Image left is of a female giant uncoverd in the Rocky Mountains older than 3,000 BCE she would stand about 9 foot*...)

Enoch lived before the Flood, during a time when the world, in ancient imagination, was very different. Human beings lived much longer, for one thing; Enoch's son Methuselah, for instance, attained the age of 969 years. Another difference was that angels and humans interacted freely — so freely, in fact, that some of the angels begot children with human females. This fact is neutrally reported in Genesis (6:1-4), but other stories view this episode as the source of the corruption that made the punishing flood necessary.

According to The Book of Enoch, the co-mingling of angel and human was actually the idea of Shernihaza, (Lucifer), the leader of the evil angels, who lured 200 others to cohabitate with women.

The offspring of these unnatural unions were giants ,(Rephiam) most being 10 to 12 feet in height, but legend and Enoch's record tell us that others of these giant Rephaim reached as hight 450 feet in height. The story goes on to tell us that the wicked angels and the giants began to oppress the human population and to teach them to do evil. (But the question remains. who was who? Who were Anunnaki who were Rephaim, who were just big fellows...)

For this reason we are told that God elected to imprison the angels and exiled them to the beneath world, a place many call today the Hollow Earth. There they would reside until the final Day of Judgment, and then God also elected to destroy the earth with a flood. Enoch supposedly set forth some supreme efforts to intercede with the heavenly hosts (?) on behalf of the fallen angels, though his attempts we apparently were unsuccessful... *See (Enoch 6-16).*

From the fragments of the Dead Sea Scrolls of Enoch. in the Testament of Amram, which may well be accurate, however they may not be genuine. Scientist disagree as to the authenticity of the text. A lot of the text found in the Dead Sea Scrolls forensics tells us, comes from a much later period then the texts are being credited as coming from...giving credence to the theory that perhaps they were written by the Templar... during the occupations of the knights of Lion Heart during the crusades

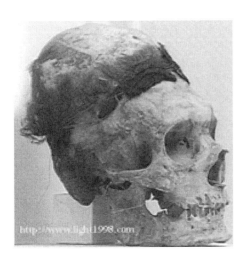 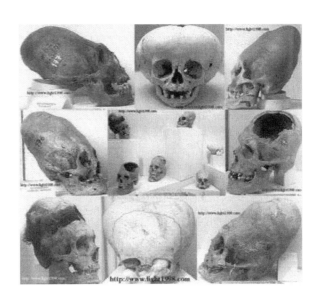

From the Testament of Amram (Dead Sea Scrolls)

Line 13 - [They (the leaders) and all ... of them took for themselves]

Line 14 - wives from all that they chose and [they began to cohabit with them and to defile themselves with them];

Line 15 - and to teach them sorcery and spells and the cutting of roots; and to acquaint them with herbs.]

Line 16 - And they become pregnant by them and bore (great) giants three thousand cubits high ...]

The Master you are

We are being pushed in this new time to employ all our spiritual teachings we have compiled over the years. They were not given to us because they were inconsequential, or as recreational tools, nor were they given to us only to be stored upon a shelf. They were given to us to use. They are powerful and divine tools and as we complete this next era, everything you learned will be summoned up at one time or another.

It is time to become the **adept**; it is time to act as **the Master you are**. For this is not a time for frolicking. The nature of the hologram is very different now. This is a time to own the responsibility for your creations, master you emotions, to control your energies and to become the sage.

As you look around you and discern the degree of madness, know that this drama to which you are witness is the real thing. Did you realize that when you began this journey you would be in school forever, dear Master? Well, all good things must come to an end; we are not play-acting with wooden swords now. Playtime and leisurely and convenient learning practices are a thing of the past. If you don't believe me, just ask Ram Dass. This time is the reason you have been in training all these years. Now you and I and everyone connected to us are being called to action.

Our addictions and dysfunctions are going to be brought to the carpet so to speak, almost on a daily basis. Every flaw you posses will be shown to you. That's why they call it **purification.** Be careful not to become cynical with yourself. Learn to see the deeper aspect of what you are about, precious entity.

Realize your physical form is merely for your use... a miraculous and perfectly designed machine. However, you are not the suit you are that which is in the suit. It is a vehicle to enable you to complete your mission in the world of sensory perception. Realize also that it is divine in its creation and is the ultimate computer. It responds to what we think and feel and it can change accordingly. So, it behooves you to put yourself to the task of being the master that is within.

If **you** who hold the fire of Creation within your soul, **O'Child of the Universe**, **Child of God**, then own your passionate dream. If this **HU-manness** is truly precious to you, then go and fight for it. For the hour is upon us. The day of awakening is here. And in a moment circumstance can change like the wind.

This reality is that which you hold so precious, so dearly to your core that you would kill your neighbor to preserve it, that you fight so hard through suffering and calamity and spend your last penny just to prolong it one more moment. (I**f you don't believe this, then please go visit a hospice.**) It is a very enlightening experience to sit with and work with other humans who are passing over. Watching their fears and realizing our own…And feeling their awakening at the moment of passing… and seeing the greater reality there is no death…just a passing through realities, like dreams in a slide show.

Humanity fights so desperately to hold on to this dream that dissolves so quickly into thin air, so to speak. And finds oh, too quickly, the reality in that truth ... only that which can be held within the Human heart will survive. Only the part of you that is eternal will carry on. Remember that is what got you here in the first place: Your desire for experience. In the end all you ever had was the dream…

In this process of awakening, abilities and powers will come to you that you may not understand at first. The only constant you wil heave will be your own inner voice, as you find out that in fact you are the one having the thoughts and experiences walking through the dream. When you find these gifts beginning to manifest within yourself.. take hold, and remember you are a powerful being... your thoughts manifest and your actions do have effect. A dark experience or an experience of the light is a matter of choice, your choice..

Use your Light to heal, use it to empower, use it to acknowledge the divine life force residing in all things, use it to lift the human spirit up, and command others respond to that octave always, by being at one with it yourself, always. Engage each situation coming across your path as a dignitary who carries that life force and as a representative of the living God within.

Now, there is a real challenge... but well worth the struggle. There is no time to dance around issues any longer. It is time to get genuine, and speak and live your truth — Your real truth. To become the being you are on the inside and express it on the outside. For if you can, you will find how quickly the gray areas between self-confidence and the imaginary world of altered-ego, all your judgment and your discernment will become clarion.

In Lak'esh   *A gift from the Maya*

The Anti-Christ is manifest, so dwelling upon the matter will not give us the solution. How else could *IT* be? Humanity has so long called it forth. However, the Anti-Christ is born of the image, and like the image will fade into its own dream of itself, it is a dream with borders and limited in substance. Nevertheless, that which is manifest will play out its drama. Be certain.... How many life times did you call the dream forth forth? How many life times did you yourself dance with the dark? And are you still doing so?

As for those who are **the innocents**, have compassion, give encouragement and always remember... **In Lak'esh**... They are a part of you... They are your other self. This understanding can be expanded to touch all aspects of our cosmic reality. For all things are connected in the web of life, all things....

In Lak'esh is a living positive action. It is much more than just a cute Mayan saying, it is an understanding of how the matrix works. It lifts us from the state of neutrality to become causal with the universe. Neutral is nowhere; it is not participating in the dance of life. Perhaps for momentary reasons, it can be a good thing to separate from a situation in order to see it clearly. But to exist in this state for too long a period has the reverse effect upon us. We are creatures of action in a participatory universe; everything in the universe is based upon the concept of **In Lak'esh**.

The very phrase **In Lak'esh** means "*I am your other self*", I am a part of you... We are connected... **In the oneness...** Like many indigenous languages it is a verb, then a noun. It describes an action or a movement of energy.

To the Mayan this greeting is an honoring for each other and a declaration of the Divine connection that exists between all things. In Lak'esh mirrors other greetings such as, Aho Mitakyue Oyasin in Lakota meaning all my relations, Namaste for East India, Viracocha for the Inca in Peru.

My understanding of the term *In Lak'esh,* as has been shared with me by my Solar Brother, Hunbatz Men, is that the term *In Lak'esh* goes beyond being just a casual greeting. To the Mayan People and those who are remembering in this awakening process *In Lak'esh* is a declaration of a spiritual codex bespeaking not only of a way to live with our fellow human beings, but with all forms of life in our cosmos!

Mayan Elder, Hunbatz Men teaches that we can express the energy of *In Lak'esh* to each other, *In Lak'esh* to the trees, *In Lak'esh* to the sky, *In Lak'esh* to the birds, *In Lak'esh* to the stars and so on. This action of *In Lak'esh* is honoring and acknowledging our intimate connection with all of life. When we live the code of *In Lak'esh* we send an essential energy that is filled with love and respect to all life forms. Being the essence of *In Lak'esh* is understanding that everything we do in this dimension, in this moment, affects all life and spirit in the whole of the cosmos, either in a positive or negative way, depending on our actions and motivations.

When we practice *In Lak'esh* we are producing and sending positive and vital life force to all other forms of life. When we practice *In Lak'esh* we quit being neutral and non-participatory and take action in a positive way. Each time we state and truly empower it with our emotion *In Lak'esh* even in the silence of our minds we are reinforcing the oneness of all that has been given life. We are acknowledging the web of life energy, which connects us all...to everything.

If you begin to exercise the principle of *In Lak'esh* in your every day life you will begin to understand very quickly that when you give your life energy to any other life form you are also giving to yourself! What causes us to lose our life force is fear and the feeling or belief of being separated from life.

This starts a cycle that actually closes down the energy of the life force able to flow through our own body. Our glands like our organs correspond to the planets of our solar system begin to close down and the life force energy becomes constricted. When you begin to understand that you are giving your life force energy to something that is connected to you, you are actually giving that energy to another part of yourself!

Remember this grand reality ... believe or choose not to believe, that is your divine option. We are all going through this process of change and transformation. We can go along and stumble into each experience of awakening or learn to take the reigns and steer our vessel through the dream

.......as you learn to walk upon shifting ground...

(want to understand this better...? Next time youa are dreaming try to touch something, or read something... There! I knew you'd get it...)

Entering the 5-D Reality

Remember to employ the principles of the **5-D reality... Discernment, Discretion, Detachment, Determination and Desire**, about which I wrote in **_Through the Eye of the Shaman._** Hold closely to your heart your family and loved ones. For in reaching out and touching each other there is great comfort and strengthening of the spirit. Compassion will be the single most empowering principle we can self-apply. Times will get strange and then they will get stranger. It is time to develop an "**anything is possible**" reality.

The energies that will begin to be released from Mother Earth as we move into the Earth Changes will be of extraordinary measure. They will alter the very physics of the air. We will, upon meeting **our cosmic brethren and sisterern** from the Star Nations, also be moving into amazing shifts of consciousness. These shifts of awareness will affect everything; remember the wisdom of **In Lak'esh**. This will be very important when this begins to occur. Consciousness sets the parameters of our reality. For so long we have existed in such a narrow band of frequency that for some, this new reality experience will be shattering.

Be prepared to form communities, extended families if you will. These will be necessary for your survival. No one can do it all alone. Eventually these little groups who break away from the corrupted matrix, will be drawn to each other. First there will be the networking of communities; there will then be alliances and then comradery. It is a very natural process, and will evolve to ever-deeper levels of communication and exchange. Many of you will navigate through some difficult times as you learn to break away from your dependencies upon the system.

Also, there will be networks for education and a new spiritual oneness will begin emerge as you learn again to reach out to each other in the principles of **In Lak'esh**, instead of the selfish pulling inwards of energy that occurs with the "**what's in it for me attitude**". These communities are also necessary for the health and care of the children who will be entering your plane and carrying on the chain of forever.

Where should I go? What should I do to survive these days

If you are able, build your hovels so that they can withstand the elements. The weather will become increasingly unstable as we continue through this process of change. Make them out of natural materials, and keep them simple…One can accomplish many things and manage to keep the spirits up when they are dry and warm and clean.

There will be many periods of martial law, and the wars of the Heavens will touch the Earth. Great fear will arise from the plagues that will begin soon to be rampant upo the land…Cities will be quarantined and If you do not take the mark of the beast, the sacred ship, if you are outside the system you will be suspect.

During times of the occupation (which will be temporary, except in urban areas), it will be necessary for some at times to head to the shelter of the Mountains and the deep woods. Keep always that which is required for three to four days stay as to keep life pleasant while enduring wilderness conditions. Also, keep your stores in various places, as during times of occupation your homes and dwellings will be searched and used by those inflicting the temporary hardships.

It would be wise to be abe to help up to 8 individuals each of us. Then there will not be the necessity of judging who wil stay, and who should go…If enough of us do this then we will move through these times with relative poise and grace.

Learn the ways of the woods, the herbs that will keep you healthy, ease pain, toothaches can make a miserable experience. Antibiotics are bountiful if one knows where and what to use. Be creative think good old Yankee ingenuity you'll need lights, water, and maintain a level of safe hygiene,

The reign of fear, and the witch hunts and military activity, will, although commonly occurring, be fairly sporadic in the rural areas, as most tactical forces will be stationed within striking distance of the urban areas and close to the military bases. The level of paranoia will be extreme in the urban areas and there will be much confusion.

It is a hard thing to be asked to impose a condition upon your own people you know is morally wrong and spiritually incorrect; it is even harder to abide by it.   The intensity of the conditions among the people dealing with the diseases and dealing with natural disasters and financial collapse will be accepted at first and then there will begin to be breakdowns within the matrix itself, which has already been established in the plan of things. This is when hysteria will set in…Love all…. trust no one..

As the situation move into a higher gear, the chief concerns will not be so much crowd control of inhabitants of the city they can easily be contained. Rather it will be defense against the raiders from above. For the masks will continue to fall, and it is a matter of frequency that dominates the expression of reality…

Those rebel pirates who have contrived all manner of trade and commerce with our corrupt governments, their games of deception and treachery, will be exposed very shortly. And as this occurs there will be struggles between groups for dominance. Again, our visitors from the stars are not that much different from you and I. Where do you think our attitudes and love for violence came from?

If you have developed the fabric of the Christos within self, and live the compassion that it brings forth You will become a very different kind of individual. For you will be as the indigenous people of Canada say **OTIPEMSIWAK** one who owns themselves. You will not be governed by fear. You will be able to maintain your own thoughts and sense of reason as the chaos around you spins…

Having this inner core affixed to the Christos…you will sense you immortality and follow the higher frequencies…You will find that you are a natural leader, and that many will flock to the energy that you exude and share with those around you who are of like mind.. Keep your ego in check; it is not you they flock to it is the light which moves through you. The God within.

If you develop this to its fullest extent no matter where you go you will always be the calm in the storm.. We are headed towards tumulus times, and the crying and gnashing of teeth, are what will be going on around you, it need not be the condition within you. To be the Christ today does not mean that you must be crucified…that has already been done…. You are aligned to a higher purpose, yours is to be the light that leads the children out of the darkness. The staff that the weary might lean on. If you feel the weakness of strength to do this, then align yourself in community, and use the energy of the group. The extended family…

The will of Mother Father God will reign supreme, and metaphysical law will prevail.. The god within you shall awaken and you will be a dancer in these Days to Come…for these are your Days Of Destiny…

"God is all things. God is the source that causes the seed to become the flower. God is the soil that the flower grows upon, as well as the Sunlight it seeks for energy.

God is the scent of the flower as well as the texture of the flower...its petals, its leaves...God is also the color of the flower. God is the flower in life as well as in death.

Mother Father God, is the source, and the thought of all that is.

And the Christos is realized as God in man....

Hu - Man GOd-Man... "

ISBN 141200726-7

9 781412 007269

Made in the USA
San Bernardino, CA
16 February 2014